REPUBLICAN EUROPE

Constitutional orders constitute political communities—and international orders deriving from them—by managing conflicts that threaten peace. This book explores how a European political community can be advanced through EU constitutional law. The constitutional role of the Union is to ensure peace by addressing two types of conflict. The first are static conflicts of interests between the national polities in the EU. These are avoided by ensuring reciprocal non-interference between Member States in the Union through deregulation in Union law. The second are dynamic conflicts of ideas about positive liberty held by the peoples of Europe. These can be resolved through regulation in a European political space. Here, EU law enables a continuous process of re-negotiating a shared European idea of positive liberty that can be accepted as its own by each national polity in the EU. These solutions to the two types of conflicts correspond to the liberal and republican models for Europe. The claim of this book is that the constitutional design of Europe presents both liberal and republican features. Taking an innovative approach, which draws on arguments from substantive law, constitutional theory, case law analysis, insights from psychology and philosophy, it identifies how best to strengthen the Union through constitutional law.

Volume 72 in the Series Modern Studies in European Law

Modern Studies in European Law
Recent titles in this series:

Fundamental Rights in EU Internal Market Legislation
Vasiliki Kosta

Uniformity of Customs Administration in the European Union
Kathrin Limbach

The Impact of Union Citizenship on the EU's Market Freedoms
Alina Tryfonidou

Equal Citizenship and Its Limits in EU Law
Päivi Johanna Neuvonen

European Law on Unfair Commercial Practices and Contract Law
Mateja Durovic

The European Union's External Action in Times of Crisis
Edited by Piet Eeckhout and Manual Lopez-Escudero

The Legitimacy of Family Rights in Strasbourg Case Law: Living Instrument or Extinguished Sovereignty?
Carmen Draghici

Strengthening the Rule of Law in Europe: From a Common Concept to Mechanisms of Implementation
Edited by Werner Schroeder

The Pluralist Character of the European Economic Constitution
Clemens Kaupa

Exceptions from EU Free Movement Law
Edited by Panos Koutrakos, Niamh Nic Shuibhne and Phil Syrpis

Reconceptualising European Equality Law: A Comparative Institutional Analysis
Johanna Croon-Gestefeld

Marketing and Advertising Law in a Process of Harmonization
Edited by Ulf Bernitz and Caroline Heide-Jörgensen

The Fundamental Right to Data Protection: Normative Value in the Context of Counter-Terrorism Surveillance
Maria Tzanou

Republican Europe
Anna Kocharov

For the complete list of titles in this series, see
'Modern Studies in European Law' link at
www.bloomsburyprofessional.com/uk/series/modern-studies-in-european-law

Republican Europe

Anna Kocharov

• HART •
PUBLISHING
OXFORD AND PORTLAND, OREGON
2017

Hart Publishing
An imprint of Bloomsbury Publishing Plc

Hart Publishing Ltd
Kemp House
Chawley Park
Cumnor Hill
Oxford OX2 9PH
UK

Bloomsbury Publishing Plc
50 Bedford Square
London
WC1B 3DP
UK

www.hartpub.co.uk
www.bloomsbury.com

Published in North America (US and Canada) by
Hart Publishing
c/o International Specialized Book Services
920 NE 58th Avenue, Suite 300
Portland, OR 97213-3786
USA

www.isbs.com

First published 2017

British Library Cataloguing-in-Publication Data
A catalogue record for this book is available from the British Library.

ISBN: HB: 978-1-50991-074-8
ePDF: 978-1-50991-076-2
ePub: 978-1-50991-073-1

Library of Congress Cataloging-in-Publication Data

Names: Kocharov, Anna, author.

Title: Republican Europe / Anna Kocharov.

Description: Oxford ; Portland, Oregon : Hart Publishing, an imprint of Bloomsbury Publishing Plc, 2017. | Series: Modern studies in European law ; volume 72 | Includes bibliographical references and index.

Identifiers: LCCN 2016058792 (print) | LCCN 2016059672 (ebook) | ISBN 9781509910748 (hardback : alk. paper) | ISBN 9781509910731 (Epub)

Subjects: LCSH: Constitutional law—European Union countries—Philosophy. | Federal government—European Union countries. | Conflict management—European Union countries. | International and municipal law—European Union countries. | Republicanism—European Union countries. | Liberalism—European Union countries.

Classification: LCC KJE4445 .K63 2017 (print) | LCC KJE4445 (ebook) | DDC 342.24—dc23

LC record available at https://lccn.loc.gov/2016058792

Typeset by Compuscript Ltd, Shannon
Printed and bound in Great Britain by Lightning Source UK Ltd

With gratitude to Miguel, Marise, Dennis, my parents, Alessandro.

Contents

Table of Cases

Court of Justice of the European Union

EFTA Court

European Court of Human Rights

US Cases

Table of Legislation

International Law

EU Treaties and International Agreements

Treaties

International Agreements between Member States of the EU

Europe Agreements

Stabilization and Association Agreements

Partnership and Cooperation Agreements

Euro-Mediterranean Agreements

Other Mixed External Agreements

Mobility Partnerships

EU Secondary Law

Decisions

Framework Decisions

Regulations

Directives

Proposals

EU Policy Documents

European Council

Council

European Commission

European Parliament

Surveys

Speeches and Declarations

Member State Documents

Austria

Finland

France

Germany

Italy

Latvia

Lithuania

Netherlands

Poland

Portugal

Spain

UK

Introduction

SEVEN DECADES AFTER the end of the WWII, the challenges facing Europe have changed dramatically. War in the EU has become materially impossible and unthinkable: Peace as the absence of military confrontation between Member States has been achieved. Instead, Europe is increasingly facing new types of conflict that may potentially prejudice Peace. Internally within the Union, disagreement is looming between Member States on policy issues that range from immigration to sovereign debt. Externally, the Union and its states are challenged by instability at their external borders, transnational private interests and powerful third states. This indicates that the threat to Peace has not disappeared but has changed in two important dimensions. First, a conquest no longer implies a war.[1] A People may now be conquered without the use of military force. Trade, financial and technological interdependence offer new means for subduing a state. Conquest extends to the capacity to govern, not mere territorial control. The promise of Peace is thereby extended to enabling governance in the pursuit of one's own goals. Second, the source of potential disruptions of governance has shifted: these are not only caused by Member States to each other but by actors not bound by Union law. Externally, these are third states, transnational private interests, individuals and organisations that find themselves outside EU and national law. Internally, the ability of a people to govern may be undermined by malfunctions in the political process. This book explores how, with the changing nature of conflicts, Union law is adjusting to ensure continued Peace.

The uniqueness of EU legal order lies in its structure, designed to advance Peace between the peoples of Europe. This structure contains a strong introvert bias aimed at eliminating threats to Peace that originate in the risk of conquest between Member States in the Union. Community law reduces this risk by empowering the individual and disempowering the state in what can be termed as a 'reciprocal disarmament of national polities'. While successful between Member States in the Union, this very structure of EU legal order renders it vulnerable to external actors who are not bound by Union law. Herein lies the potential self-subversion of EU legal order: reducing the risk of conquest between Member States may raise the risk of conquest by external actors. A tension results between what I shorthand as the liberal and republican models, the former centred on empowering the individual against the state, the latter focused on strengthening the polity against conquest. These two models are not incompatible. Every policy of the Union presents

[1] For a broader understanding of war and therefore threats to Peace, see DMC Yuen, *Deciphering Sun Tzu* (Oxford, Oxford University Press, 2014).

a mixture of both. It is shown that from the very beginning of the Communities, even policies structured on individual rights have concealed deeply republican elements. The liberal and the republican are not alternatives but two indispensable aspects of a single whole. By adjusting their proportions, EU legal order can strengthen Peace in the face of the changing nature of conflicts.

Three dimensions of constitutional adaptation are identified throughout this book. First, with the relative increase in risks of conquest by actors not bound by Union law, the introvert bias in Union powers shifts from the internal to the external. Second, the need to develop a common policy towards external actors diversifies conflict potential between Member States: not only interests but also ideas may conflict. A need emerges for Union law not only to prevent conflicts of interests, but also to offer rules for constant (re-)negotiation of conflicts of ideas. Third, the rise of conquest through governance (as opposed to the military conquest of territory) leads to expansion not only of Union powers, but also of the scope of EU constitutional law. What constitutes 'a purely internal situation' that falls outside the scope of Union law is re-conceptualised not in terms of geography and policy choices but in terms of governance and rules for making policy choices.

1. EUROPE IN CRISES

Europe today finds itself in multiple crises: the euro and fiscal crisis, the failure of the European neighbourhood policy with the wars in Syria and Ukraine, new waves of mass migration to Europe, the first instance of exit from the EU. These crises reveal new conflicts and the importance of governance for the ability to maintain Peace. In terms of governance, Europe's crises are not unrelated. The arrival in Germany of ca one million asylum seekers in 2015 (many fleeing the wars in Syria and Iraq) roughly doubles its long-term unemployment,[2] posing an economic challenge. The mass migration to Greece alone of 30,000 people per week on average in November 2015 with a total of over 800,000 in 2015[3] presents a logistical and security challenge not unlike the anti-austerity demonstrations in the same country three years earlier, in which up to 500,000 people took part. No wonder that at the end of 2015 Turkey, the major country of transit for migrants on their way to Europe, benefited from unprecedented EU funds and concessions,[4] including acceleration of its accession to the EU. In the same year, Greece almost exited the euro, the Swiss voted in a referendum to end free movement of persons,

[2] 2% of the population in 2014, with 'long-term' defined as being out of work for longer than 12 months, Eurostat http://ec.europa.eu/eurostat/statistics-explained/index.php/File:Figure_8_Unemployment_rates_by_duration_2014_(%25).png.

[3] Missing Migrants Project of the IOM (18.12.2015), http://missingmigrants.iom.int/sites/default/files/Mediterranean_Update_18_December.pdf.

[4] J Zaragoza-Cristiani, 'Analysing the Causes of the Refugee Crisis and the Key Role of Turkey: Why Now and Why So Many?' (2015) *European University Institute working paper RSCAS* 2015/95.

Iceland dropped its EU accession bid and, in June 2016, the UK voted to exit the Union. These developments have come on the heels of repeated rejections of Europe by its peoples (starting with the failed referenda on the EU constitutional Treaty, to the plummeting European Parliament (EP) elections turnout, to the rise of the so-called Eurosceptics). Union citizens not only fail to accept European policy choices but actively vent their disaccord. National constitutional courts are also in doubt.[5]

The claim of this book is that Europe's crises of governance are rooted in its constitutional design, a design that is largely based on now obsolete threats to Peace. This design needs re-conceptualisation in order to prevent and withstand future crises. This book unveils this constitutional design and the potential for revamping it, and shows to what extent this is being done already.

2. POLICY CHOICES AND CONSTITUTIONAL CHOICES

This book does not discuss substantive policy. Rather, it 'looks for the questions behind the question' of European policy choice.[6] It has been noted that Union law developed with no explicit constitutional theory.[7] The aim of this work is to render the implicit explicit. It is shown that starting from the Treaty of Rome, EU law contains implicit constitutional theory, which was used and developed by the Court of Justice of the EU. With the Treaty of Lisbon, the presence and substance of this theory comes out with new force.

This project began with the why and what questions. Why is there a difference in the individual–state relationship established in Union law between the internal market and the area of freedom, security and justice? What does this difference mean for the role of Union law? And for the structure of policy making in the EU legal order? To answer these questions, a distinction is made between constitutional choices and policy choices. The latter pertain to substantive Union policies that set a balance between competing interests in Union law. The former pertain to the rules for setting this balance. Whose interests are represented in the process of making policy choices—and whose interests are protected from the process of

[5] See EO Eriksen and JE Fossum, 'Bringing European Democracy Back In—Or How to Read the German Constitutional Court's Lisbon Treaty Ruling' (2011) 17(2) *European Law Journal*; J Komárek, 'Czech Constitutional Court Playing with Matches: The Czech Constitutional Court Declares a Judgment of the Court of Justice of the EU Ultra Vires' (2012) 8(2) *European Constitutional Law Review*; P Kiiver, 'The Lisbon Judgment of the German Constitutional Court: A Court-Ordered Strengthening of the National Legislature in the EU' (2010) 16(5) *European Law Journal*; G Beck, 'The Lisbon Judgment of the German Constitutional Court, the Primacy of EU Law and the Problem of Kompetenz-Kompetenz: A Conflict between Right and Right in Which There Is No Praetor' (2011) 17(4) *European Law Journal*.

[6] R Van Gestel and HW Micklitz, 'Why Methods Matter in European Legal Scholarship' (2014) 20(3) *European Law Journal* 311.

[7] M Poiares Maduro, 'Three Claims of Constitutional Pluralism' in M Avbelj and J Komárek (eds), *Constitutional Pluralism in the European Union and Beyond* (Oxford, Hart Publishing, 2012) 67–68.

making policy choices? Union Treaties not only contain both constitutional and policy choices but, confusingly, in Union law, some policy choices perform a constitutional function. It is the constitutional function, the rules for making policy choices, that this book identifies and brings together for a coherent constitutional theory of Union law.

The study of constitutional choices—the rules for making policy choices—in the multicultural setting of Europe requires an interdisciplinary approach. Constitutions establish and stabilise polities by rendering predictable human interaction in the course of making policy choices. They do this by creating a practice for the development of shared experiences and understandings (political culture) that renders the discussion of policy choices possible. But the practice itself is embedded in past experiences and culture. Where the experiences and the meanings derived from them diverge, as in Europe today, shared meanings can be found in two broader expressions of culture: philosophy and psychology. Elements of both are combined with institutional and constitutional elements of Union law to outline such a foundation. Further, the theoretical aspect of this book draws on theories of transnational legal systems, European integration and constitutionalism. The focus on people and groups of people (polities) as opposed to the Hobbesian state, state institutions or their officials, makes evident the relevance of psychology and philosophy to constitutional law.

To identify the constitutive elements of EU legal order and trace their adaptation to the changing nature of conflicts, a comparative constitutional approach is used. Changes in the constitutional construct of Europe are exposed and explored through the analysis of the only EU policy that spans three constitutionally different areas. These three constitutional areas diverge in the structure and type of conflicts to be resolved in Union law: conflicts between the national polities, conflicts with actors not bound by Union law, and conflicts internal to every national polity. The substance of law—European policy choices—is used in order to distil the constitutive elements of EU legal order and therefore understand the EU's constitutional choice. Comparative analysis of policy choices in the three constitutional areas highlights their constitutional implications and explains the different approaches taken by the legislator and the Court. By distinguishing between policy choices (the *what*) and constitutional choices (the *how*), this work combines theory with legal analysis to flesh out a holistic constitutional theory of EU law.

3. WHAT'S IN A POLICY?

One EU policy is chosen to illustrate and detect constitutional adaptation. This policy is migration, understood broadly to include all the provisions that regulate mobility of people to and from Member States of the EU. It is unique for the convergence of the multiple factors that evidence Europe's constitutional construct.

First, migration is a highly conflict-prone policy characterised by high heterogeneity of interests and ideas about the best policy choice. The presence of two different types of conflict—conflicts of interests and of ideas—enables comparison between the constitutional solutions adopted in Union law for each. It is also a policy where substantive policy choices are made both in Treaty law by unanimity and in secondary EU law subject to majoritarian political process. Further, migration law can be enacted under exclusive or shared competences of the EU. These features enable comparisons that reveal constitutive elements of the EU legal order.

Second, migration allows for comparative analysis between the internal and the external in the EU constitutional construct. In fact, it is the only policy that spans three constitutional areas: (1) the internal market, (2) external agreements of the EU, and (3) the area of freedom, security and justice. These areas diverge at the level of interdependence between the national polities and the type of actors involved in conflict. In terms of actors, there are three types of conflict: between Member States, between the Union and external actors, and within each national polity of the EU. These correspond to three potential sources of conquest: (1) conquest of one European people by another, (2) conquest by actors not bound by Union law, (3) conquest of a European polity by internal minority interests. In Europe, migration policy produces another deep tension: while it is used to eliminate conquest potential between Member States, it can simultaneously be used to subdue and conquer the Union.[8] This paradoxical relation requires a careful balance, enabling the discussion of how the two opposites compose the whole.

Third, comparison between constitutional and policy choices is possible thanks to the presence of three distinct groups as concerns the political process: members of Europe's polities (in their home Member State and in another Member State of the Union) and 'outsiders'. This enables a meaningful comparison between not merely the substance of rights but the reasons for the difference in substance. To the extent that migration law regulates human beings (who deserve the same basic rights) in the same situation of trans-border mobility but in a different situation as regards membership in different political communities, choosing this policy fixes one component of comparison while focusing on the differences in the other. Even when worded identically, rights provisions found in different constitutional contexts could have different constitutional functions and effects in terms of rules for making policy choices. This work reveals these different constitutional effects and the challenges to Peace that they address.

These unique features of EU migration policy allow for a highly comparative and holistic approach necessary to map how Union law regulates conflicts. One type of conflict remains outside migration policy due to its scarce reliance on technical expertise: the conflict between expert knowledge (technocracy) and politics (democracy). However, even this conflict, although not present in migration policy, can benefit from the conclusions presented in this work. Thanks to its belonging firmly within the sphere of politics, migration can showcase the

[8] On the use of migration as a tool to subdue a state, see KM Greenhill, *Weapons of Mass Migration. Forced Displacement, Coercion, and Foreign Policy* (Ithaca, NY, Cornell University Press, 2010).

difference between justice and liberty as an approach to EU constitutional law. Is the role of Europe to secure (political) liberty or (social) justice? The claim advanced in this book is that both are relevant, and that securing justice necessarily begins with liberty.

The analysis of migration law presented here explores the political as it emerges from substantive Union law. Through this analysis, the work reveals elements of EU constitutional order and their adaptation to the broader changes in and around the Union. This book compares how Union law addresses different types of conflict to advance our understanding of the legal order not in theoretical or 'desirable' terms but as it results from the legislative process and case law. Conclusions from this analysis are relevant for all Union policies and answer the question of *how* policy choices are made. The reader should not expect to learn from this book *what* immigration or asylum measures are to be put in place. Rather, a holistic understanding of EU constitutional order, where substantive justice relies on political liberty, comes to the fore.

4. ARGUMENT OVERVIEW

This book claims that the constitutional design of Europe presents both liberal and republican elements. As the nature of threats to Peace change, the balance between the two is shifting and constitutional adaptation takes place. Understanding this balance provides the foundation for a constitutional theory of EU law and is therefore key to all areas of Union law.

The book evolves in five chapters. It starts with a theoretical framework for conceptualising the constitutional in Union law. Constitutions regulate a society of people; regulating people requires understanding of how they think and act. For this reason, Chapter 1—'Liberty in the Constitutional Construct of Europe'—combines the elements of psychology and philosophy relevant for Western democratic societies. There is no claim that all the people in Europe share these ideas—merely that our political culture and way of thinking are to a large extent founded on them. A connection is made between the three aspects of liberty (negative liberty, positive liberty, liberty from domination), legitimacy of the EU legal order and loyalty between the peoples of Europe. Together, liberty, loyalty and legitimacy allow the 'quotidian character of practice' of EU law to be preserved.[9] Only a people that enjoys all the three aspects of liberty can exercise loyalty vis-à-vis other peoples. Liberty thus defines the constitutional function of EU law and acceptance of Union policies. The chapters that follow discuss each of the three aspects of liberty in turn.

[9] D Patterson, 'Methodology and Theoretical Disagreement' in U Neergaard, R Nielsen, L Roseberry (eds), *European Legal Method Paradoxes and Revitalization* (Copenhagen, DJOF Publishing, 2011) 236.

Chapter 2—'A Union of Polities: Negative Liberty'—proceeds to analyse EC law developed before the Treaty of Lisbon through a comparison between the internal market and mixed external agreements of the EC. It examines negative liberty secured in EU free movement law, reveals conflicts that this conception of liberty can and cannot address, and discusses why it is so. Substantive law and case law are analysed in order to identify what types of conflicts are being solved with the help of Union law. Internally in the Union, Peace is conceived primarily as avoiding conflicts of interests between European polities; it is achieved through reciprocal deregulation. As a result, non-interference between European polities is being enforced over their positive liberty expressed in mixed external agreements. Both, however, require liberty from dependence to be advanced in Union law.

Chapter 3—'A Political Union: Positive Liberty'—traces the emergence of positive liberty as the foundation for the area of freedom, security and justice (AFSJ). The abolition of physical borders between national polities introduced an external dimension into the internal policies of the EU, leading to reconceptualisation of Peace. Peace in Europe is now more likely to be undermined not by Member States but by external actors who are not bound by Union law. In Europe's Union defined by reciprocity of commitment, Peace through deregulation is impossible when actors are not bound by Union law. As regards such external actors, Peace between Member States is transformed from a tool for avoiding conflicts into a tool for solving them. Absence of functional objectives in Treaty legal bases reflects this constitutional change. With the abolition of functional objectives from the definition of shared powers, the European idea of positive liberty became subject to an ongoing process of policy choice in Union law. The Lisbon Treaty thus finalised the emergence of a European political space, and opened for Union law a thicker constitutional function as a regulator of politics.

Chapter Four—'Conflict in Union Law'—traces the reorientation of Union law from conflicts of interests to conflicts of ideas. This is evident in the division of powers both in the legislative process and as adjudicated by the Court. Elements of the republican model forcefully emerge. With the relative increase in the importance of external threats to the Peace of Member States, conflicts between them are increasingly about ideas rather than interests. This is translated into Union law, albeit only implicitly, with a shift from EU policy choice as an instrument of conflict prevention towards the increased role of Union law as a tool for continuous (re)solution of conflicts.

Chapter Five—'The EU Court and Liberty from Dependence'—examines recent CJEU (Court of Justice of the European Union) case law in order to trace the adjustment of general principles of Union law to the different types of conflict. Cases on citizens and third-country nationals are examined. The principles in focus are primacy, mutual recognition, solidarity and the scope of Union law. It is shown that with the changing nature of conflicts fundamental freedoms yield to constitutional principles that set shared rules for making policy choices. The major challenges for the Court are connected with the national constitutional identities of Member States, where a careful balance needs to be struck between shared EU rules for the political process and the national political identity of polities in the EU. The identity of each people of Europe as an autonomous political community able to define and pursue its own idea of ideal life in the Union is a necessary precondition for loyalty and longevity of Union law. Liberty from dependence emerges as a key feature of the EU legal order, uniting the liberal and republican models for Europe.

The book's Conclusion—'Union Law As the Pacifier of Conflicts'—draws together the elements of EU constitutional theory that have emerged throughout this book into a holistic approach to Union law. It explains how the changing nature of conflict transforms the constitutive elements of the EU legal order.

1

Liberty in the Constitutional Construct of Europe

A republic is the property of the public. But a public is not every kind of human gathering, congregating in any manner, but a numerous gathering brought together by legal consent and community of interest.
Cicero, *The Republic*[1]

1. THE CONSTITUTIONAL SOUL OF EUROPE

A CONSTITUTION WITHOUT politics is like a body without a soul.[2] In Western democracies, Constitutions organise the process by which law is made; they regulate 'the relationship among citizens and define how their sovereignty is to be expressed in the political community'.[3] A constitutional order (in contrast to international law or contract law) sets not only the institutions, substantive rights, rules on the conflict of laws and division of powers but, more importantly, establishes rules about making choices. Opinions may abound on any policy choice; plurality of choices imply a multitude of interests that potentially collide and require balancing in an acceptable way. These interests are represented through the political process and balanced in its course. By laying down rules for the political process, Constitutions provide a 'mutually agreed, stable framework within which controversial debate (and action) is to take place'.[4] By shaping the political process (rather than being a product of it), Constitutions enable future majoritarian policy choice.[5] This makes a Constitution different from international and contract law.

Not every policy choice requires a political process. A policy choice may be imposed by a tyrant; or the interests of all the participants may coincide so there is no need for balancing (unanimity); or balancing can take place in such a way that

[1] *The Republic and The Laws* (Oxford, Oxford University Press, 1998) 19.

[2] M Poiares Maduro, 'Sovereignty in Europe: the European Court of Justice and the Creation of European Political Community' in ML Volcansek and JF Stack Jr (eds), *Courts Crossing Borders. Blurring the Lines of Sovereignty* (Durham, NC, Carolina Academic Press, 2005) 58.

[3] ibid, 46.

[4] Stanford Encyclopedia of Philosophy (http://plato.stanford.edu/entries/constitutionalism/).

[5] See also S Bartolini, 'Taking "Constitutionalism" and "Legitimacy" Seriously' (2008) *European Governance Discussion Paper* 2008/01.

every relevant interest is thereby appeased (consensus). In all the three situations, there is no political process: there is either no dialogue, or there is an accord.[6] Nevertheless, policy choices made by unanimity or consensus may also be regulated by constitutional law. For instance, an interest may be protected from the process of making policy choices by withdrawing the competence to regulate certain interests or to make a certain choice (e.g. outlawing acts of aggression between states or prohibition of torture). In this minimalist sense, the European Economic Community Treaty, the European Convention on Human Rights (ECHR), the UN Charter and the General Agreement on Tariffs and Trade (GATT) are Constitutions: they bind their parties (limit their choices) and benefit from (varying degrees of) enforcement. By limiting policy choices available to the national polities, a Treaty can have a constitutional nature without, at the same time, establishing a political process and without constituting a polity.

European political process neither takes place nor is required for such a feeble constitutional soul. This, at the outset, was the constitutional construct of Europe. The binding nature of EU law achieved through primacy and direct effect limits the national political process and policy choices while at the same time leaving the crux of policy choice with the Member States. National polities enter into a Union (and, with the Lisbon Treaty, can also exit from it) and within this framework represent and negotiate their national choices in such a way that no individual Member State is bound against its will. As long as unanimity or consensus of all Member States guide the shaping of common (European) policy choices, the mere existence of regulatory powers on a European level neither requires nor creates a political process but results in diplomacy between States.[7] Any controversy, if it existed, is removed by concessions, all the interests are appeased, the outcome not contested. The choice is made by each national polity and no polity has to comply against its own policy choice.

This lifeless image was reflected in EU constitutional scholarship. EU law was said to have constitutional quality due to its 'binding' nature derived from primacy, direct effect and the role of the European Court of Justice (ECJ). The constitutional elements of EC law were limited to the division of powers, the institutional balance, the role of the ECJ. There were no constitutive constitutional elements inasmuch as the Community—and later the Union—was constituted unanimously by Member State governments, who then unanimously made European policy choices. Rather than a 'non-identified political object',[8] the European Community remained an international organisation with powers both conferred and limited by the States.

[6] A Somek, *Individualism: An Essay on the Authority of the European Union* (Oxford, Oxford University Press, 2008) 160: 'non-democratic process of decision-making … can be legitimate in relatively homogeneous societies, for these societies are marked by a common belief in the right answer'.

[7] On the distinction between diplomacy and democracy in international relations see DM Curtin, *Postnational Democracy* (The Hague, Kluwer Law International, 1997) 27–40.

[8] Speech by Jacques Delors (Luxembourg, 09.09.1985).

The situation is different with respect to majoritarian political processes, where acceptance of choices no longer relies on the satisfaction of all. Here, minorities may be bound by—and resolve to comply with—choices of the majority that contradict their preference for a particular choice. Implied in this compliance is recognition of the group by the reference to which majority is established, the interests are balanced, and majority choices made. Not every group will be so accepted. Emergence of a 'group feeling' or 'bonding'[9] among individual members within this group (a polity) enables acceptance of majority rule. This is the meaning I will attach to 'polity' in this work: a group of people who perceive themselves as a group for the purpose of identifying the majority that makes binding choices. The emergence of a majoritarian political process opens up a new dimension to a legal order, requiring that it now regulate the process of policy choice. This causes the emergence of new constitutive elements of constitutional order, making it very different from international law.

Majoritarian policy choices are a reality in the EU today. A series of developments led to this. Replacing unanimity by qualified majority vote (QMV) in the Council[10] in practice led to decisions by consensus, 'under the shadow of the vote'.[11] This shadow materialised into the vote with increasing difficulties of attaining consensus due to the expansion of the Union and its powers. This, however, was not itself a decisive difference because of the possibility of packages and reciprocal deals. Even when a genuine QMV is possible, the scope of available policy choices will be limited by the conferral of powers, defined by all national polities unanimously on ratification of EU Treaties. Thus, the scope of potential Union powers is closely linked to majoritarian policy choice. Treaty amendments culminating in Lisbon extended Union competences into more politically sensitive fields characterised by high heterogeneity of interests and policy choice preferences. These new powers are less limited by Treaty objectives, leaving ample scope for policy choice.[12] At the same time, the Union enlarged to 28 Member States, increasing the diversity of circumstances and interests across the polities that compose it. As a result, an individual European polity may now be bound by Union law without its consent through Treaty ratification or in the Council and even despite an express negative vote. The majoritarian decision-making process not only binds individual polities to a specific policy choice against their preferred choice but, through the combined operation of pre-emption and primacy, it also withdraws from the national political process competence over the passage of powers from the national level to the EU. Taken together, these changes shifted the reference group for majoritarian choice from the national polities to the Union. Such a shift in polity requires acceptance by Union citizens

[9] JHH Weiler, *The Constitution of Europe: 'Do the New Clothes Have an Emperor?' and Other Essays on European Integration* (Cambridge, Cambridge University Press, 1999) 247, 338.

[10] Introduced by the Single European Act (1987) Luxembourg: Office for Official Publications of the European Communities Vol. I+II.

[11] Weiler (n 9) 72.

[12] Discussed in detail in Chapter 3.

> that in a range of areas of public life, one will accept the legitimacy and authority of decisions adopted by fellow European citizens in the realization that in these areas preference is given to choices made by the out-reaching, non-organic demos, rather than by the in-reaching one.[13]

There is no such European polity today. Eurobarometer surveys[14] and the persistent decline in turnout for the European Parliament elections[15] clearly show this. Majoritarian decision making in policies characterised by disagreement requires—yet, also hinders—emergence of a European political community. This book explores how the self-perception of the peoples of Europe as a unified political community can be built through Union law.

Despite the birth of a political soul of Europe, EU constitutional law is puppeteered like a lifeless body. 'Very often one has the impression that though the political (in the sense of institutions) is well grasped in relation to the case law, the social (in the sense of human dimension and communities) has been far less understood'.[16] The constitutive elements of EU constitutional order identified by scholars kept distance from passions: the institutional framework,[17] Union citizenship[18] and fundamental rights,[19] division of powers,[20] substantive policies,[21]

[13] Weiler (n 9) 346.

[14] Standard Eurobarometer 81 June 2014 *European Citizenship* 10: in June 2014, 'more than half the respondents defined themselves first by their nationality and then by their European citizenship (51%, +4 percentage points); the proportion of respondents who say that they define themselves first by their European citizenship and then by their nationality is still small (6%, +1); only 2% say that they see themselves solely as European citizens (no change)'.

[15] V Cuesta Lopez, 'The Lisbon Treaty's Provisions on Democratic Principles: A Legal Framework for Participatory Democracy' (2010) 16(1) *European Public Law* 123.

[16] JHH Weiler, 'Van Gend en Loos: The Individual as Subject and Object and the Dilemma of European Legitimacy' (2014) 12(1) *International Journal of Constitutional Law* 98.

[17] See generally: P Craig, 'Integration, Democracy and Legitimacy' in P Craig and G De Burca (eds), *Evolution of EU Law* (Oxford, Oxford University Press, 2011); F Laursen (ed), *The EU's Lisbon Treaty. Institutional Choices and Implementation* (Aldershot, Ashgate, 2012); L Pech, 'The Institutional Development of the EU Post-Lisbon: A Case of Plus Ça Change…?' in D Ashiagbor, N Countouris, I Lianos (eds), *The European Union after the Treaty of Lisbon* (Cambridge, Cambridge University Press, 2012); A Biondi, P Eeckhout and S Ripley (eds), *EU Law after Lisbon* (Oxford, Oxford University Press, 2012); P Craig, *The Lisbon Treaty, Revised Edition: Law, Politics, and Treaty Reform* (Oxford, Oxford University Press, 2013).

[18] See generally: M Condinanzi, A Lang and B Nascimbene, *Citizenship of the Union and Free Movement of Persons* (Leiden, Brill, 2008); FG Jacobs, 'Citizenship of the European Union—A Legal Analysis' (2007) 13(5) *European Law Journal*; F Wollenschläger, 'A New Fundamental Freedom beyond Market Integration: Union Citizenship and its Dynamics for Shifting the Economic Paradigm of European Integration' (2011) 17(1) *European Law Journal*; J Habermas, 'Bringing the Integration of Citizens into Line with the Integration of States' (2012) 18(4) *European Law Journal*; PC Jiménez Lobeira, 'EU Citizenship and Political Identity: The Demos and Telos Problems' (2012) 18(4) *European Law Journal*.

[19] See generally: S de Vries, U Bernitz and S Weatherill (eds), *The Protection of Fundamental Rights in the EU after Lisbon* (Oxford, Hart Publishing, 2013); G De Angelis and P Barcelos (eds) *The Long Quest for Identity: Political Identity and Fundamental Rights Protection in the European Union* (Bern, Peter Lang, 2013).

[20] See especially: R Schütze, *From Dual to Cooperative Federalism* (Oxford, Oxford University Press, 2011); R Schütze, *European Constitutional Law* (Cambridge, Cambridge University Press, 2012).

[21] See especially: C Barnard, *The Substantive Law of the EU. The Four Freedoms* (Oxford, Oxford University Press, 2013).

and the role of courts.[22] Although excellent writings on EU constitutional law abound, few identify what makes EU law constitutional in terms of regulating the process of making policy choices.[23] Few authors retain the focus on polity building as a necessary prerequisite for majority rule.[24] Some deny the relevance of constituting a polity with a majoritarian political process[25] or suggest a demoi-cracy[26] as a model for politics with a plurality of constitutional orders[27] that interact, typically through courts.[28] All these accounts avoid the core issue of what makes a polity and how this understanding translates into constitutive elements of the EU as constitutional order.

This chapter unpacks the phenomenon of polity and through it identifies the constitutive elements of the EU as a constitutional order. The acquisition by the Union of a constitutional soul—a majoritarian political process in highly contestable policy fields—both enables and requires that Union law regulate the political process in such a way that the resulting choices are accepted by all the peoples of Europe. It will be argued that acceptance of majoritarian policy choice is based on Loyalty among polities and polity members, which prevents their Exit from majoritarian rule. Beyond merely Member State governments and institutions as actors of EU policy choice, the introduction of Loyalty factors in citizens as a key component of Europe's constitutional order. This more 'human' approach is required by the shift from 'a constitutional order of states'[29] towards a Union with a political process based on majority rule. Loyalty here is understood as a

22 See generally: A Stone Sweet, *The Judicial Construction of Europe* (Oxford, Oxford University Press, 2004); B de Witte and HW Micklitz (eds), *The European Court of Justice and the Autonomy of Member States* (Antwerp, Intersentia, 2012); SK Schmidt and RD Kelemen (eds), *The Power of the European Court of Justice* (London, Routledge, 2013).

23 The following do engage with the question: JHH Weiler and M Wind (eds), *European Constitutionalism beyond the State* (Cambridge, Cambridge University Press, 2003); K Tuori and S Sankari, *The Many Constitutions of Europe* (Aldershot, Ashgate, 2010); G de Burca and JHH Weiler (eds), *The Worlds of European Constitutionalism* (Cambridge, Cambridge University Press, 2012).

24 EO Eriksen (ed), *Making the European Polity* (London, Routledge, 2005); EO Eriksen and JE Possum, *Rethinking Democracy in the European Union* (London, Routledge, 2012).

25 For a critique see M Poiares Maduro, 'Where to Look for Legitimacy?' in EO Eriksen, JE Fossum and AJ Menéndez (eds), *Constitution Making and Democratic Legitimacy* (2002) ARENA Report 5.

26 BMJ Szewczyk, 'European Citizenship and National Democracy: Contemporary Sources of Legitimacy of the European Union' (2011) 17 *Columbia Journal of European Law* 151; K Nicolaidis, 'The New Constitution as European Demoi-cracy?' (2004) 7(1) *Critical Review of International Social and Political Philosophy*; S Bensson, 'Europe as a Demoi-cratic Polity' (2007) 30(1) *Jurist- og Økonomforbundets Forlag Retfaerd* 116; PL Lindseth, 'Equilibrium, Demoi-cracy, and Delegation in the Crisis of European Integration' (2014) 15(4) *German Law Journal*.

27 *Ex multis*, M Avbelj and J Komarek (eds), *Constitutional Pluralism in the European Union and Beyond* (Oxford, Hart Publishing, 2012).

28 A Stone Sweet, *Governing with Judges: Constitutional Politics in Europe* (Oxford, Oxford University Press, 2004); M. Bobek, *Comparative Reasoning in European Supreme Courts* (Oxford, Oxford University Press, 2013); A Vauchez, 'The Transnational Politics of Judicialization. Van Gend en Loos and the Making of EU Polity' (2010) 16(1) *European Law Journal*.

29 A Dashwood, *Reviewing Maastricht, Issues for the 1996 IGC* (London, Sweet & Maxwell, 1996) 7; A Arnull, C Barnard, M Dougan and E Spaventa (eds), *A Constitutional Order of States? Essays in EU Law in Honour of Alan Dashwood* (Oxford, Hart Publishing, 2011).

relational phenomenon[30] underpinned by liberty: it requires one's own idea of *positive liberty* elaborated without *domination*; *interference* with one's own *positive liberty* that results from majoritarian choice can then be accepted if it is balanced out by continuity of the relationship with the other(s) as an integral part of one's own *positive liberty*. The prerequisite of liberty for a lasting union is illustrated by analogy between Loyalty and Love: both result in a self-perceived conception of *positive liberty* in the union with the others(s). This model shows how through interest representation, balancing and protection in the course of the political process a lasting Union can be built through law.

2. LEGITIMACY OF THE UNION AND THE PARADOX OF POLITY

Where policy choices are made at the Union level (the EU has regulatory powers) and bind national polities (through primacy and direct effect) against their preferred choice, the peoples of Europe need to accept not only the expansion of powers and borders of the Union, but also the expansion of their polities from national level to the EU.

> In terms of democratic theory, the final objective of a unifying polity is to recoup the loss of democracy inherent in the process of integration. This 'loss' is recouped when the social fabric and discourse are such that the electorate accepts the new boundary of the polity and then accepts totally the legitimacy—in its social dimension—of being subjected to majority rule in a much larger system comprised of the integrated polities.[31]

Without a perception of the Union as a unified polity,[32] concerns over legitimacy of majoritarian choices soar.[33]

The reasons for the Union's 'legitimacy deficit' are two structural changes that were introduced in the Single European Act and the Maastricht Treaty and

[30] On Loyalty as a legal principle of EU law see M Klamert, *The Principle of Loyalty in EU Law* (Oxford, Oxford University Press, 2014).

[31] JHH Weiler, 'The Transformation of Europe' (1991) 100 *Yale Law Journal* 2472.

[32] Although the majority of Europeans feel that they are citizens of the EU, the overwhelming majority consistently perceive themselves first of all as nationals of their Member States—as members of their national polities. The fraction of Union citizens who see themselves first as Europeans and only then nationals of their Member States remains insignificant (and similar to the rate of mobility of Union citizens between Member States). See Standard Eurobarometer 83 (Spring 2015) *Public Opinion in the European Union*, Section IV, Standard Eurobarometer 81 (Spring 2014) *European Citizenship*, 10; Standard Eurobarometer 80 (Autumn 2013) *European Citizenship*, 29–39; Eurobarometer Qualitative Study (September 2014) *The Promise of the EU*, 12.

[33] *Ex multis*, G De Burca, 'The Quest for Legitimacy in the European Union' (1996) 59(3) *MLR*; K Lenaerts and M Desomer, 'New Models of Constitution-Making in Europe: The Quest for Legitimacy' (2002) 39 *CML Rev*; SC Sieberson, 'The Treaty of Lisbon and Its Impact on the European Union's Democratic Deficit' (2008) 14 *Columbia Journal of European Law* 445; J Priban, 'The Self-Referential European Polity, its Legal Context and Systemic Differentiation: Theoretical Reflections on the Emergence of the EU's Political and Legal Autopoiesis' (2009) 15(4) *European Law Journal*; N Walker, 'Europe's Constitutional Momentum and the Search for Polity Legitimacy' (2005) 3(2 & 3) *International Journal of Constitutional Law*; JC Piris, *The Lisbon Treaty. A Legal and Political Analysis* (Cambridge, Cambridge University Press, 2010) 112.

elaborated in subsequent Treaty amendments. The first concerns the reach of Union policies and powers and can be termed as policy interdependence.[34] Policy interdependence takes place independently from the decision-making procedure at Union level (unanimity, consensus or QMV) and refers to the factual capacity of each national polity to regulate within its jurisdiction (to implement a policy choice). This capacity can be undermined as a result of externalities and interdependence between the national polities created by European integration, whereby regulatory decisions by one polity may affect the regulatory capacity of the other. A good example of policy interdependence are the Schengen area and the euro, where immigration and budgetary decisions respectively of one Member State may produce effects on the policies pursued by another Member State. The problem caused by policy interdependence can be resolved by shifting policy making from the national level to the EU. National polities and national political processes would then lend their legitimacy to the Union and its policies (through Article 10(2) Treaty on European Union (TEU)) as long as these are adopted by unanimity or consensus. In return, the increased regulatory capacity of Member States in the Union increases the legitimacy of the national political process.

The second structural evolution of the Union that gives rise to legitimacy concerns is the method of decision making, which causes polity interdependence. The departure from unanimity in the making of policy choices[35] implies that Union policies no longer derive legitimacy from the national political process because individual Member States may find themselves bound against the preferred choice as it emerged from the national political process. This creates interdependence between the national and European levels of decision making, between the national and European political processes. On the one hand, the legitimacy of the resulting European policy choice will be linked to the legitimacy of choices made within each national polity. On the other hand, legitimacy of the national political process is undermined because the national polity can be bound against its will; an alternative source of legitimacy is needed on the Union level to compensate for this loss. Several options are available for this alternative legitimacy source:

1. *Messianic or promise legitimacy* corresponds to the original promise of Europe to deliver peace and prosperity to its peoples.[36] To the extent that this promise is fulfilled, this type of legitimacy is exhausted[37] and transformed into output or result legitimacy.
2. *Substantive or output legitimacy* links the acceptance of public power to the results that this power achieves. It is also the extent to which the polity is

[34] Chronologically, this is the second element that gained prominence with the abolition of internal borders and the introduction of the single currency.

[35] Although QMV was foreseen already in the original 1957 EEC Treaty, it was not exercised until the 1986 Single European Act.

[36] Recital 8, Preamble to the 1957 EEC Treaty; Schuman Declaration (Paris, 9 May 1950).

[37] JHH Weiler, 'The Political and Legal Culture of European Integration: An Exploratory Essay' (2011) 9(3–4) *International Journal of Constitutional Law* 683.

capable of autonomous self-governance.[38] Output legitimacy will be high for popular measures that achieve their promised results and low for unpopular policies or failure to deliver. The onset of the financial crisis and unpopular austerity measures have undermined this source of legitimacy.

3. *Formal legitimacy or consent* describes whether the powers were constituted and laws enacted following formal rules, procedures, and constitutional guarantees. It is the legalistic side of process legitimacy that does not necessarily translate into acceptance of the resulting rules.[39] Lack of compliance with the letter and spirit of the Treaties would undermine this legitimacy source.
4. *Process or input legitimacy* seeks to achieve the acceptance of public power through interest representation and participation in the political process. The idea is to give voice to polity members, whom public power is there to serve. Such reforms as citizens' initiative and subsidiarity review by national parliaments seek to further process legitimacy; low turnout of voters in the EP elections, on the contrary, undermines it. Process legitimacy, to be effective, needs to be backed up by accountability.
5. *Political legitimacy or accountability* is the capacity of citizens to remove the government from power when the latter no longer represents their voice.[40] This mechanism aims to ensure that the government acts in the interest of its citizens and does not abuse power. An example of an EU arrangement aimed to raise this type of legitimacy is the nomination of *Spitzenkandidaten* in the 2014 EP elections,[41] when 'giving a face to EP elections'[42] aimed to create a 'difference to Europe and in Europe whether and how the people vote for the European Parliament'.[43]

[38] N Walker, 'Constitutionalizing Enlargement, Enlarging Constitutionalism' (2003) 9(3) *European Law Journal* 368, citing F Scharpf, *Governing in Europe: Effective and Democratic?* (Oxford, Oxford University Press, 1999) ch 1.

[39] Weiler (n 31) 2469.

[40] JHH Weiler, U Haltern, F Mayer, *European Democracy and its Critique: Five Uneasy Pieces* (1995) EUI Working Paper RSC No. 95/11, 9: 'In its present state, no one who votes in the European elections has a strong sense at all of affecting critical policy choices at the European level and certainly not of confirming or rejecting European governance'.

[41] On the constitutionality of this arrangement see A Kocharov, 'Constitutional Complexities of European Democracy in Light of the 2014 EP Elections', Europa-Institut der Universität des Saarlandes, *Zeitschrift für Europarechtliche Studien* 4/2014.

[42] J Borrell Fontelles, 'The Future Role of the European Parliament' in L Tsoukalis and JA Emmanouilidis (eds), *The Delphic Oracle on Europe: Is There a Future for the European Union?* (Oxford, Oxford University Press, 2011) 54.

[43] For analysis of the 'opportunities and possible risks related to prospect of turning the European elections into personalized contest for the presidency of the European Commission' see JHH Weiler, 'Challenges to Electoral Participation in the European Elections of 2014. Restoring Electoral Faith: Prospects and Risks' in *Strengthening European Democracy: Citizens' Participation. Which Challenges Do We Face at the European Elections of 2014?* (2013) Brussels, European Parliament AFCO Report doc. PE 493.036.

6. *Adjudicative legitimacy* corresponds to the capacity of polity members to enforce limited government in court, in particular through the protection of the individual from the state and minorities from majorities.[44] It can also be linked to the principle of limited government, whereby the exercise of public power is thus restricted so as to ensure 'that the few do not rule over the many but, at the same time, … guarantee that the many will not abuse of their power over the few'.[45] Directly effective rights of Union citizens secured in the Treaties raise this type of legitimacy in the EU.
7. *Social legitimacy* is the result of all the previous methods of increasing the authority of public power and corresponds to 'the overall support for and stability of the polity in question as a self-standing "political community"'.[46] It is reflected in public opinion surveys[47] and in the actual acceptance of the resulting norms.[48] Here, the surveys are worrying: in 2013, only 39 per cent of Europeans expressed trust in the European Parliament while 48 per cent distrusted it; 12 per cent said that they expect nothing from the EU.[49]

The first two types of legitimacy require convergence across the European polities as to the purpose and desired outcomes of European integration. However, even when such a convergence is present (for less controversial and politically sensitive policies), attainment of the promise or failure to deliver, unpopularity of measures (no matter how necessary and beneficial in the long run) or disagreement over equally viable options undermine these types of legitimacy.

The three types of legitimacy that follow—formal, process and political legitimacy—require self-perception of citizens as a polity, a group by the reference to which they accept majority rule. Two alternatives for constructing these types of legitimacy in the Union can be envisaged. First, through institutional arrangements EU law could further representation of national polities in the Union. This, however, does not address the deeper problem posed by QMV: even if representation of Member State polities in the Union were perfect, the members of these

[44] Poiares Maduro (n 2); G de Búrca and O Gerstenberg, 'The Denationalization of Constitutional Law' (2006) 47(1) *Harvard International Law Journal*.

[45] Poiares Maduro (n 25), citing N Komesar, *Imperfect Alternatives. Choosing Institutions in Law, Economics, and Public Policy* (Chicago, IL, University of Chicago Press, 1994).

[46] Walker (n 38) 369.

[47] Weiler (n 31) 2469; JHH Weiler, 'Europe in Crisis—On "Political Messianism", "Legitimacy" and the "Rule of Law"' [2012] *Singapore Journal of Legal Studies* 248.

[48] What Tuori calls 'empirical legitimacy', see K Tuori, *Critical Legal Positivism* (Aldershot, Ashgate, 2002) 244; H Haukeland Fredriksen, 'Bridging the Widening Gap between the EU Treaties and the Agreement on the European Economic Area' (2012) 18(6), *European Law Journal* 876. See also FW Scharpf, *Interdependence and Democratic Legitimation* (1998) MPIfG working paper no 98/2: 'when we speak of "democratic legitimacy," the reference must be to arguments that can be used to justify the exercise of governing authority—i.e., of the authority to adopt collectively binding decisions, to implement these with resources taken from the members of the collectivity, and ultimately by resort to the state's monopoly of legitimate coercion'.

[49] Standard Eurobarometer 80 (n 32) 7.

polities would still need to accept that on some occasions they would be bound against their preferred choice: 'The legitimacy crisis does not derive principally from the accountability issue at the European level, but from the very redefinition of the European polity'.[50] Second, and alternatively to representation through national polities, a unified European political process could be built in order to ensure these three types of legitimacy directly at Union level, bypassing the compromised national political processes. Progressive empowerment of the EP, Union citizenship, and citizens' initiative are all examples of such attempts. These efforts fail because they are based on the presumption that a European polity already exists. Only when there is a polity will a well-functioning political process further acceptance of majoritarian rule. Yet, the peoples of Europe do not perceive that they 'belong to the Union' and that the Union belongs to them.[51] This mismatch between the institutional mechanisms for interest representation and the self-perception of people undermines the authority of governance both at Union and national level. There appears to be no way around the national polity.

Adjudicative legitimacy of the Union is based on an even greater presumption about the nature of Union law. Beyond mere primacy and direct effect, and in addition to there being a European polity with a corresponding European political process, for Union law to secure adjudicative legitimacy it would need to have a constitutional soul: it would need to regulate and restrict the political process as opposed to being shaped by it. Only if such a soul is present, can adjudicative legitimacy be ensured through the operation of Union law. If, on the other hand, the substance of Union law is but a product of the political process then both primacy and direct effect can be overridden by changing the rules; no more constitutional nature, this is mere international law.

Social legitimacy encapsulates the paradox of polity. On the one hand, it is based on all the previous forms of legitimacy, the combined function of which is to ensure that the political process furthers the interests of all polity members; on the other hand, it describes the acceptance of majority rule by a minority whose preference for policy choice diverges. Social legitimacy thus reflects the self-perception of polity members as a legitimate unified group—a polity—for the purpose of majority rule: an agreement on 'which constituency is appropriate and apt to put things in common' and the extent and domains in which it is prepared to do so.[52] Acceptance of polity by all polity members is linked to the capacity of this polity to further their interests—yet, this acceptance results in the minority forgoing its own interest in favour of majority choice. This paradox of Loyalty (to a polity) was captured by Hirschman in the Voice-Exit-Loyalty model.

[50] Weiler (n 31) 2473.

[51] Weiler (n 9) 333; see also: G Palombella, 'Whose Europe? After the Constitution: A Goal-based Citizenship' (2005) 3(2-3) *International Journal of Constitutional Law* 357–82.

[52] Walker (n 33) 215; see also J Habermas, 'Citizenship and National Identity: Some Reflections on the Future of Europe' in B van Steenbergen (ed), *The Condition of Citizenship* (London, Sage Publications, 1994).

3. CAPTURING THE PARADOX: VOICE, EXIT AND LOYALTY

The Voice-Exit-Loyalty model by Hirschman captures acceptance of groups, organisations and states.[53] The model is based on the presumption that individuals value their own interest and their ability to further it within a group leads to continued membership and to acceptance of the group's choices. The foreclosure of Exit (for instance, the lack of alternatives) will cause higher propensity to exercise Voice (efforts to further one's own interest within the group). Conversely, decreasing ability to influence policy choice (Voice) may cause disengagement or partial Exit from the group and the choices it makes. Impossibility or inefficacy of Voice will cause complete Exit. In the words of Weiler, 'Exit is the mechanism of organizational abandonment in the face of unsatisfactory performance. Voice is the mechanism of intraorganisational correction and recuperation'.[54]

Loyalty forecloses Exit in the face of a decrease in Voice. As a result of Loyalty, the 'decisional changes affecting Voice will not cause a corresponding adjustment to Exit'.[55] Unsatisfactory performance in terms of furthering one's own interest will no longer trigger immediate Exit but it will see Exit postponed through the onset of Loyalty.

This accurately describes acceptance of majority rule. Participants in the political process seek to promote their own interest within the polity or opt out of the resulting rules when they do not further their interest. Thus, when a polity fails to further the interests of its members (messianic and output types of legitimacy), to protect these interests (adjudicative legitimacy or withdrawal of interests from the political process through constitutional rights), and to take them into account (formal and input types of legitimacy that correspond to interest representation), polity members will seek Exit from the resulting policy choice by refusing to condone those who made it (accountability) and to comply with the resulting rules (social legitimacy). We can therefore associate partial Exit with accountability of public power;[56] complete Exit with low social legitimacy and non-participation in the political process, the legal system and policy choice; Voice with all the interest-centred types of legitimacy (messianic, process, output, formal and adjudicative); and Loyalty with acceptance of majority rule. A series of choices that consistently undermine the interests of all or some polity members will affect legitimacy of the corresponding polity and its political process as a whole. The contrary is also true: when a polity and its political process are perceived as providing Voice (input, formal and adjudicative types of legitimacy), the outvoted minority does not exercise Exit from the majority choice despite its interest being defeated (low output legitimacy).

53 AO Hirschman, *Voice, Exit, Loyalty* (Cambridge, MA, Harvard University Press, 1970).

54 Weiler (n 31) 2411. Weiler used this model to explain behaviour of Member States in the Council as primacy and direct effect of Union law led to a partial closure of Exit.

55 ibid 2466.

56 JHH Weiler, '60 Years since the First European Community—Reflections on Political Messianism' (2011) 22(2) *European Journal of International Law* 303.

With the expansion of polity (the group by the reference to which majority is determined) to include additional members, each member's Voice is bound to fall. In the EU, this happened in two ways. First, the abolition of veto in the Council and the changing role of the Commission[57] caused a fall in interest protection for each individual European polity, while the passage to QMV decreased Voice or input legitimacy for polities in the Council.[58] Second, the passage of new policy fields from national to the European level reduced the Voice of individual polity members, while the arrangement under which the party winning the EP elections nominates the president of the Commission annihilated the Voice of those citizens who come from small Member States or vote for minority parties.[59] At the same time, the possibilities of Exit, either complete (from the Union)[60] or partial (from individual policy areas and choices),[61] increased, rendering Exit not only possible but likely as the ability to satisfy the interests of all the 28 diverse polities (output legitimacy) falls. All this increased the importance of Loyalty for the legitimacy of EU law.

Hirschman does not link Loyalty to legitimacy. He understands Loyalty in cost-benefit terms: 'the most loyalist behaviour retains an enormous dose of reasoned calculation'.[62] For Hirschman, Loyalty is a cost on Exit, and he suggests is can be an *external* cost: 'High fees for entering an organization and stiff penalties for exit are among the main devices generating or reinforcing loyalty in such a way as to repress either exit or voice or both'.[63] For him, 'usefulness of loyalty depends on the closeness of available substitutes',[64] leading to the conclusion that 'Loyalty to one's country … is something we could do without, since countries can ordinarily be considered to be well-differentiated products'.[65] Applying this logic to the EU, heterogeneity among European polities in linguistic, cultural and other terms will increase the propensity to exercise Voice on the national level and lower the propensity of Exit from the national polities towards other European polities

[57] Which is being transformed from being an impartial safeguarding of Community interest and the interest of small Member States into a political body shaped by the outcome of elections to the EP, see A Wille, 'The Politicization of the EU Commission: Democratic Control and the Dynamics of Executive Selection' (2012) 78(3) *International Review of Administrative Sciences*.

[58] Weiler (n 9) 348–49.

[59] A Kocharov, 'In the Image of State: Constitutional Complexities Of Engineering a European Democracy' in F Fabbrini, E Hirsch Ballin and H Somsen (eds), *What Form of Government for the European Union and the Eurozone?* (Oxford, Hart Publishing, 2015).

[60] Article 50 EU.

[61] eg Ireland, the UK and Denmark enjoy derogations from the Area of Freedom, Security and Justice; instruments of international law are being used to solve problems of Union policies such as the euro and sovereign debt, which both amount to Exit from the EU legal order and leave Exit from the compact more open as compared to the possibility of Exit from EU law, see A Kocharov (ed,) *Another Legal Monster? An EUI Debate on the Fiscal Compact Treaty* (2012) European University Institute working paper LAW 2012/09.

[62] Hirschman (n 53) 79.

[63] ibid 93.

[64] ibid 80.

[65] ibid 81.

(or, indeed, towards European polity) despite the facilitation of such Exit in EU law through free movement rights and institutional arrangements for exercising Voice at Union level. Loyalty to the national polities will remain high while the possibility of Loyalty among polities (cross-polity Loyalty of Union citizens or acceptance by Union citizens of a unified European polity as a reference group for majoritarian choice) is uncertain.

Limiting Loyalty to functional non-Exit rather than substance (the interest it protects) explains neither acceptance of immediate loss of interest occurring to the outvoted minority as a result of majority rule nor acceptance of groups from which Exit is 'unthinkable' even in the face of a decrease in Voice.[66] As to the former, while exercising Voice instead of Exit may fulfil the hope of 'reform from within' sometime *in the future*—to influence the outcome and further one's own interest the next time a policy choice is made—this does not explain why Exit should not occur *now*, on the particular instance of losing one's own interest to majority rule. Concerning the latter, if Loyalty is a mere practical impossibility of Exit, then what if Exit becomes possible even from a family, tribe or state? Will Loyalty to a family or tribe always translate into acceptance and non-Exit no matter how limited the Voice—and does it then amount to unconditional acceptance?

Hirschman's model does not explain the paradox of Loyalty. On the one hand, the cost-benefit conception recognises the importance for Loyalty of one's own interest; on the other hand, it sees Loyalty as reluctance to pursue one's own interest elsewhere even as the ability to pursue it within the group fades. From this tension, Loyalty emerges as an alternative to the interest that is lost through the decline in Voice and output legitimacy, suggesting it is another form of interest: interest in group membership and relationship with the other(s). The value of this interest, perceived subjectively by the individual who is loyal, places an additional cost on Exit delaying it vis-a-vis the decline in Voice. For a mere hope of gain in the future cannot explain a loss in interest now. Rather, Loyalty must exist at every moment when majoritarian choice is accepted: at each opportunity to Exit from this choice. This is why a thicker understanding of Loyalty involves seeing it as the pursuit of the individual's interest and as an exercise of Liberty, tied to legitimacy through Liberty and inseparable from it. Indeed, the central role reserved to the individual's interest in the Voice-Exit-Loyalty model indicates the conception of individuals as rational beings who value their autonomy and seek to further it in their relationships with each other. This is, in effect, one of the main tenets of liberalism, which 'is now broadly endorsed in some form or other by the vast majority of citizens and politicians in all European democracies—indeed, in all democratic

[66] Hirschman does not explain how Loyalty works in families, tribes and states; he mentions that some of these groupings limit Voice by instituting rules for expulsion or excommunication—this creates a system where Exit is unthinkable and Voice is limited—Hirschman then concludes that for the purposes of his analysis he needs 'an organization where exit and voice both hold important roles', ibid 76–77.

states worldwide'.[67] The Voice-Exit-Loyalty model describes majoritarian liberal democracy. All EU Member States are liberal democracies and it is reasonable to expect that what gives legitimacy to the national political process will be required for legitimacy of the European political process, too. Liberty is therefore central to understanding Loyalty. Without valuing Liberty, Loyalty is impossible and the legitimacy question does not arise.

4. THE THREE ASPECTS OF LIBERTY

Drawing on the history of Western political thought, Skinner identifies three aspects of liberty that complement one another: negative liberty, positive liberty, and liberty from domination.[68] For the purposes of this analysis, it makes sense to invert Skinner's order and begin with positive liberty, which is most closely linked to what was understood as 'interest' in the Voice-Exit-Loyalty model and to the legitimacy overview that preceded it.

Positive liberty is the ability to achieve one's own ideal or most fulfilling way of life, one's own subjective interest. 'Positive liberty is the belief that human nature has an essence, and that we are free if and only if we succeed in realizing that essence in our lives'.[69] 'Liberty consists of following that way of life in which, all passion spent, we finally achieve harmony with our nature'.[70] To comply with positive liberty 'the action freely chosen is one that the agent can own, thinking: this bears my signature, this is *me*'.[71] It follows that 'there will be as many different interpretations of positive liberty as there are different views about the moral character of humankind'.[72] However, 'the attraction of a specific way of life' can create 'an interest in and affective attachment to a particular ethos'.[73]

Negative liberty or *non-interference* is freedom from interference and restriction by others. The very idea of *interference* implies two things. First, that the individual has her own interest or her own idea of *positive liberty*: one cannot interfere with something that does not exist. Second, that the interference is external to the individual and restricts her ability to exercise *positive liberty*: not only does the individual not follow the choice she made in the pursuit of her ideal life, but she does so as a result of circumstances external to herself. This can be force majeure or, in a society, circumstances that are derived from the relationship with the other(s). In the latter case, negative liberty will be regained by Exit from the relationship of interference; the main function of law is to prevent Exit or render it unnecessary

[67] R Bellamy and C Attucci, 'Normative Theory and the EU: between Contract and Community in European Integration Theory' in A Wiener and T Diez (eds), *European Integration Theory* (Oxford, Oxford University Press, 2009) 201.

[68] Q Skinner, *A Third Concept of Liberty* [2002] Proceedings of the British Academy 117.

[69] ibid 242.

[70] ibid 243.

[71] P Pettit, *Theory of Freedom. From the Psychology to the Politics of Agency* (Cambridge, Polity Press, 2001) 6: Pettit calls it *liberty from domination* (rather than *liberty from dependence*).

[72] Skinner (n 68) 242.

[73] J Habermas, 'Why Europe Needs a Constitution' (2001) 11 *New Left Review* 8.

by limiting interference of individuals with each other's interests in acceptable ways. Voice can also remedy interference by negotiating the action of the interfering agent in a way that respects the individual's own *positive liberty*. Even in the absence of interference, its very possibility—impossibility of Voice and Exit—constitutes another impediment to liberty: dependence or domination.

Liberty from dependence on the arbitrary will and power of other(s)—*liberty from domination*—is independent of whether any interference actually takes place: a mere possibility of interference may limit the capacity of the individual to achieve her perceived *positive liberty*,[74] her conception of 'ideal life'.[75] 'Freedom is restricted not only by actual interference or the threat of it, but also by the mere knowledge that we are living in dependence on the goodwill of others'.[76] This way, *liberty from domination* is linked to the rule of law and coherence of the legal order. Domination occurs in the presence of a potential external power that may be exercised to interfere with *positive liberty* in an arbitrary way, without taking the individual's interest into account; it is, in essence, the absence of Voice or of the risk of being arbitrarily deprived of the possibility to influence the outcome.

Hirschman connects Loyalty to all the three aspects of Liberty. First, the very existence of Loyalty 'is predicated on the possibility of exit', of being disloyal.[77] In other words, Loyalty is a choice to forgo *non-interference* with one's own *positive liberty*. Second, the Exit option is exercised when 'the individual member is likely to have a low estimate of his influence on the organization'—there is no Voice.[78] The essence of Voice is to ensure that the individual's interests are taken into account, linking to *liberty from domination*. Third, if the dissatisfied individual continues to value the 'output' of the group even when absence of Voice would prescribe Exit she will seek to avoid the 'prospective damage which would be inflicted on [the exiting individual] as a prospective nonmember' by exercising 'loyalist behavior'.[79] In this third case, the individual places an additional value on membership in a group, on her relationship with the other(s). This value—Loyalty—places a cost on Exit when membership in the group is seen as a separate benefit, a part of the individual's perceived *positive liberty*. The individual seeks a balance between the three aspects of liberty so that when membership in a group or relationship with the other(s) constitutes a part of individual's *positive liberty*, this value of the relationship may compensate, at least to a degree, for *interference* with another aspect of *positive liberty* (the individual's preference for a particular policy choice). Exit from the group represents a loss of the part of one's own *positive liberty* that is associated with Loyalty, which is compared to staying in the group at the cost of the other part of one's own *positive liberty*, associated with

[74] P Pettit, *Republicanism: A Theory of Freedom and Government* (Oxford, Oxford University Press, 1999).

[75] This idea is traceable to Aristotle; here borrowed from CJ Galipeau, *Isaiah Berlin's Liberalism* (Oxford, Clarendon Press, 1994) 70.

[76] Skinner (n 68) 247.

[77] Hirschman (n 53) 82.

[78] ibid 83.

[79] ibid 100–03.

policy choice (short-term loss of Voice or ability to attain preferred policy choice). The area inside the triangle (Figure 1.1) represents liberty or absence of domination, when all the three aspects of liberty are present to various degrees.

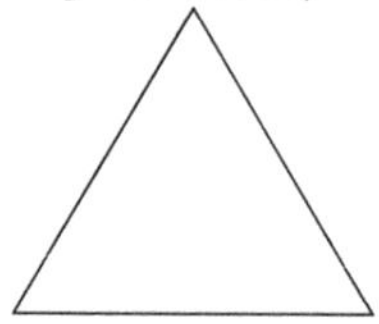

Figure 1.1: Voice, Exit, Loyalty and the three aspects of liberty

The link between Loyalty and liberty finally explains majoritarian rule. For the outvoted minority within a polity, the combination of political rights and constitutional guarantees may secure attainment of their interest (a component of *positive liberty*) only *in the future*, the next time a choice is made; in the particular instance, majority rule implies that minority will lose *liberty from domination* (effectiveness of Voice) to pursue its preferred vision of ideal life. At least in the short run, abstention from Exit (which would secure *negative liberty*) in a situation of decreasing Voice (resulting in *domination*) cannot be explained by mere hopes for 'another chance'. It can, however, be explained by Loyalty—that part of one's own *positive liberty* that sees preserving one's relationship with the other(s) (with the majority, in this case) as an integral part of one's own ideal life. In situations of majoritarian rule, the only way to preserve liberty without Exit (thus forgoing *negative liberty*) and without Voice (amounting to *dependence* of the outvoted minority on the majority), is if the majority choice coincides with *positive liberty* of the minority in such a way that gains in *positive liberty* resulting from non-Exit at least compensate for the loss of Voice. If continued relationship with the majority is an integral part of the ideal life as perceived by the minority, the latter can accept majoritarian choice as its 'own'. The minority will then balance between two components of its own *positive liberty*: a particular preference for policy choice versus continuing relationship with the majority.[80]

[80] Other authors have noted the trade-off between one's own policy preference and continuity of relationship with the other, albeit not constructing it as an integral part of one's own *positive liberty*, see A Somek, *Individualism* (Oxford, Oxford University Press, 2008) 17: 'political authority derives from the mutual realization that inasmuch as one lives communally, that is together with others, one has to conceive of oneself from the perspective of all others and, indeed, as a stranger to oneself'; Weiler (n 9) 338: Loyalty 'is not only a passive value: to be accepted. It is also active: to accept'. Similarly to love, Loyalty implies respect for the liberty of the other.

Note that Loyalty is not a penalty on Exit imposed externally (which would amount to *interference* rather than *positive liberty*) but a cost of Exit that originates in one's own vision of ideal life. Loyalty is a part of one's own subjective *positive liberty* whereby the ideal life includes a continued relationship with the other(s). It is this internalisation of balance between the three aspects of liberty that gives legitimacy to non-Exit in situations characterised by a decrease in Voice, which leads to the acceptance of majority rule. Loyalty to a group, state or an individual helps me 'internalise' their interference as my own *positive liberty*: interference is no longer an external choice, no longer an interference, but *my* choice and *my positive liberty*.[81] The premium value I place on my relationship with those to whom I am loyal leads me to make a choice not to exercise Exit. This implies *my* choice not to pursue my earlier chosen alternative in favour, instead, of majority rule; it is no longer an interference because it corresponds to the other part of my ideal life, the part that associates me with those who made the choice. Both *negative liberty* (real possibility of Exit) and *liberty from domination* (identification of my own ideal way of life with the choice made by the other(s)) are retained.

Loyalty, on this view, requires individual liberty: perceived *liberty from domination* (Voice or the ability to represent and protect one's own interest), real possibility of *negative liberty* (not only should it be possible to Exit from a relationship of interference or domination but there need to be alternatives to this relationship, it must be possible to pursue *positive liberty* elsewhere), and one's own idea of *positive liberty* that is based on the relationship with other(s). Constitutions of liberal democracies are premised on the recognition that we all share one fundamental aspect of *positive liberty*: our preference for life in a community with others. A relationship with the other(s) is central to constitutional orders; only within such a relationship (between two or more individuals) do all the three aspects of liberty fully make sense. Without one's own conception of *positive liberty*, *liberty from interference* and *liberty from domination* cannot exist; without the particular conception of *positive liberty* as relationship with the other(s) (Loyalty), *non-interference* and *non-dependence* become preconditions for *positive liberty*: there can be no legitimate majoritarian rule.

This particular conception of *positive liberty* as ideal life in relationship with the other(s) links Loyalty to legitimacy. In liberal democracies, legitimacy of majoritarian political process, public power and institutions derives from Loyalty among polity members. Only when individual polity members see themselves as a group, a polity, that forms the foundation for each member's subjective vision of ideal life, will the outvoted minority follow the choice made by the majority as part of its own *positive liberty* and without the need for coercion. In order to ensure legitimate majoritarian political process in Europe (and legitimacy of its institutions and public power), European peoples and individual members of European

[81] In other words, the 'willingness to pay and costs *jointly* determine the aggregate level of civic acts', R Cooter, 'Do Good Laws Make Good Citizens? An Economic Analysis of Internalized Norms' (2000) 86(8) *Virginia Law Review* 1590.

polities need to share the conception of *positive liberty* as a continued relationship in the Union. There needs to be Loyalty among the peoples of Europe in order to ensure legitimacy of majoritarian rule. Mere cost-benefit analysis does not create legitimacy because as the interest of the individual (the effectiveness of Voice) declines, the individual will abstain from Exit only where Exit is followed by an externally imposed sanction: without the internalisation that comes with Loyalty, the non-Exit option amounts to domination, which will not be accepted and will therefore lack legitimacy.

The conclusion that Loyalty is connected to subjectively perceived relationships between individuals points to the relevance of psychology for constitutional law. The frequent allegory in constitutional law of passion with politics and constitution with reason[82] corroborates this finding. And while the purpose of law is to infuse reason in passionate humans, understanding the psychology behind human passions is indispensable for reasoning about them.[83] The study and design of constitutional law—the shaping of reason that tames passions—necessarily requires insights into psychology.[84] To the extent that constitutional law regulates politics, ie passions between people, the study of human relationships acquires centre stage.

5. EUROPE'S LOVE TRIANGLE

The deeper sense of attachment or belonging to a shared project that borders our sense of identity arises not only in polities, but also in nations, families and tribes.[85] Perhaps the most intense attachment is the relationship of love. Both Love

[82] J Madison, *The Federalist No 10* (1787); Weiler (n 9); M Poiares Maduro, 'Passion and Reason in European Integration' (2010) lecture Humboldt-Universität, Berlin on 10 February 2010, Walter Hallstein-Institut für Europäisches Verfassungsrecht (FCE 03/10); A Sajó, *Constitutional Sentiments* (Newhaven, CT, Yale University Press, 2011); A Sajó, 'Emotions in Constitutional Design' (2010) 8(3) *International Journal of Constitutional Law* 354–84; in particular, the marriage analogy has been used in relation to integration between states through law, see S Peers, 'Living in Sin: Legal Integration Under the EC-Turkey Customs Union' (1996) 7 *EJIL* 411.

[83] See generally on law and emotions (though none applied to the constitutional realm or the EU): EA Posner, 'Law and the Emotions' (2001) 89 *Georgetown Law Journal* 1977; H Li Feldman, 'Foreword: Law, Psychology, and the Emotions' (2000) 74 *Chicago-Kent Law Review*; DJ Arkush, 'Situating Emotion: A Critical Realist View of Emotion and Nonconscious Cognitive Processes for Law and Legal Theory' [2008] *Brigham Young University Law Review*; K Abramst and H Kerentt, 'Who's Afraid of Law and the Emotions?' (2009–2010) 94 *Minnesota Law Review*; R. Tushnet, 'More Than a Feeling: Emotion and the First Amendment' (2014) 127 *Harvard Law Review*; and C Mala Corbin, 'Emotional Compelled Disclosures' (2014) 127 *Harvard Law Review*.

[84] A Gibbs, 'Taking Agency Seriously: An Examination of Legal Integration and Constitutionalism' in D Augenstein (ed), *Integration Through Law Revisited: The Making of the European Polity* (Aldershot, Ashgate, 2012) 59: the agency of law in European integration is relational and reflects 'the experience we have of our collective political and legal lives'. For a parallel between, on the one hand, relations between humans and, on the other hand, relations between states, albeit from a different angle, see also P Bobbitt, *The Shield of Achilles: War, Peace and the Course of History* (New York, Knopf, 2002) 78–79.

[85] Weiler talks about the 'emotional and psychological attachment' of citizens to a nation, Weiler (n 9) 333.

and Loyalty are connected to the identity of both persons and imply identification between the people. Love causes a 'state of intense longing for a union'[86] or the desire 'to form and constitute a new entity in the world, what might be called a *we*'.[87] Loyalty is based on a sense of belonging to the same group, 'one of the agent's own'.[88] The privileged relationship of reciprocity with the other(s) as a crucial part of one's own *positive liberty* underlies equally the relationship of loyalty to a polity[89] and love between people.[90] In both cases, what is relevant are the perceptions and self-identification by people as part of smaller or larger groups. And while Loyalty to a family member or friend and Loyalty to a polity or a group are different, accepted social (and legal) norms on love reflect the balance between the three aspects of liberty prevailing in the society at any given time. The same balance of liberty must be respected in polities, if this type of union is to last. Identifying the elements that balance between the three aspects of liberty in a smaller group (marriage) could illuminate a more complex one (polity).

Emotional psychology explains the phenomenon of Love. In his triangular theory of love,[91] Sternberg distinguished three components of a loving relationship: intimacy, passion and commitment. These components form a triangle, the area of which represents 'consummate love'. All the three components must be present; with all the three absent, there is no love or 'non-love'.

Passion for Sternberg refers to 'the drives' of physical attraction between people; applied to peoples, it makes sense to talk about *attraction* more generally. According to findings of social psychology, attraction increases with physical proximity, familiarity and similarity between people.[92] Without intimacy and commitment, attraction alone, or 'infatuated love' as Sternberg calls it,[93] is bound to wither. *Passion* with *intimacy* (but no commitment) for Sternberg is 'romantic love' such

[86] RJ Sternberg, 'Construct Validation of a Triangular Love Scale' (1997) 27 *European Journal of Social Psychology* 315.

[87] R Nozick, 'Love's Bond' in *The Examined Life* (New York: Simon and Schuster, 1989) 70.

[88] P Pettit, 'The Paradox of Loyalty' (1988) 25(2) *American Philosophical Quarterly* 168–69.

[89] A Sangiovanni, 'Global Justice, Reciprocity and the State' (2007) 35(1) *Philosophy & Public Affairs* 20: 'obligations of egalitarian reciprocity to fellow citizens and residents in the state, who provide us with the basic conditions and guarantees necessary to develop and act on a plan of life'.

[90] P Pettit, 'Love and its Place in Moral Discourse' in R Lamb (ed), *Love Analyzed* (Boulder, CO, Westview Press, 1997) 153: 'When people develop a relationship as partners in love, one aspect of what happens is that each becomes aware not just of loving, but of being loved, and not just of loving and being loved, but of this being itself a matter registered by both of them'. Reciprocity will become relevant in the following chapter.

[91] RJ Sternberg, 'A Triangular Theory of Love' (1986) 93(2) *Psychological Review* 119–35; 'Triangulating Love' in RJ Sternberg and ML Barnes (eds), *The Psychology of Love* (Newhaven, CT, Yale University Press, 1988) 119–38.

[92] M Hewstone, W Stroebe and K Jonas, *An Introduction to Social Psychology* (British Psychological Society and John Wiley & Sons Ltd, 2012) 368–69; RE Olmstead and PM Bentler, 'Structural Equations Modeling: A New Friend?' in FB Bryant, J Edwards, RS Tindale, EJ Posavac, L Heath, E Henderson-King and Y Suarez-Balcazar (eds), *Methodological Issues in Applied Social Psychology* (New York, Plenum, 1992) 143–44.

[93] RJ Sternberg and K Sternberg, *The Nature of Hate* (Cambridge, Cambridge University Press, 2008) 56.

as between Romeo and Juliet when they first met:[94] through *intimacy*, it may develop Loyalty and lead to *commitment*.

Intimacy for Sternberg 'refers to feelings of closeness, connectedness, and bondedness in loving relationships'.[95] More than familiarity and similarity of circumstance, a relationship based on intimacy is a friendship: similarity of interests and mutual trust lead us to share secrets and do things together both now and in the future: it is an ongoing process. Supplemented by *commitment*, *intimacy* results in a relationship between best friends. Such relationships bear trust and the exercise of Voice between people who are confident they can find solutions and accommodate each other.

Commitment for Sternberg is the willingness to make the relationship binding and maintain it in time by (partially) closing Exit. It can take the form of marriage (a legal bond) or simply a decision that one is in a relationship. A relationship based on commitment alone Sternberg calls 'empty love': this can be the first stage of an arranged marriage or the last stage of a marriage initially based on love. A commitment without intimacy and attraction may develop—if not in love—then in friendship between the spouses. This is so if, once committed, ie with the foreclosure of Exit, intimacy is developed between the partners through the exercise of Voice, so that shared interests and a shared vision of their joint 'ideal life' are developed. 'Greater intimacy may lead to greater passion or commitment, just as greater commitment may lead to greater intimacy, or with lesser likelihood, greater passion'.[96]

By contrast, perpetuating *passion* through foreclosure of Exit is not likely to work. *Passion* with *commitment* (but without intimacy) is fatuous love: without a shared vision of the future and common interests, it is short lived like a 'celebrity marriage'. Here the power of analogy becomes apparent: few would expect longevity from a 'celebrity marriage'; more are ready to see viability in a Union based solely on attraction. Neutralisation of the political process that leads to policy choices about *positive liberty* is equivalent to neutralising intimacy. In the words of Joseph Weiler:

> This neutralization of ideology has fostered the belief that an agenda could be set for the Community, and the Community could be led towards an ever closer union among its peoples, without having to face the normal political cleavages present in the Member States.[97]

The more heterogeneous the interests and opinions of parties to a union, the more problematic the absence of intimacy or politics. Expanding EU policies into the fields where national polities diverge on their perceptions of positive liberty and

[94] Example borrowed from P Salovey, Yale Courses, available at www.youtube.com/watch?v=kZoBgX8rScg.

[95] Sternberg (n 86) 315.

[96] ibid.

[97] Weiler (n 31) 2476.

the circumstances that shape these perceptions necessarily requires a political process for the development of shared—and accepted—policy choice.

One possible reason for this failure is the conflation of attraction with intimacy. So for instance Habermas writes:

> Democratic self-determination can only come about if the population of a state is transformed into a nation of citizens who take their political destiny into their own hands. The political mobilization of 'subjects,' however, depends on a prior cultural integration of what is initially a number of people who have been thrown together with each other. This desideratum is fulfilled by the idea of the nation, with whose help the members of a state construct a new form of collective identity beyond their inherited loyalties to village, family, place, or clan. The cultural symbolism of 'a people' secures its own particular character, its 'spirit of the people,' in the presumed commonalities of descent, language, and history, and in this way generates a unity, even if only an imaginary one. It thereby makes the residents of a single state-controlled territory aware of a collective belonging that, until then, had been merely abstract and legal. Only the symbolic construction of 'a people' makes the modern state into a nation-state.[98]

Yet, there is a difference between the factors that form a nation (descent, language, history, etc) and 'cultural integration' that enables 'political mobilization' and collective taking of their own 'political destiny into their own hands'. The former are elements that create 'attraction' while the latter (the political culture) is the element that enables 'intimacy' and can, indeed, be built through law:

> [T]he empirical circumstances necessary for an extension of [the] process of identity formation beyond national boundaries ... are: the emergence of a European civil society; the construction of a European-wide public sphere; and the shaping of a political culture that can be shared by all European citizens.[99]

Harmonisation through law and the setting of common standards without a shared vision of *positive liberty* developed through Voice (intimacy) result in the negation of liberty—and in Loyalty that fails to arise—leaving Exit as the only alternative that would at least secure *negative liberty*.

Applying these principles of psychology to a union among peoples, a perfect 'Union among the peoples of Europe', would have the participants voluntarily abstain from Exit and accept legitimacy of each other's choice. The European Communities were born out of *attraction* rooted in geographic proximity and similarity of goals. The bases for *attraction* among the peoples of Europe are listed in the preambles to the Treaties establishing the European Coal and Steel Community (1951) and European Economic Community (1957): the founding 'countries' shared a history of war and broken economies in need of reconstruction; their 'destiny henceforward shared' was based on a common 'ideal' of peace, liberty and economic development, to be attained 'by establishing a common market'.[100]

[98] J Habermas, *The Postnational Constellation* (Cambridge, Polity Press, 1998) 64.

[99] Habermas (n 73) 16.

[100] All these found as late as EC Treaty (2000), eg Article 2 EC; some changes were made in the Lisbon Treaty, see Chapter 3.

Development of primacy and direct effect (the binding nature of EC law) turned this relationship into a *commitment*, although only in 'limited fields'.

Geographic proximity and similarity of circumstances uniting the founding Member States can be contrasted with the diversity of peoples in the Union after the 2004 enlargement; war between Member States has become unthinkable, and economies, however fragile, are nowhere close to the devastation following WWII. This change in circumstances withers *attraction* and increases conflict potential between the peoples of Europe, who remain united through their *commitment* in law. Especially for smaller polities, Exit is limited due to the limited possibilities to pursue *positive liberty* elsewhere: there is no real alternative to the EU. Europe's Union thus becomes an arranged marriage, based on commitment and high Exit costs that are independent of one's own *positive liberty*. In traditional cultures, arranged marriage may be a first step on the road to intimacy because it forecloses Exit through high societal costs of divorce. However, in liberal Western societies, the opposite is true: commitment without intimacy and passion is the last stage of unions that persist only due to externally imposed cost of Exit (eg higher costs of living alone, the perceived convenience of raising children together, etc). The Treaties commit Member States and their peoples, yet more is required to make the Union last. Through a dialogue of *intimacy*, whereby their own subjective ideas of *positive liberty* are negotiated and furthered, peoples may develop new shared visions of ideal life; this builds up Loyalty and prevents Exit in situations of diluted Voice. Developing Loyalty requires retention of their own *positive liberty* and elaboration of shared ideas of ideal life that enrich, not annihilate, their own liberty.

Loyalty in the sense of willingness to abstain from Exit, thereby forgoing our own interest, is related to how dear the other is to us.[101] Pettit successfully argued that Love attachment relates to the identity of the beloved rather than any virtue that Love may represent.[102] We do not love a person because s/he is worthy or because we believe in love as such—if it were so, all those who share same ideals of worthiness or dedication to Love would love the same person(s), which is clearly not the case. Neither Love nor Loyalty arise 'on the neutral ground that this will testify to the value of love, or on the neutral ground that this will help the most attractive person in the area, or on the agent-relative ground that it will help someone that [we] happen to love'.[103] Rather, we are loyal to and love a particular person, not any abstract concept such as the Union, marriage, Loyalty or Love. Because of the irrelevance of virtues for Loyalty and Love, this aspect of *positive liberty* is compatible 'with severe reservations' about the worth of the person(s) to whom we are attached. Herein lies the special value of such relationships, which justifies a preferential attitude towards a particular person as a universally accepted

[101] The degree to which we are willing to compromise our own interest for the interest of our loved one might also be genetically determined: D Schoebi, BM Way, BR Karney and TN Bradbury, 'Genetic Moderation of Sensitivity to Positive and Negative Affect in Marriage' (2012) 12(2) *Emotion*.

[102] Pettit (n 90) 158.

[103] Pettit (n 88) 168.

and understandable phenomenon.[104] Both Love and Loyalty lead to union as a universally recognised value—as opposed to virtue.

This conclusion has far-reaching consequences for polity-like relationships construed in law. A good European parallel between commitments based on virtue and on value is the contrast between the Council of Europe with its ECHR and the EU with its Treaties. The former is a union of virtue, a commitment to human rights as such, independently of who happens to be their holder. No preferential relationship is thereby established among the peoples of the Council of Europe but they all commit to a shared virtue, namely the protection of human rights. The ECHR is based on commitment to virtue and does not give rise to any significant degree of Loyalty among the parties. EU Treaties, on the other hand, establish an 'autonomous legal order',[105] a special relationship that is recognised as a value by others. The existence of such a union among the peoples of Europe justifies, including to the external observer,[106] a difference between the treatment that the peoples in this union accord each other versus the treatment of outsiders. Europe's Union must be a value, a part of a self-perceived *positive liberty* linked to its own identity and that of the other peoples of Europe.

Unions are different from virtues. We do not rationalise our desire to form a union with other person(s) because we like unions as such; it might be practical to have a union but this practical understanding will not create a preferential attitude, a desire to 'form a we', a special bond of Loyalty to another. Practicality of the Union (or output legitimacy) imposes an external cost on Exit, not necessarily integrating the Union into one's own perception of ideal life. The failure of Europe to instil Loyalty in its citizens[107] has as much to do with disinterest in psychology as with the 'marketing' of the 'Europe brand'. Similar to what happens with Love, the preferential relationship of Loyalty between the peoples of Europe cannot be constructed as a virtue or duty. There can no more be a 'duty of loyalty to a polity'[108]—or a Union—than a duty of love in a marriage: as a duty of love in a marriage too easily conceals rape, so duty of loyalty to a polity is the veil for domination. As there can be no Loyalty to Love or marriage, so can there be no Loyalty to the Union or the idea of Europe. This is simply not the way human psychology works. People are inherently social beings, relationships with the others are part of our nature. We are Loyal to other people(s), not to the idea of a union as such. The true object of Loyalty is not the Union but its peoples united under

[104] Pettit (n 90) 160: 'The reason that moves the lover must essentially involve the identity of the beloved'.

[105] Case 14/64 *Costa v ENEL*.

[106] ECtHR, *Bosphorus v Ireland* (30.06.2005).

[107] Weiler (n 9) 333–34.

[108] JHH Weiler and JP Trachtman, 'European Constitutionalism and Its Discontents' (1997) 17(1) *Northwestern Journal of International Law and Business*. Only when loyalty is a part of one's own subjective perception of *positive liberty*, can the individual be truly loyal. See also JHH Weiler, 'European Citizenship—Identity and Differentity' in M La Torre (ed), *European Citizenship. An Institutional Challenge* (The Hague, Kluwer Law International, 1998); Weiler (n 9).

the commitment of the Treaties. We do not 'market' a marriage when we court our desired partner; we market ourselves to convince the person to marry us. Promoting European integration as a virtue, for the sake of itself, is doomed to fail; promoting it as a value requires *attraction*, *intimacy* and *commitment* that build the sense of a 'we' and a shared idea of ideal life together that translates into Loyalty.

6. EUROPE AS A LIBERTY-PRESERVING CONSTRUCT

The analysis in this chapter has come full circle back to the concept of polity for the purpose of majority rule. A polity is 'not any mass gathering, but a multitude bound together by a mutual recognition of rights and a mutual cooperation for the common good'.[109] It is 'a multitude of reasonable beings bound together by a common agreement as to the objects of their love'.[110] Individuals in a polity are

> united among themselves by common sympathies, which do not exist between them and any others—which make them cooperate with each other more willingly than with other people, desire to be under the same government and desire that it should be government by themselves, to a portion of themselves, exclusively.[111]

Existence of such a polity gives rise to Loyalty, enabling legitimate political process and acceptance of majority rule. Thanks to the onset of Loyalty, the *interference* with one's own liberty that results from majoritarian political process can be offset by the other aspects of liberty: *positive liberty* and *non-domination*. European political process, its success and its very existence, depends and requires Loyalty among the people(s) of Europe. Building Loyalty and ensuring its continuity in the political process is the constitutional function of EU law.

Building Loyalty at Union level is by no means an easy task. On the one hand, EU enlargement and expansion of EU powers into new policy fields require majoritarian rule; on the other hand, a greater diversity of interests and situations across the Union weakens Loyalty, the prerequisite for accepting majoritarian choice. In this emerging political process of majoritarian policy choice,[112] Loyalty is required not only from Member States and their governments in the Council, not only from the people within each national polity, but also from the peoples of Europe. This is a qualitative change from a relationship between governments and organisations to a relationship between human beings. The larger the polity or decision-making group and the smaller the Voice of its individual members, the more crucial Loyalty becomes for ensuring Voice and preventing Exit. The

[109] Cicero, *De re publica* 1.25 quoted in W Harmless (ed), *Augustine in His Own Words* (Washington, DC, Catholic University of America Press, 2010) 337.

[110] St Augustine, *The City of God* (XIX, 24).

[111] JS Mill, *Considerations on Representative Government* (New York, Harper & Brothers, 1862) 287—this definition was used by J Rawls, *The Law of Peoples* (Cambridge, MA, Harvard University Press, 1999) 23–24.

[112] See Chapter 3 for a detailed discussion of features pointing towards the emergence of a European political space.

more politically contested the policy, the more diverse the interests involved, the greater the Loyalty that is required to legitimise majority choice. Beyond a mere cost-benefit analysis (messianic and output legitimacy), remaining in the Union with the other peoples of Europe must form part of one's own self-identified ideal way of life.

Continuous availability of Exit is an important prerequisite for Loyalty: only a free individual (she who has other options) can be truly Loyal. According to Hirschman, Loyalty with a partial closure of Exit will increase the propensity to exercise Voice—but the possibility of Exit must still remain present. This is why 'One-party states, even where there is an election and a vote, are not considered democratic because of the absence of choice'.[113] This is how legitimacy and Loyalty are a function of the three aspects of liberty. Legitimacy for Europe and its law are determined by its capacity to further each polity's liberty.[114] On the one hand, *non-interference* and *non-domination* between the polities are necessary to ensure *positive liberty* of individual polities; on the other hand, inability to advance one's own *positive liberty* is more likely to cause aggression towards others.[115] The passage from unanimity to majoritarian policy choice in the Union implies *interference* with the *positive liberty* of some European polities. Acceptance of such *interference* requires a shared idea of *positive liberty* the value of which would offset the benefit of minority Exit from EU policy choice. Sharing a vision of *positive liberty* that places a value on continuity of the Union creates Loyalty and thus acceptance (social legitimacy) of the policy preference made by majority.

Europe is founded on a shared idea of *positive liberty*: Peace between the peoples of Europe. This is a twofold commitment: to preserve the different European peoples and to ensure Peace among them. This shared commitment to Peace among the founding Member States is reflected in the preamble to the 1957 EEC Treaty;[116] Peace is at once the rationale for the creation of Europe[117] and for its continued existence.[118] For the first time in the Lisbon Treaty, Peace is placed not

113 Weiler (n 43) 5.

114 Understood as individual and collective liberty of citizens that compose each polity and therefore the EU. For more detail and examples from case law see the discussion in Chapter 2.

115 J Dollard, NE Miller, LW Doob, OH Mowrer and RR Sears, *Frustration and Aggression* (Newhaven, CT, Yale University Press, 1939) 22; the more important the aspect of *positive liberty*, the more aggression is likely to result from its denial. For the link between *positive liberty* as economic wellbeing and aggression in twentieth-century European history, see G Soros, *The Tragedy of the European Union* (New York, NY Public Affairs, 2014) 32–33 and 112–13.

116 Although Peace as the purpose of integration in Europe featured already in the EEC Treaty of 1957, prior to the Lisbon Treaty, Peace remained in the preamble, while Treaty articles only mentioned Peace in the context of the Common Foreign and Security Policy (CFSP) (Article 11(1) TEU Amsterdam) and Member State obligations 'for the purpose of maintaining peace and international security', see Article 224 EEC Treaty (1957), Article 297 EC Treaty of Amsterdam.

117 *Declaration by the French Foreign Minister, Robert Schuman* (Paris, 09.05.1950) Selection of texts concerning institutional matters of the Community from 1950 to 1982. Luxembourg: European Parliament—Committee on Institutional Affairs (1982); for analysis of the role of Peace in European legal and political culture see also Weiler (n 37) 678–94.

118 M Eilstrup Sangiovanni and D Verdier, 'European Integration as a Solution to War' (2005) 11(1) *European Journal of International Relations*.

only in Treaty text but in one of its foremost articles, ahead of the main policy areas: promotion of Peace 'of its peoples' is the 'aim' of the European Union in Article 3(1) EU. Union policies and powers are instrumental to achieving this aim. Despite interfering with the national political processes and preferred national policy choice, Union law enjoys legitimacy due to its unique capacity to ensure Peace between the peoples of Europe.

Construing legitimacy as Peace through liberty—the constitutional construct of the Treaties—furthers Loyalty between the European polities.[119] Just as people brought together in a union remain distinct individuals rather than merge into one, so the peoples brought together in the Union do not and need not become one people or polity; they need not abandon their own *positive liberty* or the practice of its identification and pursuit in the course of the national political processes; on the contrary, their ability to do so in and with the help of the Union will determine social legitimacy of both the national and European political processes. A Union that secures and helps advance its own *positive liberty* will foster Loyalty between the peoples of Europe. Loyalty between polities attained in the Union thanks to ensuring liberty in Union law can thus enable and legitimise majority rule.[120] No European polity is required. Liberty of peoples in the Union will determine whether the Union lasts.

7. CONSTITUTIVE ELEMENTS OF EU CONSTITUTIONAL ORDER

This book presents and defends a model for the political soul of Europe based on the conception of Union law that furthers liberty (see Figure 1.2).

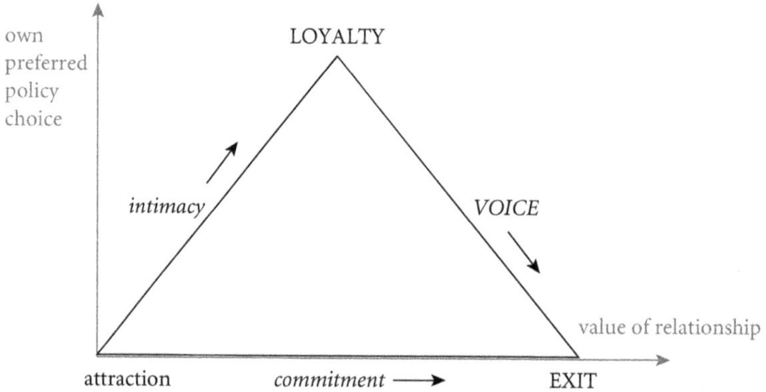

Figure 1.2: Liberty in the constitutional construct of Europe

[119] As opposed to Loyalty between Union citizens as individual members in a unified European polity, see Chapter 3.

[120] Liberty (freedom) is recognised in Article 2 TEU as one of the Union's founding values.

The vertical and horizontal axes in Figure 1.2 correspond to the two components of one's own subjective *positive liberty*: specific preference for policy choice and the value placed on the continuity of the relationship with the other(s). At the point of Loyalty, the self-perceived value of the components of *positive liberty* associated with continuing the relationship with the other(s) balances out the loss created by *interference* through majoritarian choice with the self-perceived value of another component of *positive liberty*, that associated with certain policy choices. Liberty is represented by the area of the triangle. Flipping the triangle down along the *value* axes and to the left along the *preferred-policy* axes would represent the absence of one's own idea of *positive liberty*. *Liberty from interference* lies outside the triangle: it exists outside the relationship with the other(s). The *attraction* point is the ideal start of the relationship; *Loyalty* is its maximum strength, *Exit* is a tool to prevent *dependence* and *domination*, which can be represented by flipping the triangle downwards in continuation of the Voice axis.

Starting the Union from shared circumstances (*attraction* point where the positive values of the two components of *positive liberty* start), there are two possible routes. One route proceeds along increasing commitment towards the right and, as the circumstances change with the passage of time (including the strengthening of commitment and the degree that it limits one's own idea of *positive liberty*), may arrive at the point of Exit (where attraction or shared vision of *positive liberty* fades). This is the model of *non-interference*, whereby liberty of the national polity to further its own idea of *positive liberty* is limited by Union law to secure *non-interference* with the liberty of other European polities. Alternatively, the Union may proceed from shared circumstances along the *intimacy* line upwards, elaborating a vision of *positive liberty* shared by all the peoples of Europe. The upward shift will be a vertical line if this vision is elaborated unanimously. When one's own idea of *positive liberty* is negotiated with others, trading some aspects of preferred policy choice for one's own preference to abstain from Exit, the *intimacy* line will slope between the vertical and the horizontal axes. This process of developing a shared idea of ideal life builds Loyalty, the point at which majoritarian choices become accepted as one's own. Loyalty allows majoritarian choices along the line of declining Voice (policies unpopular with some national polities) without an immediate exercise of Exit.

Both *intimacy* and Voice refer to the political process and the elaboration of a shared idea of ideal life. Their legitimacy depends on Peace as liberty from domination. *Intimacy* corresponds to the interaction with others in a union that begins with identification of one's own subjective *positive liberty*, which is then negotiated with others in a consensual way. The legitimacy of this process and its outcome is premised on the preservation of liberty of all the participants. Each participant in the political process needs to be able to identify her own *positive liberty* in the conditions of *liberty from domination*: our own identity is essential for our capacity to interact and form unions with others.[121] The ability to identify and further

[121] The importance of this is recognised in Title II TEU (Provisions on Democratic Principles) and in the Copenhagen criteria (European Council Conclusions of the Presidency 21–22 June 1993 SN 180/1/93 REV 1) for joining the EU.

our own *positive liberty* is fundamental for integration to succeed: 'solo una chiara consapevolezza della propria identità consente di aprirsi al dialogo con … "culture diverse"' (only a clear understanding of own identity allows dialogue with … "other cultures").[122] Without an idea of our own *positive liberty*, interaction with other(s) may lead to domination and therefore Exit from such a Union. Our own identity can only be self-determined.[123] Identification of our own *positive liberty* and its negotiation with others in the Union then takes place for each policy choice. *Liberty from domination* in the process of *intimacy* is secured as *non-interference* with our own idea of ideal life.

In the second part of the political process characterised by a decrease in Voice, shared *positive liberty* is pursued through the enactment of law. Respect for liberty of each participating polity (output legitimacy) and internalisation of the ideas of *positive liberty* developed in the process of *intimacy* between polities in the Union build Loyalty, which enables a reduction in Voice without immediate Exit. Legitimacy of this majoritarian process (Voice) requires *liberty from domination*; without liberty, Loyalty does not arise and does not endure. However, under majority rule, non-domination cannot be secured as *non-interference* since, by definition, some polities will end up being bound against their preferred policy choice. The alternative is to secure *liberty from domination* as one's own *positive liberty* by securing two forms of Exit. First, immutable minority interests need a permanent Exit by having their interests withdrawn from majoritarian policy choice similar to the withdrawal of interests of insular minorities[124] from the political process in national constitutional law. Second, for non-minority interests, representation of interests must be secured. Because the participants in the European political process are individuals bound in national polities, individual citizens need to be factored in. The ability of the national political process to develop its own idea of *positive liberty* is fundamental for internalising the shared idea of *positive liberty* negotiated in Europe. Accountability in the national political process for the identification, negotiation and pursuit of this shared idea must not be undermined by the shift of policy choice to Europe. The possibility of sanctioning national governments through European elections (partial Exit) without removing them from power (complete Exit) furthers Voice and liberty on the national level,[125] stabilising national polities and enhancing legitimacy of the national political process. Union law could enhance availability of partial Exit further through other rules

[122] M Cartabia and A Simoncini, *La Legge di Re Salomone. Ragione e diritto nei discorsi di Benedetto XVI* (Milan, Edizioni Rizzoli BUR, 2013) 7.

[123] M Poiares Maduro, 'Contrapunctual Law: Europe's Constitutional Pluralism in Action' in N Walker (ed), *Sovereignty in Transition* (Oxford, Hart Publishing, 2003) 526.

[124] ie interests that form an integral and immutable part of one's own identity—an equivalent to insular minorities in US constitutional law. In the European political process these would be formed where the interests of national polities are strongly affected by permanent characteristics such as geography, population size or climate.

[125] Similar to how national courts referred to the ECJ in order to acquire Voice against the national institutions, see Weiler (n 31).

that enhance accountability of national governments in the national political process for policies that are subject to majoritarian choice in Europe. *Positive liberty* of each polity would increase were Union law to ensure that the shift of policy choice to Europe decreased accountability of national governments in the national political process. Liberty from domination (with the resulting Loyalty and legitimacy) would thus be secured both during *intimacy* and (the decline in) Voice.

Legitimacy and longevity of Europe's constitutional construct is inseparable from the capacity of each European polity to identify and pursue its own *positive liberty*. Neither the Union, its law and institutions, nor the European polities and national political processes possess an independent source of legitimacy. Rather, the two levels are intertwined and necessarily support each other. *Liberty from* (actual and potential) *interference* secured with the help of Union law furthers legitimacy of the national political processes through boosting their capacity to develop and pursue their own *positive liberty*. Loyalty thus furthered at the national level and the legitimacy of the national political process can then support the European political process in the course of which a shared vision of *positive liberty* is elaborated between the peoples of Europe. Unless and until Union citizens perceive themselves as a single polity, reliance on legitimacy of national polities and the Loyalty between their members is fundamental for the pursuit of Peace. Stability and legitimacy of the national polities are crucial for building European Loyalty through *intimacy* among them. In order to further Loyalty in the Union, the constitutional function of Union law needs to ensure that each European polity can identify its own idea of *positive liberty* and negotiate it with others in *liberty from domination*. Building Loyalty as a value by furthering *liberty from domination* is the constitutional role of Union law.

The constitutional soul of Europe combines two models for Peace. The first model is based on elimination of interference between the polities, which furthers their ability to pursue their own *positive liberty* individually. Chapter 2 illustrates how this takes place. Securing Peace as *non-interference* encounters the limits of messianic legitimacy: once the mechanism to secure *liberty from interference* is established (success)—or once the Union fails to secure *non-interference* (failure)—this source of legitimacy is equally exhausted.[126] Peace as *non-interference*, however necessary, is insufficient. The second model for Peace comes in where reciprocal *non-interference* is impossible. Peace is secured through shared *positive liberty* (as opposed to *positive liberty* of each European polity separately) that is identified by all European polities in the Union. This is the model discussed in Chapter 3. It allows the transformation of Europe's constitutional construct from a static model premised on *non-interference* as the ultimate aim of integration in Europe, into a dynamic continuous process of elaborating and achieving a vision of *positive liberty* shared among the peoples of Europe.[127] Interpreted in

[126] Weiler (n 47) 248–268.

[127] On the connection of politics and liberty see also H Arendt, *Between Past and Future* (New York, Penguin Books, 1968) ch 4.

this dynamic manner, Peace as a source of Europe's legitimacy is a process that can only end together with the dissolution of the Union. It is here, in the second model, that the *European* political process takes place. Chapters 4 and 5 discuss the implications of this dynamic model for some of the key concepts of EU constitutional law. At least to an extent, cases decided by the CJEU reflect the birth of the political soul of Europe.

2

A Union of Polities: Negative Liberty

HIS MAJESTY THE KING OF THE BELGIANS, THE PRESIDENT OF THE FEDERAL REPUBLIC OF GERMANY, THE PRESIDENT OF THE FRENCH REPUBLIC, THE PRESIDENT OF THE ITALIAN REPUBLIC, HER ROYAL HIGHNESS THE GRAND DUCHESS OF LUXEMBOURG, HER MAJESTY THE QUEEN OF THE NETHERLANDS,

RESOLVED by thus pooling their resources to preserve and strengthen peace and liberty, and calling upon the other peoples of Europe who share their ideal to join in their efforts,

HAVE DECIDED to create a European Economic Community

Thus began the Treaty Establishing the European Economic Community (EEC) in 1957. After the destruction and horrors of two World Wars, both initiated in Europe, the heads of state and government of European nations shared an ideal of peace and liberty, for the attainment of which they promulgated the Treaty. Beyond a mere peace Treaty that 'terminates one war', the bond between states in the European Community would secure 'perpetual peace' and 'end all wars for good'.[1] To 'further the works of peace'[2] and make 'any war between France and Germany not merely unthinkable, but materially impossible',[3] the founding Member States pooled together resources that could be used for the conduct of war. Three Communities were created, the most important being the European Economic Community, which evolved into the EU. Powers were conferred by Member States on the EEC in order to achieve as follows:

ARTICLE 2 EEC

The Community shall have as its task, by establishing a common market and progressively approximating the economic policies of Member States, to promote throughout the Community a harmonious development of economic activities, a continuous and balanced expansion, an increase in stability, an accelerated raising of the standard of living and closer relations between the States belonging to it.

Article 3 EEC thereafter listed the powers conferred on the Community by Member States in limited fields.[4] The powers in these fields were to further 'the

[1] I Kant, 'Perpetual Peace' in *Political Writings* (Cambridge, Cambridge University Press, 1991) 104.
[2] Preamble to the Treaty establishing European Coal and Steel Community (1951).
[3] *Schuman Declaration* (Paris, 09.05.1950).
[4] Case 14/64 *Costa v ENEL.*

purposes set out in Article 2' EEC. The Titles and Chapters of the Treaty that followed contained a detailed subject-by-subject list of the legal bases and specific objectives for each policy field. One of these powers was 'the abolition, as between Member States, of obstacles to freedom of movement for persons'[5] defined further in Article 48 EEC as 'freedom of movement for workers' and 'the abolition of any discrimination based on nationality between workers of the Member States', in Article 52 EEC as 'freedom of establishment of nationals of a Member State in the territory of another Member State' and in Article 59 EEC as 'freedom to provide services within the Community'. This Union freedom is well known and has been analysed at length.[6] As a result of free movement rights, Member States largely lost their ability to implement immigration policy vis-a-vis nationals of other Member States.

Liberalisation of migration in the internal market came about through the combined operation of four aspects of Union law. First, *direct effect* of Union law in the national legal orders, in particular of Treaty provisions that are 'sufficiently clear, precise and unconditional' such as Articles 48, 52 and 59 EEC,[7] empowered individuals to enforce a Treaty concluded between states directly in the national courts without having to rely on state action for protecting their rights. Second, and predicated on direct effect,[8] the principle of *primacy* of Union law precludes provisions of national law that conflict with the Treaties and EU secondary law.[9] Primacy and direct effect of EC law made it 'real' law or '"hard" in the sense of being binding not only on but also in states'.[10] Third, in terms of substance of Union law, Article 7 EEC[11] *outlawed* provisions of national law that either directly or indirectly *discriminate on the grounds of nationality*.[12] Fourth, in the substance of market freedoms, the principle of *abolition of obstacles to free movement* precludes non-discriminatory national laws the effect of which is to de facto discourage or obstruct mobility in the internal market.[13] The first two aspects relate to the modus operandi of integration between states, while the latter two aspects concern the degree to which EC law secured *non-interference* by the state with the individual's migration choice.

[5] Article 3(c) EEC.

[6] See C Barnard and S Peers, *European Union Law* (Oxford, Oxford University Press, 2014) ch 13; EF Isin and M Saward (eds), *Enacting European Citizenship* (Cambridge, Cambridge University Press, 2013); N Nic Shuibhne, 'EU Citizenship after Lisbon' in D Ashiagbor, N Countouris and I Lianos (eds), *The European Union after the Treaty of Lisbon* (Cambridge, Cambridge University Press, 2012); P Minderhoud and N Trimikliniotis (eds), *Rethinking the Free Movement of Workers: The European Challenges Ahead* (Nijmegen, Wolf Legal Publishers, 2009).

[7] Current Articles 45, 49 and 56 TFEU; Case 32/84 *Van Gend en Loos*.

[8] M Dougan, 'When Worlds Collide! Competing Visions of the Relationship between Direct Effect and Supremacy' (2007) 44 *CML Rev*.

[9] Case 14/64 *Costa v ENEL*; For a different conception of primacy in Union law see M Avbelj, 'Supremacy or Primacy of EU Law—(Why) Does it Matter?' (2011) 17(6) *European Law Journal*.

[10] JHH Weiler, 'The Transformation of Europe' (1991) 100 *Yale Law Journal* 2426.

[11] Current Article 18 TFEU.

[12] Save for the exceptions listed in Directive 2004/38/EC Union Citizenship.

[13] *Ex multis*, Case 186/87 *Cowan*, Case C-415/93 *Bosman*, Case C-281/98 *Angonese*.

Constitutionally revealing yet much less explored, is the reason for excluding third-country nationals from free movement in the internal market. Although Article 48 EEC (currently Article 45 TFEU) did not mention nationality, the nationality criterion for free movement of workers was introduced as early as the following year.[14] Only nationals of the Member States were covered. Articles 52 and 59 EEC (currently Articles 49 and 56 TFEU) specifically excluded third-country nationals and despite a possibility of extending free movement of services to third-country nationals 'who are established within the Community' contained in Article 59(2) EEC, this power has never been used.[15] Third-country nationals could derive rights from their Community employers or Member State national family members without which rights nationals of the Member States would be obstructed in exercising their market freedoms[16] but they could not benefit from market freedoms in their own right.[17] Despite proposals to extend free movement in the internal market to legally resident third-country nationals,[18] this has never been done.[19]

Nor were other internal market provisions used to regulate third-country nationals. Article 137(1)(g) EC (currently, Article 153(1)(g)TFEU) authorised the Union to 'support and complement the activities of the Member States' in the field

[14] Regulation No 3 of the Council of the European Economic Community concerning social security for migrant workers (OJ 16 December 1958) applies to 'wage-earners or assimilated workers who are or have been subject to the legislation of one or more of the Member States and are nationals of a Member State or are stateless persons or refugees permanently resident in the territory of a Member State, as also to the members of their families and their survivors' (Article 4 (1)); subsequently reiterated in Article 1 Regulation 1612/68/EC.

[15] The Commission proposed such an extension (COM (1999) 3 final OJ C/1999/67/17, amended COM (2000) 271 final OJ C E/2000/311/197) but the proposal failed in the Council and was withdrawn (COM (2004) 542 final OJ C/2005/75/ 10).

[16] Third-country national family members of Union citizens who have exercised free movement as workers or service providers enjoy residence (Case C-60/00 *Carpenter*), employment (Article 23 Directive 2004/38/EC) and non-discrimination (Case 40/76 *Slavica Kermaschek*) rights similar to nationals of the Member States, as denying them rights would constitute an obstacle to the exercise of market freedom by EU national workers. Under Article 56 TFEU, third-country nationals enjoy residence and employment rights as employees of EU service providers posted to another Member State for the provision of services; although not benefiting from formal access to the labour market of the host Member State, authorities of the host Member State may not subject posted third-country national employees of EU service providers to the requirement of national work and residence permits (Case C-43/93 *Van der Elst*). Joined Cases C-297/88 & C-197/89 *Dzodzi*; Joined Cases 35 & 36/82 *Morson*.

[17] Case 238/83 *Meade*, Case C-230/97 *Awoyemi*.

[18] For proposals to this effect as regards third-country nationals who reside legally in the EU and have a valid work permit, see K Hailbronner and J Polakiewicz, 'Non-EC Nationals in the European Community: the Need for a Coordinated Approach' (1992–1993) 3 *Duke Journal of Comparative International Law* 55. For an excellent overview of the failed attempts to do so see S Peers and N Rogers (eds), *EU Immigration and Asylum Law* (The Hague, Martinus Nijhoff, 2006) 19–45.

[19] Not under EU immigration law under the AFSJ either: A Skordas, 'Immigration and the Market: The Long-Term Residents Directive' (2006) 13 *Columbia Journal of European Law*; A Kocharov, 'What Intra-Community Mobility for Third-Country Workers?' (2008) 6 *European Law Review*; S Iglesias Sanches, 'Free Movement of Third-Country Nationals in the European Union?' (2009) 15(6) *European Law Journal*.

of 'conditions of employment for third-country nationals legally residing in Union territory'. As early as 1985, the ECJ confirmed that immigration policy could fall under this article to the extent that 'the employment situation and, more generally, the improvement of living and working conditions within the Community are liable to be affected by the policy pursued by the Member States with regard to workers from non-member countries'.[20] The Council legal service opined that this article could even serve as a legal basis to regulate *access* to employment by third-country nationals.[21] Yet, this power has never been so used.

Instead, the institutions opted for a more general legal basis under the Area of Freedom, Security and Justice (AFSJ).[22] After the introduction of Community powers over third-country nationals (Amsterdam) and the passage of this power from unanimity to majority (Lisbon), Directive 2009/50/EC Blue Card and Directive 2011/98/EU Single Permit were adopted under Article 79(2)(b) TFEU. Article 79(2)b TFEU provides for the adoption of measures that cover 'definition of the rights of third-country nationals residing legally in a Member State'—a much broader power subject to majority vote. While it is generally possible to base Union measures on several different Treaty articles, combining Article 79 TFEU with Article 153 TFEU is problematic because of the Danish, Irish and British opt-outs from common immigration policy.[23] In case of different legislative procedures, preference should be given to the legal basis that provides for the full involvement of the European Parliament in the legislative process.[24] After the passage to ordinary (co-decision) legislative procedure under the Lisbon Treaty, Article 79 TFEU gains preference over Article 153(1)g TFEU, which remains limited to consultation of the EP.

Articles 100 and 235 EEC (later Articles 94 and 308 EC, now Articles 115 and 352 TFEU)[25] were equally refuted. Article 100 EEC provided for approximation of national laws that directly affect the common market, while Article 235 EEC did not require such a direct link and allowed the introduction of common rules

[20] Joined Cases 281, 283, 284, 285 and 287/85 *Germany v Commission*.

[21] Regarding Directive 2001/55/EC Temporary Protection, see Council Document 6736/01 of 1 March 2001 (not on the issue of access to legal status but as regards rights of third-country nationals who had already received the status); regarding Directive 2003/9/EC Reception Conditions, see Council Document 9077/02 of 22 May 2002 (same as the previous directive); regarding the 2001 proposal for a Directive on Legal Economic Migration, see Council Document 14150/02 of 12 November 2002. See also G Brinkmann, 'The Immigration and Asylum Agenda' (2004) 10(2) *European Law Journal* 188.

[22] See Regulation 1231/2010 and Council Regulation 859/2003.

[23] See opinion of the Council legal service on the 2001 proposal for a directive on economic migration, Council doc. 14150/02.

[24] Case C-300/89 *Titanium Dioxide*.

[25] Article 235 EEC was changed with the Lisbon Treaty. Its successor, current Article 352 TFEU, provides the legal basis whenever Union action 'should prove necessary, within the framework of the policies defined in the Treaties' when 'the Treaties have not provided the necessary powers'. This broader all-encompassing formulation is no longer limited to the internal market or to only one Treaty. See A Rosas and L Armati, *EU Constitutional Law. An Introduction* (Oxford, Oxford University Press, 2010) 21. This competence is not likely to be used to regulate immigration due to the requirement of unanimity in the Council, see Peers and Rogers (eds) (n 18) 19–45.

and even a new right.[26] In 1976, the Commission proposed a directive on illegal employment of third-country nationals[27] based on Article 100 EEC,[28] arguing that conditions of their employment were liable to affect the living and working conditions in the Community as a whole and thus necessitated supranational action. The proposal did not succeed.[29] While not rejecting the idea of such a measure being adopted under Community competence over the common market, the Council reconfirmed its previous position that Article 235 EEC, not Article 100 EEC, was the proper legal basis for such action.[30] This implied that the powers to harmonise national laws concerning unauthorised stay and employment by third-country nationals[31] were not comprised in Community powers to regulate the internal market under all other legal bases, making recourse to Article 235 EEC necessary.[32] Although the 'residual competence' in Article 235 EEC was used extensively,[33] it was never used to regulate third-country nationals. The ECJ pronounced that Article 235 EEC could not be used 'as a basis for the adoption of provisions, whose effect would be, in substance, to amend the Treaty without following the procedure which it provides for that purpose'.[34] Would regulating third-country nationals under the internal market amount to such a case? My argument is that it would.

1. THE NATURE OF EUROPE'S UNION: *NON-INTERFERENCE* BETWEEN NATIONAL POLITIES

The fact that numerous internal market provisions that could be used to regulate migration by third-country nationals had not been so used[35] indicates that free movement of workers seeks to establish not merely the internal market but a

[26] Case C-376/98 *Tobacco Advertising*.

[27] COM (76) 331 final, amended in 1978 COM (78) 86 def.

[28] Then Article 100 EC, currently Article 115 TFEU.

[29] A Evans, 'Third Country Nationals and the Treaty on European Union' (1994) 5 *European Journal of International Law*.

[30] Council Resolution of 21 January 1974 concerning a social action programme, OJ C013, 12/02/1974 pp 1–4.

[31] On the link between illegal and legal immigration, though in the context of Title IV EC, see S Peers, 'The EU Institutions and Title IV' in Peers and Rogers (eds) (n 18) 60–62.

[32] Article 308 EC: 'If action by the Community should prove necessary to attain, in the course of the operation of the common market, one of the objectives of the Community, and this Treaty has not provided the necessary powers, the Council shall, acting unanimously on a proposal from the Commission and after consulting the European Parliament, take the appropriate measures'.

[33] By 2002, 'Article 308 has been used in close to 700 instances', A Vergés Bausili, *Rethinking the Methods of Dividing and Exercising Powers in the EU: Reforming Subsidiarity and National Parliaments*, Jean Monnet Working Paper 9/02 (NYU) 5.

[34] Opinion 2/94 *ECHR*.

[35] With the exception of cases where third-country nationals derive rights from Union citizens see further in this chapter—and, later, specific Union competences under the AFSJ—Chapter 3.

different kind of Union. The purpose of this Union is to unite peoples[36] with the help of but also beyond markets. By ratifying the Treaties, the peoples of Europe bound themselves not merely to a Community but to a policy choice unanimously shared by all.[37] This choice was set in Treaty objectives that defined the conferred powers of the EEC. Functional Treaty objectives limited the reach of all political process by limiting the scope of available policy choices. The Community legislator enacting secondary law could not promulgate policies that diverged from the Treaties. Nor could the national polities, in the course of their political processes, make and advance choices that undermined the achievement of EEC objectives.[38] Functional Community powers such as Articles 48, 52, 59 EEC and others did not confer general power to regulate the internal market or interstate trade.[39] Their upshot was precisely the opposite: to restrain regulatory powers, not create them. All political processes, national and European, were pre-empted through this constitutional choice.[40] No passage of powers from Member States to the Community took place in the sense that the limit on powers of the national political processes to regulate migration between Member States was not replaced by the creation of any powers to make policy choices in Europe. The exercise by QMV of functional Community powers did not change the fact that the policy choices this exercise was to further were fixed in the Treaty by all the peoples of Europe unanimously. Without unanimous Treaty amendment, this vision of *positive liberty* was subject neither to change nor to challenge.

Peace as a constraint on the political process is clearly traceable in free movement law. Free movement of workers and service providers creates interdependence between the national polities in policy terms. However, this equally generates new potential for cross-polity interference in terms of the political process.[41] This happens because free movement in the internal market creates new insular minorities[42] whose interests are not only under-represented in their host polity's political process but potentially conflict with the interests of its majority.

[36] J Monnet, *Mémoires. Nous ne coalisons pas des états, nous unissons des hommes* (Paris, Fayard, 1976).

[37] The Treaties are ratified unanimously by all the peoples of Europe.

[38] Article 4(3) TEU; for detailed analysis see M Klamert, *The Principle of Loyalty in EU Law* (Oxford, Oxford University Press, 2014).

[39] Case C-376/98 *Tobacco Advertising.*

[40] Some claim that this is still the case today: G Davies, 'Democracy and Legitimacy in the Shadow of Purposive Competence' (2015) 21(1) *European Law Journal* 2–22; but see JHH Weiler, 'On the Distinction between Values and Virtues in the Process of European Integration' (3 March 2010) draft presented at the IILJ International Legal Theory Colloquium, *The Turn to Governance: The Exercise of Power in the International Public Space*, NYU Law School, 1–2.

[41] M Poiares Maduro, *We the Court* (Oxford, Hart Publishing, 1998); M Poiares Maduro, 'Contrapunctual Law: Europe's Constitutional Pluralism in Action' in N Walker (ed), *Sovereignty in Transition* (Oxford, Hart Publishing, 2003).

[42] The term 'insular minority' is borrowed from US law and refers to immutable characteristics of an individual that she cannot change—similar to the characteristics that form grounds for the right to asylum under the 1951 Geneva Convention.

Under-representation of out-of-polity interests in the national political process generates new potential for cross-polity interference as a direct result of Europe's 'ever closer union'—exactly the opposite of achieving Peace.[43] This danger arises in three situations; in all of them, political interdependence is minimised through directly effective rights in Union law.

First, mobile Union citizens are under-represented in their host polity. Because the peoples of Europe do not identify themselves as one people, no European polity can be created and there are no European polity membership rules.[44] Each national polity determines its own membership.[45] Decisions on membership enjoy mutual recognition and bind other polities in the EU.[46] At the same time, participation in the national political process (the right to vote in legislative elections) remains reserved exclusively to members of each national polity.[47] The result is comparable to integration between the American states under the Articles of Confederation: although free movement is established, the right to participate in the host state's political process is not extended to nationals of other states.[48] When polity members and resources move between jurisdictions they become subject to regulation by the political processes of other states. National political process does not represent out-of-state interests even though these interests are governed by it. This causes a 'mismatch between citizenship and the territorial scope of legitimate political authority' with 'citizens living outside the country whose government is supposed to be accountable to them and inside a country whose government is not accountable to them'.[49]

[43] For an analogy with the role of US constitutional law in 'promotion of peaceful relations among the states', see eg JM Gonzales, 'Comment: the Interstate Privileges and Immunities: Fundamental Rights or Federalism' (1986) 15 *Capital University Law Review* 493.

[44] Union citizenship introduced in Maastricht is based on nationality of Member States, which retain exclusive powers to grant and withhold it subject to only sparse criteria in Union law, Case C-369/90 *Micheletti*, Case C-135/08 *Rottmann*. The EU accession process did not place any requirements regarding nationality rules in candidate states, G Guliyeva, 'Lost in Transition: Russian-speaking Non-citizens in Latvia and the Protection of Minority Rights in the European Union' (2008) 33 *European Law Review*.

[45] Article 9 TEU, Article 20(1) TEU, Case C-369/90 *Micheletti* §10, Case C-192/99 *Kaur* §19, Case C-179/98 *Mesbah* §29, Case C-200/02 *Zhu and Chen* §37, Case C-135/08 *Rottmann* §39.

[46] The grant of nationality by one Member State triggers obligations of other Member States regarding free movement, Case C-369/90 *Micheletti*.

[47] Although Article 25 TFEU allows the extension of voting rights of Union citizens unanimously by the Council with EP consent and constitutional ratification by all Member States, such an extension could come into conflict with Article 4(2) TEU, particularly as concerns ensuring the equality of Member States before the Treaties and respect of their national identities inherent in the political structures.

[48] AR Amar, 'Of Sovereignty and Federalism' (1987) 96 *Yale Law Journal*. Still today, see Ely's analysis of the famous footnote in *United States v Caroline Products* Co. 304 U.S. 144 (1938), n 4, 152–53: JH Ely, *Democracy and Distrust* (Cambridge, MA, Harvard University Press, 1980) 83. On the principle of indirect representation see *Toomer v Witsel* 334 U.S. 385, 395 (1948): '[The privileges and immunities clause of Article IV of the US Constitution] was designed to insure to a citizen of State A who ventures into State B the same privileges which the citizens of State B enjoy'.

[49] R Bauböck, *Stakeholder Citizenship: An Idea Whose Time Has Come?* (Migration Polity Institute, 2008) 2.

A good example are migrant workers. A national of state A who moves to state B cannot participate in the latter's political process (legislative elections on the national level) because this participation is reserved to nationals of state B (members of polity B). If labour unions of state B wish to protect their national labour market from foreign workers, they could use their voice in the national political process to pass protectionist laws against foreign workers, the latter having no right to vote. Union law resolves this potential under-representation by withdrawing the interests of mobile Union citizens from the political process of their host polity through directly effective rights. Migrant Union citizens, whether or not workers,[50] benefit from non-discrimination vis-a-vis host Member State nationals[51] and from the abolition of obstacles to free movement[52]—rights that they can enforce directly in national courts over conflicting national law. As a result, interests that belong to one European polity are withdrawn from the political process of another.

Protecting the interests of workers from polity A could also correct an internal interest bias where under-representation of interests that belong to different polities coincides with under-representation of interests within a single polity. Suppose that unlike the workers in polity B, consumers in polity B are interested in migrant labour, for instance because greater labour supply reduces production costs and prices of goods and services. Because consumers tend to be less organised than workers (the stakes per person are lower for consumers than for workers, translating into a lower incentive to invest in information, organisation and lobbying), the interest of consumers in the political process of polity B will tend to be under-represented compared to the interest of polity B workers.[53] However, if correction of internal interest representation were the aim of EU free movement law, it would lead to dependence and prejudice liberty and legitimacy of the EU and national polities.

Second, mobile Union citizens who return to their home polity after the exercise of their free movement rights also become an insular minority by virtue of this experience.[54] It may be difficult to change nationality but it is impossible to

[50] Cases on free movement rights of citizens as opposed to economically active persons include: C-140/12 *Brey*, C-138/02 *Collins*, C-184/99 *Grzelczyk*, C-209/03 *Bidar*, C-158/07 *Förster*.

[51] Case 186/87 *Cowan*.

[52] In Joined Cases C-356/11 and C-357/11 *O&S* §§59–60, the ECJ ruled that a refusal of a Member State to grant a third-country national family member of a Union citizen a residence permit could only amount to an obstacle to free movement where the Union citizen settles in the host Member State as opposed to residing there for periods of less than three months: 'short periods of residence such as weekends or holidays spent in a Member State other than that of which the citizen in question is a national, even when considered together, fall within the scope of Article 6 of Directive 2004/38 and do not satisfy those conditions'. This illustrates the difference between the prohibition on discrimination and the requirement of the abolition of obstacles: discrimination constitutes a self-standing element of free movement law, separate from and additional to the abolition of obstacles.

[53] N Komesar, *Imperfect Alternatives* (Chicago, IL, University of Chicago Press, 1994).

[54] Only ca 2% of Union citizens exercise their right to reside in another Member State, K Vasileva, 'Population and Social Conditions: Nearly Two-thirds of the Foreigners Living in EU Member States Are Citizens of Countries Outside the EU-27 (2012) 31 *Eurostat: Statistics in Focus*.

change one's past. While in a minority, the interests of returnees may be prejudiced in majoritarian political process. Placing the interests of returnees to their state of nationality within the scope of EU free movement law prevents their becoming an insular minority in their own polity.[55] In contrast, purely internal situations are left outside the scope of Union law because internally the individual can uphold her interest through the national political process by exercising the right to vote. European integration does not affect her Voice in the national political process. Member State nationals who reside in their state of nationality and do not exercise free movement rights, as well as double nationals who exercise free movement between their Member States of nationality, fall outside the scope of EU law.[56] Likewise, third-country national family members of Member State nationals fall outside the scope of free movement rights even when the Member State national herself exercises free movement but her third-country national family member remains in her Member State of nationality.[57] The same is true also vice versa: once a Member State national returns to her state of nationality, her third-country national family members can no longer derive rights from EU free movement law.[58] In such situations, 'the purely hypothetical prospect' of the right of freedom of movement being obstructed 'does not establish a sufficient connection with European Union' law.[59] Reverse discrimination does not occur because participation in the national political process of those who do not exercise free movement rights is not prejudiced by European integration.

Third, an insular minority with immutable characteristics can also arise within national polities without any mobility between Member States. We cannot choose our birthplace and parents nor can we change these facts. Non-mobile Union citizens who are minors and whose parents are not nationals of the host Member State[60] (whether Union citizens or third-country nationals) have neither the Voice in its political process (even if these minor Union citizens are themselves nationals of their host Member State) nor are represented in this process by their parents (who, not being nationals, cannot vote in the host state's national elections). Not only these Union citizens—members of one of the EU polities—cannot make

[55] Case C-370/90 *Singh*, Case C-18/95 *Terhoeve*, Case C-385/00 *De Groot*, Case C-371/04 *Commission v Italy*; situations where a Member State national acquires nationality of her new host state also belong here, see Case C-419/92 *Scholz*, Case C-542/08 *Barth*.

[56] Although such movement has the same potential to give a polity member an insular minority status, it is not a consequence of EU free movement law but of holding double nationality. Thus, there is no effect on the legitimacy of the Union and its legal order. Case C-434/09 *McCarthy*: free movement rights do not arise in a situation where a national of two Member States moves between these, such as if Mrs McCarthy, who had dual UK and Irish nationality, moved from the UK to Ireland—see §§32, 34 and 37 Case C-434/09 *McCarthy*; also Joined Cases 35 & 36/82 *Morson and Jhanjan*, Joined Cases C-297/88 & C-197/89 *Dzodzi*, Joined Cases C-64 & 65/96 *Uecker & Jacquet*, Case C-256/11 *Derici*.

[57] Case C-40/11 *Iida*.

[58] Case C-218/14 *Singh* §61. After the return to her Member State of nationality, a Union citizen does not need virtual representation (see below) in other Member States because she is no longer subject to the regulatory reach of their national political process.

[59] Case C-40/11 *Iida* §77 citing by analogy Case C-299/95 *Kremzow* §16.

[60] Case C-456/12 *O&S*.

independent choices as to whether they exercise free movement rights, but such exercise would not necessarily increase their Voice in the political process of any Member State. It is only if her parents are nationals of one Member State and decide to move back to that state that the interest of a minor Union citizen may be represented indirectly in that Member State's political process via the participation in this process of her parents. When both parents are third-country nationals, moving between Member States pursuant to Case C-200/02 *Zhu and Chen* does not solve the under-representation problem.[61] This creates a risk that the national political process may 'deprive the child's right of residence [under EU law] of any useful effect'.[62] Indeed, it may also prejudice other rights of such children. For instance, as regards a child with dual Spanish-Belgian nationality born in Belgium, the application of Belgian law concerning surnames

> had the effect that those Union citizens had different surnames under the two legal systems concerned, [which] situation was liable to cause serious inconvenience for them at both professional and private levels resulting from, inter alia, difficulties in benefiting, in one Member State of which they are nationals, from the legal effects of diplomas or documents drawn up in the surname recognised in the other Member State of which they are also nationals.[63]

Such serious inconvenience 'constituted an obstacle to free movement'.[64]

Even in their own state of nationality, minor Union citizens who reside outside the state of nationality of their parents constitute an insular minority that is under-represented in the national political process. If national law, which results from the national political process, expels these children from its territory and from the Union, minor Union citizens may also lose Voice in the political process at national and European levels *in the future*.[65] This is so because, absent from the Treaties 'provisions stating expressly and precisely which persons have the right to vote and to stand as a candidate in elections to the European Parliament',[66]

> there is nothing which precludes the Member States from defining, in compliance with Community law, the conditions of the right to vote and to stand as a candidate in elections to the European Parliament by reference to the criterion of residence in the territory in which the elections are held.[67]

[61] Case C-34/09 *Zambrano*. On the contrary, having a Union citizen parent who is a national of the host Member State apparently does, Case C-456/12 *O & B*.

[62] Case C-200/02 *Zhu and Chen* §45.

[63] Case C-434/09 *McCarthy* §51 summarising Case C-148/02 *García Avello*.

[64] See also Case C-353/06 *Grunkin and Paul* §§23, 24, 29.

[65] Union citizen children of third-country nationals who reside in a Member State other than their Member State of nationality should nevertheless comply with all the requirements of Directive 2004/58/EC, Case C-86/12 *Alokpa*.

[66] Case C-145/04 *Spain v UK* §79.

[67] Case C-300/04 *Eman* §61. See also Case C-650/13 *Delvigne* and J Shaw, 'The Political Representation of Europe's Citizens: Developments Court of Justice of the European Communities' (2008) 4 *European Constitutional Law Review*.

This is even more the case for national elections. Through the operation of national law, Union citizen minors who are expelled with their parents to a third state may remain excluded from the political process (at both national and European levels) even after reaching the age of majority in a third state.[68] It is *this* denial of political rights that amounts to a 'denial of the genuine enjoyment of the substance of the rights conferred by virtue of Union citizenship'.[69] Without Union competence over participation in the political process, whether national or European, protecting the rights of Union citizen minors in cross-polity situations is the only alternative for ensuring that Union law does not result in diminished liberty and legitimacy.[70] The fact that Union law protects the position of minor Union citizens in their own state of nationality[71] indicates that EU law regulates the national political process even in situations that are purely internal to one Member State; the fact that Union law does not protect the position of minor Union citizens in their own state of nationality when at least one of their parents is a national of this Member State[72] indicates that EU law regulates the national political process based on the presumption of *virtual representation.*

In all the three situations listed above, *substantive equal treatment* rights in Union law secure *liberty from interference* for members of European polities through virtual representation, whereby 'foreigners are self-determining in any national polity by virtue of being represented through the representation of citizens'.[73] Each European polity is subdivided into identical or similar groups, and all the groups are represented in each national political process.

> The concept looks at the polity from a very traditional lens. Societies are made up of different groups ('descriptions'); such as trades, professions, or estates. In order to have their interests in a polity represented, even only virtually, it is sufficient to have representative samples of these descriptions participate in the political process. This means that as long as at least one representative of a group is given a voice, the interests of the group are represented.[74]

The presumption behind virtual representation is that interests of members of all European polities will be roughly the same or equivalent; any conflict between the interests results only from their belonging to different national polities. Within their host polity, nationals of other Member States remain dependent on this polity in terms of *positive liberty*: even the right to vote in local elections is given to them

[68] This would be contrary inter alia to Article 21(1) of the Universal Declaration of Human Rights: 'Everyone has the right to take part in the government of his country, directly or through freely chosen representatives'.

[69] Case C-256/11 *Derici* §66.

[70] Case C-413/99 *Baumbast & R*, Case C-60/00 *Carpenter*, Case C-200/02 *Zhu and Chen*, Case C-34/09 *Zambrano*.

[71] Case C-34/09 *Zambrano*.

[72] Case C-356-7/11 *O & B*.

[73] A Somek, *The Cosmopolitan Constitution* (Oxford, Oxford University Press, 2014) 27.

[74] ibid 26.

at the discretion of each national polity, as a result of the national political process. This logic fails to factor in cultural differences or differences in ideas about *positive liberty* that may exist between national polities; rather, it is presumed that, even if differences exist, those Member State nationals who move to another polity accept the host polity's vision of 'ideal life'.[75] This is a plausible presumption as regards migration between the polities undertaken as a free choice of polity members; in Chapter 5 we will see how this presumption and the whole system fail once migration is no longer free and external interests are at stake.

Protection against discrimination on the grounds of nationality and 'a system of human rights protection that meets the mark of international peer review' are the necessary preconditions for enabling this 'cosmopolitan self-determination'.[76]

> [C]osmopolitan self-determination is not primarily about having the interests of outsiders somehow represented inside a national polity. It is about the opportunity of representation that foreigners would have if the polity were theirs. If this is guaranteed, they are virtual members.[77]

On this understanding of free movement law as an instrument of virtual representation, even the most contradictory cases such as *Akrich*[78] and *Metock*[79] become compatible and coherent. Both cases involved illegally resident third-country nationals who married Union citizens and the latter exercised free movement rights; third-country family members then claimed a right to reside legally as spouses of Union citizens. However, if in *Akrich* the right was claimed upon the return of a Union citizen to her Member State of nationality, in *Metock* it was claimed in another Member State. In terms of representation it makes a decisive difference. In *Akrich*, the right of lawful residence upon return of a Union citizen to her Member State of nationality was denied—and the Court upheld this rejection. Indeed, the Union citizen spouse in this case had full representation rights in the national political process and could use them to shape the national idea of *positive liberty* expressed in national immigration law. In *Metock*, however, the situation was different. The right to reside was claimed by third-country nationals in the Member State where their Union citizen spouse was not a national. In this situation, virtual representation was necessary and non-domination requires

[75] At least when the constitutive elements of the national political community are concerned, this corresponds also to the ECtHR case law: ECtHR Case *Lautsi v. Italy* (18.3.2011), ECtHR Case *S.A.S. v France* (1.7.2014).

[76] Somek (n 73) 26.

[77] ibid 27.

[78] Case C-109/01 *Akrich*.

[79] Case C-127/08 *Metock*; S Currie, 'Accelerated Justice or a Step Too Far?' (2009) 34(2) *European Law Review* 310–26; D Martin, 'Comments on Förster (Case C-158/07 of 18 November 2008), Metock (Case C-127/08 of 25 July 2008) and Huber (Case C-524/06 of 16 December 2008)' (2009) 11 *European Journal of Migration and Law*; N Cambien, 'Case C-127/08, Blaise Baheten Metock and Others v Minister for Justice, Equality and Law Reform' (2009) 15 *Columbia Journal of European Law*; C Castello, 'Metock: Free Movement and "Normal Family Life" in the Union' (2009) 46 *CML Rev*.

that *non-interference* with the interest of a Union citizen be protected in Union law.

Yet, free movement law goes beyond 'cosmopolitan self-determination' and gives all Union citizens an equal *right* to virtual *representation* through the abolition-of-obstacles doctrine. This is a right to have one's interests balanced, even if only virtually, against the interests of others, and as such implies the need for reciprocity between the holders of this right. National polities are not eliminated,[80] yet the boundaries of national polities stretch. On the one hand, European integration creates policy interdependence between the national polities; this interdependence ensures that no individual European polity is in a position to dominate the other(s), which in turn enables each national polity to pursue *positive liberty* without domination by other European polities. On the other hand, this policy interdependence causes interdependence between the national political processes and potential for interference with *positive liberty* of individual polity members, which risks undermining the legitimacy of the EU. Union law minimises this interference through directly effective rights to non-discrimination on the grounds of nationality, ie polity membership. These rights withdraw interests of an insular minority created by European integration from the regulatory reach of the national political process. *Abolition of obstacles* to free movement means that no national polity can exclude members of other polities from virtual representation. Reciprocity of *non-interference* between national polities can thus be enforced by individual citizens without reliance on power of the state—EU law becomes more effective or 'binding' in comparison to international law.[81]

Taken together, abolition of obstacles to free movement and non-discrimination on the grounds of nationality—key rights of Union citizenship—protect national polities as reference groups for majoritarian political process. Political liberty of citizens in a polity—their ability to identify and act on their own idea of *positive liberty*—is shielded from interference by other polities in the Union and, for insular minorities within each polity, from dependence on the majority. EU law rights of Union citizenship advance the liberty of citizens not merely as individuals but as members of their national polities, thus (1) recognising the value of Loyalty in the national political community, and (2) advancing legitimacy of the national polity through the duty of its individual members to participate in the political process. The latter is done by preventing Exit from the national political process by those polity members whose immutable characteristics turn them into insular minorities—Exit that could occur were there a risk that the national political process could result in a permanent loss for the insular minority. EU free movement law secures liberty on two levels: *liberty from interference* between national polities in the Union and *liberty from dependence* within

[80] Indeed, the ECJ recognised that Member States preserve foreign relations between them, in other words polity independence, even in the face of Union freedoms, see Case C-364/10 *Hungary v Slovakia*.

[81] See Section 3 below.

each national polity.[82] Free movement of Union citizens thus strengthens liberty and legitimacy of national polities.

National polities thus emerge as the basic building blocks of Europe. Their liberty is the essence of the founding conception of Peace in Europe. National polities trade some of their ability to pursue their own *positive liberty* in exchange for *liberty from interference* by others. So long as the overall balance of liberties is respected no legitimacy problem ensues. National polities remain the forum for policy choice, yet, all members of other polities have a right to virtual representation in it. This structure of legitimacy neither enables nor requires identification and pursuit of *positive liberty* by the European polities jointly: identifying a new idea of *positive liberty* in Europe that would differ from the ideas of all and each European peoples is not what this arrangement does. Rather, free movement in the internal market protects the national political process, its legitimacy and the liberty of its members; it does not dismantle nor substitute it.[83] This can be likened to the arrangement in EU law regarding social security, in relation to which the Court reiterated that 'the exercise of the right of residence for citizens of the Union can be subordinated to the legitimate interests of the Member States'.[84] In other words, deregulation of migration between European polities does not unconditionally override the capacity of each European polity to determine *positive liberty: non-interference* goes both ways (by host polity with interests of members from other polities and by members of other polities with the capacity of the host polity to determine *positive liberty*).

The 'same advantages' granted in Union law by all Member States to each other[85] and each other's nationals[86] amount to equal *liberty from interference*. Equality of Member States under the Treaties implies equality of their polities, their political processes, and the interests of which they are comprised. Between the national polities in the Union, their unanimous commitment to the internal market as a policy choice established the 'circumstances of justice': a binding agreement

[82] Although Member States may limit *non-interference* with cross-polity interests, these are reviewed and interpreted by the ECJ: the balance between non-domination (through interdependence) and *non-interference* (with cross-polity interests) is established in Union law; in establishing this balance, EU law protects the interests of separate national polities, in particular as regards: (1) nationality requirements for employment that involves the exercise of public authority: Case 149/79 *Commission v Belgium*, (2) loss of residence rights as a result of 'unreasonable burden' on the national welfare system: Case C-333/13 *Dano*, and (3) loss of residence rights on the grounds of public security, Case C-348/96 *Donatella Calfa*; Joined Cases C-482/01 and C-493/01 *Orfanopoulos*; Case C-348/09 *P.I.*; Case C-300/11 *ZZ*. In the latter case, a dual EU and third-country national was expelled to his third state of nationality (as opposed to his Member State of nationality) even without any criminal conviction.

[83] Not substituted to the extent that a power to deregulate immigration—ensure free movement—is not the same as a power to regulate. Case C-376/98 *Tobacco Advertising*.

[84] Case C-140/12 *Brey* §§43 and 55.

[85] Article 351 TFEU: 'the advantages accorded under the Treaties by each Member State form an integral part of the establishment of the Union and are thereby inseparably linked with the granting of the same advantages by all the other Member States'.

[86] Article 18 TFEU: 'Within the scope of application of the Treaties, and without prejudice to any special provisions contained therein, any discrimination on grounds of nationality shall be prohibited'.

establishing the 'conditions under which human cooperation is both possible and necessary'.[87] Such an agreement was undoubtedly enabled by the unique post-WWII situation, where, inter alia, all national polities were equally weakened by the war, so that 'no one among them can dominate the rest', all were 'vulnerable to attack', 'subject to having their plans blocked by united force of others' in 'the condition of moderate scarcity'.

> Thus while the parties have roughly similar needs and interests, or needs and interests in various ways complementary, so that mutually advantageous cooperation among them is possible, they nevertheless have their own plans of life. These plans, or conceptions of the good, lead them to have different ends and purposes, and to make conflicting claims on the natural and social resources available.[88]

It is these conflicting claims that were pre-empted by the policy choices in the Treaties. The 'circumstances of politics'[89] were carefully precluded. At the level of polity members, either the situation remained governed by national law (the so-called 'purely internal situations') or the policy choice was fixed unanimously by all national polities in the Treaties through Treaty objectives (abolition of obstacles to free movement) and Treaty rights (non-discrimination on the grounds of nationality), preventing subsequent disagreement.

Although functional Treaty objectives and Treaty rights enjoy high formal legitimacy that stems from being ratified unanimously by each national polity, they present an insurmountable problem for politics, and a problem should the situation change. They limit policy choices available at the European and national levels to the ideas of *positive liberty* shared by all the peoples of Europe *at the moment of unanimous ratification of the Treaties.* By directing the exercise of Union powers, they restrict the political process and render rigid the idea of *positive liberty* that they prescribe. After the ratification of the Treaties, this shared vision of ideal life is no longer subject to debate, question or amendment other than by means of Treaty reform.

A similar commitment to abstain from politics is found in EC external agreements, some of which contain clauses on the treatment of workers coming to the Community from third contracting states. The study of these agreements illuminates the boundaries of Europe's Union and abstention from politics in it: they illustrate where the commitment to a shared idea of 'ideal life' or 'circumstances of justice' in Europe comes to an end and yields space to politics. Regulation of third-country nationals under these agreements provides a useful contrast to EC free movement law because it allows comparison between two types of foreigners: Member State nationals who are members of polities bound by the EC legal order and third-country nationals who are members of polities not so bound.

[87] J Rawls, *A Theory of Justice* (Cambridge, MA, Harvard University Press, 1999) 109–10.
[88] ibid.
[89] J Waldron, *Law and Disagreement* (Oxford, Oxford University Press, 1999) 159–60: the 'elementary circumstances of politics' are characterised by a disagreement about the idea of justice and 'the felt need for a common decision notwithstanding the disagreement'.

2. *NON-INTERFERENCE* vs *POSITIVE LIBERTY* IN EC EXTERNAL AGREEMENTS

From 1963 onwards, Member States and the Community concluded association and partnership and cooperation agreements with third states, many of which contained provisions on equal treatment of third-country nationals who pursue economic activities in the Member States. On the Community side, the participation of both the Community and Member States was required due to the lack of Community powers to conclude the agreements in their entirety, these clauses in particular. The Treaty contained no express external power for the Community in this regard, while internal powers of the Community as regards regulation of third-country nationals in the framework of the internal market were not exercised, resulting in the absence of implied powers.[90] The ECJ nevertheless established its jurisdiction to interpret the agreements in their entirety, including the provisions on third-country nationals for the conclusion of which the Community lacked powers. Clear, precise and unconditional provisions of these agreements were found to have direct effect in the Community legal order and enjoy primacy over conflicting provisions of national law. To the extent that the aim and context of these agreements coincided with those of the EC Treaty, migration-related clauses contained therein were interpreted along the identically worded provisions of free movement law.[91] Before the analysis of this case law, a brief overview of the agreements follows.[92]

The most far-reaching integration between the Community and third states is foreseen under the Agreement on the European Economic Area (EEA).[93] The agreement 'establishes a close association between the European Union and the EFTA States based on special, privileged links between the parties concerned'[94] with the aim 'to provide for the fullest possible realisation of the free movement of goods, persons, services and capital within the whole EEA, so that the internal market established within the European Union is extended to the EFTA States'[95] and 'to promote a continuous and balanced strengthening of trade and economic relations between the Contracting Parties with equal conditions of competition, and the respect of the same rules, with a view to creating a homogeneous European Economic Area'.[96] The agreement creates an obligation of

[90] Nor was external action of the Community necessary for the establishment of free movement in the internal market, see Opinion 1/94 §86: 'attainment of freedom of establishment and freedom to provide services for nationals of the Member States is not inextricably linked to the treatment to be afforded in the Community to nationals of non-member countries or in non-member countries to nationals of Member States of the Community'.

[91] Current Articles 45, 49 and 56 TFEU.

[92] For an exhaustive overview see K Eisele, *The External Dimension of the EU's Migration Policy. Different Legal Positions of Third-Country Nationals in the EU: A Comparative Perspective* (The Hague, Brill Nijhoff, 2014) ch 4.

[93] (3.1.1994) OJ L1/3.

[94] Case C-431/11 *UK v Council* §49.

[95] Case C-452/01 *Ospelt* §29.

[96] Article 1(1) EEA.

homogeneous interpretation of its provisions and corresponding provisions of Union law,[97] while simultaneously seeking to preserve the autonomous character of the Union legal order.[98] Article 4 EEA provides: 'Within the scope of application of this Agreement, and without prejudice to any special provisions contained therein, any discrimination on grounds of nationality shall be prohibited'. The ECJ interpreted free movement provisions of the EEA Agreement in line with the European Treaties, including direct effect and primacy over Member State law.[99]

A lower level of integration between the Community and third states was foreseen in Europe Agreements,[100] which paved the way for the 2004 enlargement of the EU to the East. The agreements, concluded individually with each East European state, were modelled on the EC agreement with Poland, the aim of which was to develop 'close political relations between the parties' and 'promote the expansion of trade' between them, so as 'to foster the dynamic economic development and prosperity in Poland'; an explicit objective was to provide 'financial and technical assistance to Poland', as well as to create 'an appropriate framework for Poland's gradual integration into the Community', for which Poland was required to fulfil 'the necessary conditions'.[101] Article 37 of the agreement provided for non-discrimination of migrant Polish workers on the grounds of nationality, while Article 44 secured the right of Polish nationals 'to take up and pursue economic activities as self-employed persons and to set up and manage undertakings'

[97] Article 58 EEA regarding competition; generally Part VII, Chapter 3, section 1 of the EEA—also in court interpretation (Article 106 EEA) and in decisions of the EEA Joint Committee (Article 105 EEA). See W Van Gerven, 'The Genesis of EEA Law' [1992] *Fordham International Law Journal*; HP Graver, 'Mission Impossible: Supranationality and National Legal Autonomy in the EEA Agreement' (2002) 7(73) *European Foreign Affairs Review*; H Haukeland Fredriksen, 'One Market, Two Courts' (2010) 79 *Nordic Journal of International Law*; S Magnusson, 'Judicial Homogeneity in the European Economic Area and the Authority of the EFTA Court' (2011) 80 *Nordic Journal of International Law*.

[98] Opinions 1/91 and 1/92; on the tension between these two objectives see M Cremona, 'The "Dynamic and Homogeneous EEA": Byzantine Structures and Variable Geometry' (1994) 19 *European Law Review* 508; J Forman, 'The EEA Agreement Five Years On: Dynamic Homogeneity in Practice and Its Implementation by the Two EEA Courts' (1999) 36 *CML Rev* 751; H Haukeland Fredriksen, 'Bridging the Widening Gap between the EU Treaties and the Agreement on the European Economic Area' (2012) 18(6) *European Law Journal* 868–86; S Magnusson and O Hannesson, 'State Liability in EEA Law: Towards Parallelism or Homogeneity?' (2013) 38(2) *European Law Review*.

[99] Case C-452/01 *Ospelt* §29. For more on uniform interpretation of EEA and EU law see Haukeland Fredriksen (n 98).

[100] Europe Agreements concluded with Bulgaria OJ 1994 L358, the Czech Republic OJ 1994 L360, Estonia OJ 1998 L68/3, Hungary OJ 1993 L347, Latvia OJ 1998 L26/3, Lithuania OJ 1998 L51/3, Poland OJ 1993 L348, Romania OJ 1994 L357, Slovenia OJ 1999 L51/3, Slovakia OJ 1994 L359. For a detailed discussion see E Guild, 'The Europe Agreements: The Right to Establishment in the Central and Eastern European Agreements' in E Guild (ed), *The Legal Framework and Social Consequences of Free Movement of Persons in the European Union* (The Hague, Kluwer Law International, 1999) Stabilisation and Association Agreements are worded in similar terms: Croatia (28.01.2005) OJ L26/3, Yugoslav Republic of Macedonia (20.03.2004) OJ L084, Albania (28.04.2009) OJ L107/166, Serbia (18.10.2013) OJ L278/16, Bosnia and Herzegovina (30.06.2015) OJ L164/2, the Republic of Montenegro (29.04.2010) OJ L108/3.

[101] Article 1(2) Europe Agreement with Poland (1993).

within the Community. The Court of Justice found that, to the extent that these agreements seek 'to promote the expansion of trade and harmonious economic relations' and closer ties between the Union and the third state, the worker clauses of these agreements should be interpreted along the identically worded provisions of Union Treaties, in particular Article 45 TFEU.[102] Non-discrimination provisions produce direct effect,[103] while as regards migration rights in the context of the freedom of establishment in Article 44 of the Agreement, Member States could require a permit to enter and reside as part of 'a system of prior control' in order to determine whether the applicant 'genuinely intends to take up an activity as a self-employed person without at the same time entering into employment or having recourse to public funds'.[104]

The Ankara Agreement[105] aims

> to promote the continuous and balanced strengthening of trade and economic relations between the parties, while taking full account of the need to ensure an accelerated development of the Turkish economy and to improve the level of employment and the living conditions of the Turkish people.[106]

The agreement thus foresees 'progressively securing freedom of movement for workers'[107] and progressive abolition of restrictions on freedom of establishment and freedom to provide services[108] while taking into account 'the special economic and social circumstances of Turkey'.[109] Further to the agreement, subsequent decisions of the EU–Turkey Association Council[110] constitute a 'stage in securing freedom of movement for workers on the basis of Articles [45, 49 and 56 TFEU]'.[111] The Court interpreted the non-discrimination and residence rights contained in these decisions in line with its case law on free movement of workers in the internal market,[112] preserving, however, Member State powers to regulate first access by Turkish nationals to their territories and labour force.[113]

The Euro-Mediterranean Agreements contain non-discrimination clauses for migrant workers who are nationals of the contracting states.[114] The agreements

[102] Case C-257/99 *Barkoci and Malik*.

[103] *Ex multis*, Case C-63/99 *Gloszczuk*; Case C-257/99 *Barkoci and Malik*; Case C-235/99 *Kondova*; Case C-162/00 *Pokrzeptowicz-Meyer*.

[104] Case C-268/99 *Jany* §31.

[105] 1963 Agreement establishing an Association between the European Economic Community and Turkey (29.12.1964) OJ P217/3687.

[106] Ankara Agreement Article 2(1).

[107] ibid Article 12.

[108] ibid Articles 13 and 14.

[109] Second subparagraph of Article 41(2) of the Additional Protocol.

[110] In particular Decisions 1/80 and 3/80, the latter amended, as regards social security, by Council Decision 2012/776/EU, see also Case C-81/13 *UK v Council*.

[111] Case C-36/96 *Günaydin* §21.

[112] Case C-1/97 *Birden*, Case C-98/96 *Ertanir*, Case C-294/06 *Payir*.

[113] Case C-237/91 *Kus*, Case C-36/96 *Günaydin*, Case C-434/93 *Bozkurt*, Case C-4/05 *Guzeli*, Case C-188/00 *Kurz*, Case C-192/89 *Sevince*, Case C-355/93 *Eroglu*.

[114] Euro-Mediterranean Agreements concluded with Algeria (10.10.2005) OJ L265/2 Article 67, Morocco (18.03.2000) OJ L70/2 Article 64, and Tunisia (30.03.1998) OJ L98/2 Article 64;

aim inter alia to 'provide an appropriate framework for political dialogue between the Parties', 'establish the conditions for the gradual liberalisation of trade in goods, services and capital', 'promote trade and the expansion of harmonious economic and social relations between the Parties' and 'encourage integration of the Maghreb countries'.[115] Freedom of movement of workers and freedom of establishment are not foreseen in the agreements. The ECJ interpreted both the concept of worker and the modus operandi of non-discrimination rights contained in these agreements by reference to Community workers under the relevant internal market law.[116] Regarding the right to reside, however, the picture is radically different. In the absence of any mention of free movement in the agreements, the only occasion on which a right to reside may exist is where a Member State grants a third-country national worker 'specific rights in relation to employment which [are] more extensive than the rights of residence conferred on him by that State'.[117] Non-discrimination provisions will not confer residence rights where a refusal to renew a residence permit would force the worker to discontinue otherwise lawful employment. It is for the host Member State to decide when access to the national labour market will cease or commence.

Partnership and Cooperation Agreements were concluded with the former republics of the USSR. The Agreements contain standard clauses on non-discrimination of workers from the contracting states without any reference to free movement or the common market.[118] Modelled on the original agreement with Russia, the objectives of these Agreements include the establishment of a framework for political dialogue between the parties and 'a basis for economic, social, financial and cultural cooperation founded on the principles of mutual advantage, mutual responsibility and mutual support', promotion of trade and harmonious economic relations, support to the third country involved, especially as regards its 'gradual integration' into 'a wider area of cooperation in Europe' and the creation of 'the necessary conditions for the future establishment of a free trade area' that would cover cross-border trade in services and 'freedom of establish-

Euro-Mediterranean Agreements were also concluded with Lebanon (30.5.2006) OJ L143/1, Israel (21.06.2000) OJL 147/3 and Jordan (15.05.2002) OJ L129/3 without, however, any clauses on migrant workers or freedom of establishment for natural persons. They are therefore excluded from the present overview.

115 Article 1 of the Agreements with Algeria, Morocco and Tunisia respectively.

116 For instance, a Moroccan national who carried out military service in a Member State army was found to be a worker by analogy with a Member State national under current Article 45 TFEU (Case C-336/05 *Echouikh* referring to Case C-248/96 *Grahame & Hollanders*) except where eligibility of benefits in the country of origin was concerned (Case C-18/90 *Kziber*); see also Case C-103/94 *Krid*, Case C-113/97 *Babahenini*.

117 Case C-41/96 *El Yassini*; Case C-97/05 *Gattoussi*.

118 Partnership and Cooperation Agreements concluded with Armenia (1999) Article 20, Azerbaijan (1999) Article 20, Georgia (1999) Article 20, Kazakhstan (1999) Article 19, Kyrgyz Republic (1999) Article 19, Moldova (1998) Article 23, Russia (1994) Article 23(1), Tajikistan (2004) Article 17, Uzbekistan (1999) Article 19, Ukraine (1998) Article 24; Association Agreement with Ukraine (2014) Article 17.

ment of companies'.[119] The ECJ interpreted both the concept of worker and the modus operandi of non-discrimination rights (primacy and direct effect) in line with EC free movement law while leaving each Member State discretion as regards admission to its territory and labour force.[120]

Finally, the Cotonou Agreement between the EU and its Member States on the one side and 79 African, Caribbean and Pacific states on the other[121] differs from the previous agreements in its multilateral nature and the general scope of objectives, which seek 'to promote and expedite the economic, cultural and social development of the ACP States' and 'comprehensive, balanced and deep political dialogue leading to commitments on both sides' including on migration.[122] Establishing of any special trading area is not foreseen by the agreement. Article 13(3) provides that each EU Member State accord 'to workers of ACP countries legally employed in its territory [treatment] free from any discrimination based on nationality, as regards working conditions, remuneration and dismissal, relative to its own nationals'. There is no ECJ case law on this provision and, given the nature and objectives of the agreement on the one hand and the clear wording of the provision on the other, it is uncertain to what extent it may result in directly effective rights along the free movement case law.[123] At any rate, this provision will not affect the regulatory autonomy of Member States as regards admission of ACP nationals to their territories and labour force.

Case law of the ECJ on mixed external agreements raises a question of what is enforced: (1) an agreement between Member States and a third state? (2) an agreement between the Community and a third state? Or (3) an agreement between Member States in the Community? The answer to these questions will determine the political and constitutional nature of the Community and its boundaries. The first alternative can be discarded: the ECJ does not have jurisdiction to enforce an international agreement between a Member State and a third country.[124] The remaining options are key to understanding the boundaries of Europe's Union.

[119] Article 1 PCA Russia 1994; these objectives are much more far-reaching than those of all other PCAs: compare the much shorter Article 1 of the 1998 PCA Ukraine, changed in Article 1(2) Association Agreement with Ukraine 2014.

[120] Case C-265/03 *Simutenkov*, where the Court explicitly referred to case C-415/93 *Bosman*, which concerned a Member State national employed in another Member State.

[121] OJ L317, 15.12.2000 as amended OJ L209, 11.8.2005 and OJ L287, 4.11.2010.

[122] Articles 1, 8 and 13 accordingly.

[123] At least some provisions of the Agreement have direct effect: Case C-469/93 *Chiquita Italia*; though the content of rights will not necessarily be interpreted along free movement rights, Case 65/77 *Razanatsimba*. In Case C-230/97 *Awoyemi* no agreement was pleaded. The extent of rights will also depend on the existence of bilateral agreements between Member States and Cotonou states, eg mobility partnerships: Joint Declaration on a Mobility Partnership between the European Union and the Republic of Cape Verde (21.05.2008) Council doc. 9460/08 ADD 2 (mobility partnerships were also signed with the Republic of Moldova (21.05.2008) Council doc. 9460/08 ADD 1, Georgia (20.11.2009) Council doc. 16396/09 ADD 1, Armenia (6.10.2011) Council doc. 14963/11 ADD 1, Azerbaijan (30.11.2009), Morocco (03.06.2013) Council doc. 6139/13, Tunisia (03.03.2014) Council doc. 16371/13, and Jordan (09.10.2014) European Commission IP/14/1109).

[124] Article 230 EC (current Article 263 TFEU).

If the provisions regulating third-country nationals under the agreements were concluded by Member States in their sovereign capacity (3), then it is they who made policy choices, including both substantive rights of individual migrants and, as a consequence, the limits imposed on future regulatory capacity of their national political processes. No problem of democratic accountability and legitimacy would arise at the European level since the choice is made in the national political process. Interdependence through the internal market creates a union between European polities—and between them only. By enforcing provisions on third-country nationals in mixed external agreements, the Court is first and foremost enforcing an agreement *between Member States* to pursue a certain policy choice. Unilateral deviations by Member States from this choice would undermine the Community legal order by interfering with the interests of other Member States (who rely on the policy choice sealed in the agreement). On this reading, enforcing substantive rights of third-country nationals under these agreements would thus be equivalent to enforcing the agreement between Member States to limit their national political processes in this regard. This is equivalent to enforcement of EC Treaties: substantive policy choice is an instrument to secure non-interference between the European polities.

If, conversely, these provisions were concluded by the Community under *its* power, then a problem of legitimacy and accountability would arise at the European level because the decision would be withdrawn from the national political process, requiring alternative European political process and an alternative European polity with reference to which majority rule is accepted.[125] By enforcing such an agreement in Union law (2), the ECJ would enforce not merely obligations of Member States to each other but an obligation of the Community vis-a-vis a third state.[126] To the extent that the substance of rights under external agreements coincides with free movement rights in the EC Treaty, the identical modus operandi of these rights would *extend* the relationship between Member States in *the Community to the third state*. I will now show why the second option is not the case and outline what delimits Europe's deregulatory union.

3. THE BOUNDARIES OF EUROPE'S UNION: RECIPROCITY OF COMMITMENT

To various degrees, provisions on third-country workers contained in *mixed external agreements extended all the four aspects of free movement law* (direct effect, primacy, non-discrimination, abolition of obstacles) *to members of non-EU polities* in Union law. Nevertheless, this fell far short of deregulation of immigration characteristic of EU free movement law. The legal formula for market integration

125 The ECJ recognised that this is not the case: Case 12/86 *Demirel*.

126 Case 253/83 *Kupferberg*, Case C-239/03 *Etang de Berre*, Case C-459/03 *MOX Plant*.

between states in Europe—both the modus operandi of Union law (primacy and direct effect) and its substantive provisions (non-discrimination and the abolition of obstacles to free movement)—have been only partially transposed to the relations between the European Community and third states.[127] There is a constitutional reason for this.

European integration is political in nature. Within the legal orders of Member States, directly effective Treaty provisions and functional objectives thereof limit the capacity of the national political processes to regulate the interests of members from other European polities—interests without a Voice in the political process of their host Member State. The power of the state is thus abolished both in relation to other European polities and in relation to its own polity members who, as a result of free movement in the internal market, become dependent on their national polity. National polities of Member States may no longer regulate migrant workers from other Member States in a manner that deviates from the Treaty; nor can EU Member States exit from the Treaty by disapplication or partial implementation in national law. Once the provisions are directly effective and binding, national politics are disempowered. Commitment in Union law becomes binding without and despite the political process.

The ECJ is crucial for enabling deregulation. Deregulation of free movement in the internal market, this modus operandi of EC law, was only possible thanks to a sole source of final binding interpretation. Reciprocity of commitment to self-restraint by the national political processes[128] would be at risk were the integrating polities to determine its substance, scope and effect. Exit would not be limited for all national polities to the same degree; not all Member States would be prompted to participate in joint governance through the exercise of Voice. A shared court with a preliminary reference procedure and binding rulings that constitute the only source of interpretation of Union law[129] ensures reciprocity by limiting Exit and thus encouraging the exercise of Voice—crucial for joint governance.[130] This role of the ECJ transformed Europe from an alliance based on international law into a Union of polities.

The combination of primacy and direct effect with the role of the ECJ made unnecessary the retention of state powers in order to enforce commitments of other Member States under the Treaties by (the threat of) retaliation or, alternatively, by exiting from the Treaties should other Member States fail to perform their obligations and break the Treaties. The *modus operandi* and the role of the

[127] In particular, the abolition of obstacles to free movement only extends to the EEA states, see below.

[128] Article 351 TFEU: 'the advantages accorded under the Treaties by each Member State form an integral part of the establishment of the Union and are thereby inseparably linked with the granting of the same advantages by all the other Member States.

[129] Articles 267 and 344 TFEU.

[130] Weiler (n 10) 2427; JHH Weiler, *Van Ghend en Loos: the Individual as Subject and Object and the Dilemma of European Legitimacy* (2014) NYU Jean Monnet Working Paper 10/14.

ECJ made the Treaties 'unbreakable': they foreclosed Exit and ensured reciprocity. EC legal order allows and requires Member States to abandon the international law understanding of reciprocity based on retaliation[131] in favour of reciprocity based on a single source of final and binding interpretation. Regulatory powers of Member States are at once abolished and rendered redundant for enforcing commitments in EC law. The enforcement of this commitment can now be done not by the state but by individual polity members almost in a role of 'representing' their state. The interests of Member State nationals in having the Treaty enforced coincided with the interest of at least one Community polity, furthering equality of polities before EC law. Community legal order was thus proclaimed new and autonomous:[132] *non-interference* (actual and potential) between Member States established in the EC Treaty no longer depended on the national political process for its enforcement and interpretative evolution. This eliminated the potential for *interference* and contributed to non-domination between the European polities: reciprocity of commitment to *non-interference* no longer depended on the capacity of each national polity (and its political process) to protect itself from domination (either passive or active) through retaliation, diplomacy or international law.

The situation differs as regards third states, where the ECJ has no jurisdiction. There is no similar mechanism to ensure reciprocity between the EU and third states. The EEA comes closer than other external agreements to the EU integration model with the establishment of the EFTA Court, bound by the principle of uniform interpretation of EEA law in line with EU free movement law. Pursuant to this principle, similarly worded provisions of the EEA have been interpreted by the EFTA Court analogously to the ECJ case law on the internal market.[133] Nevertheless, neither direct effect nor a shared court with compulsory jurisdiction and binding rulings feature in EEA law. Jurisdiction of the EFTA Court is limited to the EFTA states, while interpretation of the EEA in EU Member States remains the exclusive jurisdiction of the ECJ; and while the EFTA Court is bound by the

[131] Hence, prohibition of retaliation between Member States in Union law, Case 90 & 91/63 *Commission v Luxembourg and Belgium*, Case C-5/94 *Hedley Lomas* §20, Case 232-78 *Commission v France* §9. W Phelan, 'The Troika: The Interlocking Roles of *Commission v. Luxembourg and Belgium*, *Van Gend en Loos* and *Costa v. ENEL* in the Creation of the European Legal Order' (2015) 21(1) *European Law Journal*.

[132] Also recognised by external actors: ECtHR Case *Bosphorus v. Ireland* (30.06.2005) Application no 45036/98.

[133] EFTA Case E-2/06 *EFTA Surveillance Authority v Norway (Norwegian Waterfalls)* (26.06.2007), Case E-4/01 *Karlsson v Iceland* (30.05.2002), Case E-1/07 *Criminal proceedings against A* (03.10.2007), Case E-9/97 *Sveinbjörnsdóttir v Iceland* (10.12.1998). Although in the latter case the EFTA Court extended the principle of state liability under *Frankovich* to the EFTA states, this does not limit their national political process in the same way as the limits placed in EC law due to the difference in the binding force of the EFTA Court and CJEU rulings. Indeed, also under the ECHR there is a system of awarding damages paid by the state which, however, does not result in a political union between the states of the Council of Europe. C Lebeck, 'General Principles' in The EFTA Court (ed), *The EEA and the EFTA Court* (Oxford, Hart Publishing, 2014).

principle of uniform interpretation, it is questionable to what extent uniformity is at all possible or even compatible with the EEA.[134] In any event, the extent to which the *substantive* provisions of the EEA in the EFTA states correspond to the ECJ case law depends on the institutions *external* to the EU and its Member States, be they the EFTA Court or national authorities, political institutions or courts of the EFTA states. In terms of the modus operandi, neither the EEA itself nor the rulings of the EFTA Court produce direct effects in the national legal orders of the EFTA states.[135] The absence of a single source of interpretation and a common modus operandi of the EEA law between the EU and the EFTA states shows that there is no common autonomous legal order between them nor a corresponding union of polities.[136] From this perspective, the argument that uniform interpretation of EEA law by the EFTA Court is destined to find a boundary in Union citizenship becomes especially compelling.[137]

The same is true under other external agreements. In one of its early judgments, the ECJ stated that 'in ensuring respect for commitments arising from an agreement concluded by the Community institutions the Member States fulfil, within the Community system, an obligation in relation to the Community, which has assumed responsibility for the due performance of the agreement'.[138] The Court seemed to presume that the Community did have powers to regulate third-country nationals, including their entry and residence, under the internal market provisions.[139] Nevertheless, more recently as regards the Agreement with Turkey, the Court drew a boundary to uniform interpretation: interpretation and enforcement of this agreement in Turkey was left to the national authorities and the national political process of this third state, and uniform interpretation of similarly worded provisions (free movement of passive service recipients) in line with EC internal market law was not envisaged by the contracting parties and would therefore be misplaced.[140] This is how the 'object and purpose' that guide the interpretation

[134] Cremona (n 98); Forman (n 98); Graver (n 97); Haukeland Fredriksen (n 97); Magnusson (n 97); K Almestad, 'The Essentials' in The EFTA Court (ed) (n 133). Temporal limitations on the principle of uniform interpretation by the EFTA Court were de facto removed.

[135] Magnusson and Hannesson (n 98).

[136] A shared court whose rulings are final and binding is a clear borderline between the EU and the EEA (the closest integration is provided in an external agreement after the integration between Member States in the EU), see Opinion 1/91 *EFTA* and Opinion 1/92 *EFTA*.

[137] Haukeland Fredriksen (n 98).

[138] Case 12/86 *Demirel*.

[139] Even if these powers had not yet been exercised; Member States vehemently denied it. Case 12/86 *Demirel*: 'since freedom of movement for workers is, by virtue of Article [39 EC] et seq., one of the fields covered by the Treaty, it follows that the commitments regarding the freedom of movement fall within the powers conferred on the Community by Article [310 EC]'. The Court reached a similar conclusion as regards mobility of third-country nationals for the purpose of provision of services: it rejected the argument that this fell within the Community powers on common commercial policy because the Treaty contained 'specific chapters on the free movement of natural and legal persons' as part of the internal market, implying that 'the treatment of nationals of non-member countries on crossing the external frontiers of Member States' could be à *contraire* to what was proposed, regulated under the internal market powers of the Community, see Opinion 1/94.

[140] In Case C-221/11 *Demirkan* §61, the ECJ examined 'the practice of the contracting parties' with regard to whether the contracting parties 'intended' to include passive freedom to receive services under

of similarly worded provisions[141] differ within the EU and between the EU and Turkey.[142] A similar conclusion was reached for other external agreements.[143]

The jurisdiction of the ECJ emerges as the boundary of Europe's Union: together with the principle of direct effect (developed by the Court!), the role of the ECJ secures reciprocity of commitment and self-restraint of all Member State polities and their political processes under the Treaties. It is this function of the Court that enables reciprocal deregulation. The ECJ has jurisdiction to interpret EC external agreements within the Union and national legal orders but not as regards their legal effect in the third states parties to the agreements. Effectiveness and scope of seemingly reciprocal provisions of EC external agreements outside the EC legal order hinge on the political process of the third-country polity. There is no limit on the national political process as far as the third-country party to the agreement is concerned; on the contrary, the implementation of external agreements in the third state entirely depends on its political process alone—and so does Exit from the agreement, partial or even complete. Preconditions for Voice or higher political engagement by third states with the Community are not created. Unlike what happens between Member States under the Treaties, third-country polities and their political processes retain full regulatory autonomy under the agreements. Vis-a-vis third states, considerations of reciprocity in a traditional international law mode of retaliation and Exit from broken Treaties are alive and well. Binding reciprocity of commitment developed by the Court through primacy and direct effect doctrines requires acceptance by each national polity that it is party to a privileged relationship based on reciprocity of commitment to a shared vision of 'ideal life'—life in the Union.[144] Having one's own idea about *positive liberty* developed in each national polity in *liberty from dependence* and *from interference* is required for this to take place.

4. CONSTITUTIONAL DILEMMA OF INTERNAL OVER EXTERNAL

If reciprocity is the key and nothing guarantees reciprocity in the third contracting state, why did the ECJ repeatedly give migration-related clauses of mixed external

the freedom of provision of services under the EU–Turkey Association Agreement, explicitly referring to the fact that Turkey had introduced tourist visas for some Union citizens and some Member States had done likewise for Turkish nationals. Hence, the Court concluded, internal market case law on free movement for receiving services could not be extended to Turkish nationals under the Agreement.

[141] Article 31(1) of the Vienna Convention on the Law of Treaties requires that Treaties be interpreted in light of their context, object and purpose; Case C-416/96 *El Yassini* §47.

[142] Case C-371/08 *Ziebell* §74.

[143] Case C-416/96 *El Yassini*, Case C-268/99 *Jany*.

[144] This reciprocity and self-perception of bondedness is similar in nature (though not in intensity) to that between citizens in a polity in that it creates a closed community based on shared self-determined identity and an idea of positive liberty that is shared within the group. See A Sangiovanni, 'Global Justice, Reciprocity and the State' (2007) 35(1) *Philosophy and Public Affairs* 20: 'obligations of egalitarian reciprocity to fellow citizens and residents in the state, who provide us with the basic conditions and guarantees necessary to develop and act on a plan of life'.

agreements direct effect in Community law? To answer this question of *modus operandi* of mixed external agreements *in Union law* requires a perspective *internal* to Europe's Union. The function of enforcing worker clauses of mixed external agreements by the ECJ within the Union is to secure the autonomy of the EU legal order both internally and externally. Autonomy of the Union's legal order and integration between European polities require that the commitment assumed by Member States between themselves in the Union remains unaffected by the implementation of external agreements in third countries and their interpretation by non-EU courts.[145] This is what the Court means by emphasising the need 'to guarantee commitments towards non-member countries in all the fields covered by the Treaty'.[146] From this *internal* perspective and despite the external agreements being concluded between the EU and its Member States on the one hand and third countries on the other, their actual effect between Member States is to withdraw certain interests from their national political processes, thus requiring the same effect—and the same modus operandi—as other polity-restraining provisions of Union law. This does not mean, however, that the Community may not thereafter regulate these interests—quite the contrary.

Two elements of ECJ case law on mixed external agreements can be distinguished: the *substance of rights* that they secure to the individual (non-discrimination and other substantive rights) and the *effect of these provisions in national law* (primacy and direct effect). The former is connected to the type and level of integration foreseen with the third contracting state and is set out in the agreements: it is a matter of policy choice made by each national polity in the exercise of its external power to conclude the agreement. However, since all the Member States are bound thereby, within the framework of the Community, the resulting mixed external agreement acquires an additional value. It is not only an agreement with a third state, but also an agreement *between Member States* to regulate certain aspects of immigration as regards nationals of third contracting states in a certain way, to accord the third state a privilege. Similar to the EC Treaty, 'clear, precise and unconditional' wording in EC external agreements reflects an accord between Member States about the idea of *positive liberty* they share unanimously in their relationship with the third contracting state. A mixed external agreement amounts to an agreement between Member States (reciprocal self-restraint by the European polities) as much as between them and the third signatory state. Once this accord is reached in the framework of the Community, the nature of the EC legal order prevents Member States from defecting *vis-a-vis each other*. Hence the modus operandi of the agreements in Union and national law, primacy and direct effect: it is a matter of constitutional choice in the EC legal order. In the case of mixed external agreements, enforcing primacy and direct effect of an agreement between Member States withdraws the immigration-related provisions

[145] Opinion 1/91 *EFTA* and Opinion 1/92 *EFTA*.
[146] Case 12/86 *Demirel*.

of these agreements from the regulatory autonomy of the national political process; this incidentally gives rights to third-country nationals and limits the power of each Member State to retaliate against the third contracting state or withdraw from the agreement. But this is regulation, not deregulation.

A constitutional dilemma arises. On the one hand, there is a need to preserve regulatory powers vis-a-vis third states in order to ensure the individual and collective capacity of European polities to pursue *positive liberty* externally without dependence on third states. On the other hand, there is a need to abolish regulatory powers of Member States' political processes in order to preserve an agreement reached among them (the idea of *positive liberty* that Member States identified in the external agreement) and ensure their reciprocal *non-interference*. If the agreements were accompanied by a shift in external regulatory power from Member States to the Community the problem would be resolved: it would be possible to secure both external independence and the binding nature of internal accord. This may be a long-term aspiration.[147] However, where external regulatory powers are not passed to the Community, preserving the binding nature of Member States' obligations towards each other in the Community can only come at the expense of their external independence. The latter is the dilemma faced by the Court in all cases involving third-country nationals.

5. *NON-INTERFERENCE* BETWEEN MEMBER STATES PREVAILS OVER EXTERNAL *POSITIVE LIBERTY*

The solution to this dilemma adopted by the ECJ was to prioritise internal accord between Member States in the Community over their capacity to regulate third-country nationals in external agreements. Direct effect and primacy of mixed external agreements was not interpreted as an incidence of the Community regulating third-country nationals or of Member States conferring powers to the Community. Rather, the Court enforced the policy choice *agreed between Member States*. By agreeing to grant rights to the nationals of third contracting states, Member States agreed among themselves to withdraw this subject matter from their national political processes and, as a result, to limit their own autonomy to regulate third-country nationals to the extent provided by the agreements. This was an unavoidable trade-off: either the agreement between Member States would be enforced and primacy of EC legal order protected or Member States would preserve their regulatory autonomy as regards regulation of third-country nationals—*liberty from dependence*—both vis-a-vis third states and vis-a-vis each other in the Community. The latter would weaken the Community legal order internally. In the dilemma between the two, the ECJ consistently chose the former. Reciprocal *non-interference* between Member States thus prevailed over

[147] eg Case C-246/07 *Commission v Sweden*.

their external independence. This is so even in the absence of any corresponding regulatory powers of the Community that could replace external powers of the Member States sacrificed to *non-interference* in EC law.[148]

The preference for internal accord that secured *non-interference* between Member States over their capacity to advance *positive liberty* externally was previously established by the Court in free movement case law. There, the same choice was made between, on the one hand, the deregulatory concessions agreed between Member States in the internal market and, on the other hand, the power of Member States to regulate third-country nationals in national immigration law.[149] This is consistent with the doctrine of primacy and necessary for the autonomy of Community legal order. In the event of conflict between Member State obligations to each other in the Community and their national law, freedom to provide services and free movement of workers override national law, including national law on immigration by third-country nationals.[150] In Case C-43/93 *Van Der Elst*, the French authorities were not allowed to require that third-country nationals, employed by a Belgian service provider under Belgian immigration law and posted by their employer in France, comply with the requirements of French immigration law as concerns work permits. As long as 'the national legislation applicable in the host State concerning the immigration and residence of aliens had been complied with', any further requirements or fees imposed by the French authorities on third-country national employees of a Community service provider amounted to 'a restriction on the freedom to provide services within the meaning of Article 59 of the Treaty'.[151] A similar conclusion was reached as regards

[148] For an account of how the ECJ counterbalances this effect by forging 'an arena that makes possible the political engagement of European states, institutions and individuals' in 'the circumstances in which the unity of external politics was necessary in order to safeguard the conduct of internal politics' see R Post, 'Constructing the European Polity: AETR and the Open Skies Judgments' in M Poiares Maduro and L Azoulai (eds), *The Past and Future of EU Law* (Oxford, Hart Publishing, 2010).

[149] After the introduction of shared Community powers to regulate third-country nationals under the AFSJ into the EC Treaty (Amsterdam), all secondary law adopted under this power excludes from its scope third-country nationals who derive rights from Member State nationals' freedom of movement, see eg Article 3(3) Directive 2003/86/EC Family Reunification, Article 2(e) Directive 2003/109/EC Long-Term Residents, Article 3(1)(e) Directive 2009/50/EC Blue Card.

[150] Case C-43/93 *Van Der Elst*, Case C-445/03 *Commission v Luxembourg*, Case C-219/08 *Commission v Belgium*, Case C-60/00 *Carpenter*, Case C-291/05 *Eind*, Case C-457/12 *S & G*: derived rights of third-country nationals from their connection with Member State nationals and companies who exercise free movement rights.

[151] Prior to the abolition of internal borders between France and Belgium, France was entitled to require short-stay visas from such posted workers but not to apply its immigration law as regards residence and employment rights. After the abolition of internal borders, the national authorities of the state where the service is provided may require that 'the service provider furnishes a simple prior declaration certifying that the situation of the workers concerned is lawful, particularly in the light of the requirements of residence, work visas and social security cover in the Member State where that provider employs them' Case C-445/03 *Commission v Luxembourg* §46 and Case C-244/04 *Commission v Germany* §§41 and 42; conversely, insisting 'on an authorisation prior to the exercise of economic activity where workers who are nationals of non-member States are posted by Community undertakings in the framework of a provision of services' would run counter to the freedom to provide services, see Case C-219/08 *Commission v Belgium*.

third-country national family members of Member State national migrant workers.[152]

The *Metock*[153] case marked a decisive turn in favour of internal *negative liberty*. Previously, in *Akrich*,[154] the Court concluded that derived rights of third-country national family members in the host Member State served to remove obstacles to free movement by their Member State national sponsors, benchmarking residence rights at the level of those enjoyed in the previous Member State. However, in *Metock* the Court ruled that it was a matter of an absolute right and Member States were thus obliged to regularise third-country national family members of Union citizens even if these third-country nationals had previously broken national immigration law. The *Metock* judgment appears to presume that, since free movement of Union citizens between Member States is lawful by definition without derived equal rights for their third-country national family members, Union citizens would be obstructed in their exercise of this right unless reciprocal deregulation between Member States extended to third-country national family members of Union citizens. Thus, non-interference between European polities requires a limit on their capacity to regulate third-country nationals who are family members of Union citizens.[155] *Negative liberty* within the Union requires a sacrifice in the ability to advance *positive liberty* vis-a-vis non-Community interests.

[152] Case C-413/99 *Baumbast & R*, Case C-60/00 *Carpenter*, Case C-370/90 *Singh*. Residence and employment rights of family members are part of the worker's free movement right, irrespective of their family members' nationality (Articles 10–12 Regulation 1612/68/EC superseded by Directive 2004/38/EC, in particular Articles 5–7, 9–10, 12–14, 16–18, 20, 23–24, 28). Family members therefore benefit from the same rights as the Member State national worker, including access to the labour market (Article 23 Directive 2004/38/EC) and social security (Article 24 Directive 2004/38/EC, Case 40/76 *Slavica Kermaschek*), and Member States are under an obligation to 'grant family members who are not nationals of a Member State leave to enter their territory with a valid passport' and 'every facility to obtain the necessary visas' (Article 5 Directive 2004/38/EC).

[153] Case C-127/08 *Metock*.

[154] Case C-109/01 *Akrich* §53. Case C-456/12 *O & B* might mark a return to *Akrich*, see §63: this wording suggests that the right of residence that a third-country national derives from the free movement right of her Union citizen spouse depends on whether the third-country national in question enjoyed lawful residence in another Member State.

[155] The Lisbon Treaty reform for the first time introduced into the Treaties an explicit power and objective for the Union to 'combat illegal immigration' (Article 79 TFEU). It is, however, unlikely that setting such an explicit objective, even in Treaty text, will change the principle established in *Metock*. No matter how clear, precise and unconditional, Treaty objectives cannot prevail over Treaty rights such as free movement of Union citizens (Articles 20(2)a and 21(1) TFEU); even were the Council and the European Parliament to adopt secondary law to the contrary (an amendment to Directive 2004/38/EC proposed by some national governments after the judgment in *Metock*, see *Migration News Sheet* (September 2008) 1–4 and (January 2009) 2, cited in S Barbou des Places, 'Droit communautaire de la liberté de circulation et droit des migrations ou est la frontier?' in C Boutayeb, JC Muscatel, S Rodrigues and H Ruiz-Fabri (eds), *Mélanges en l'honneur de Philippe Manin. L'Union européenne: union de droit, union des droits* (Paris, Pedone, 2010) 343), it would be trumped by directly effective rights contained in the Treaty. Unless the Court changes its mind once more (which is not very likely because the *Akrich* position could increase its caseload), the only way to reinstitute Member State or EU powers to combat illegal immigration in *Akrich-Metock* situations could be by an explicit Treaty provision limiting this aspect of the rights inherent in Union citizenship.

These cases emphasise the central importance of enforcing reciprocal limits on the national political processes of Member States for the legitimacy of the Community legal order. Voluntary unions of states come about as a response to sufficiently serious, symmetrical and lasting threats.[156] Differently from other cases of unions among states, such as the United States of America (including the Articles of Confederation) or Switzerland, the main threat motivating unification in Europe did not originate from outside the Member States but from within: the threat of war in Europe, especially between France and Germany. Even before the end of WWII, the need to neutralise first of all this *internal* threat sparked off the idea of a Community of states,[157] whose design placed Member States both in interdependence and in a position to check each other's actions.[158] A tension emerged between two schools of thought.[159] On the one hand, a vision of Europe with a legitimacy in its own right that stems directly from the people(s); armed conflict between the peoples of Europe will be avoided by ultimately creating a single European people that can elect a single European government. On the other hand, a vision of Europe that places a check on the direct link between the peoples and their governments by obliging them to govern jointly in the Community; no matter how legitimate the government with its people, it cannot materially wage a war without the consent of its neighbours. Both visions result in prioritising *non-domination* between Member States in the Community—neutralisation of an internal threat to Peace—over their ability, individual or collective, to pursue *positive liberty* externally. In other words, EC law has a strong in-built internal-oriented bias that prevails over the ability to ascertain regulatory independence externally.[160]

Nowhere is the internal-oriented bias more evident than in the regulation of third-country nationals. To the extent that enforcing an agreement between Member States de facto results in withdrawing the interests of members of a third-country polity from the political processes of both Member States and the Community—at least until the Community exercises its powers to regulate third-country nationals—the limits on the regulatory capacity of national polities negotiated by Member States among themselves as regards regulating the interests that belong to their national polities are de facto extended, at least in part, to regulating interests of people from third-country polities. This creates a void in the regulatory power and the ability of Member States to pursue *positive*

[156] J Parent, *Voluntary Union in World Politics* (Oxford, Oxford University Press, 2011) 8–14.

[157] A Spinelli and E Rossi, *The Ventotene Manifesto* (Ventotene, The Altiero Spinelli Institute for Federalist Studies, 1941) 75–96.

[158] S Cassese, 'Is There Really a "Democratic Deficit"?' in S Cassese and G della Cananea (eds), *Institutional Reforms in the European Union: Memorandum for the Convention* (Rome, EuropEos, 2002).

[159] A Wiener and T Diez, 'Introducing the Mosaic of Integration Theory' in A Wiener and T Diez (eds), *European Integration Theory* (Oxford, Oxford University Press, 2009).

[160] For the 'foreign affairs' rationale for plenary federal power over immigration developed by the US Supreme Court and a comparison with the rise of the EU powers over immigration and foreign policy see EF Delaney, 'Justifying Power: Federalism, Immigration, and "Foreign Affairs"' (2013) 8(1) *Duke Journal of Constitutional Law & Public Policy*.

liberty on the international scene.[161] On the one hand, no mechanism to ensure reciprocity in enforcement is created in EU law vis-a-vis third states; on the other hand, the mechanism that existed in international law (retaliation and withdrawal from broken Treaties) is dismantled. Enforcement of reciprocity in relations with a third state, where it is relevant,[162] requires an accord between all Member States and possibly a joint Community measure; in policy areas so contested as immigration, not only are joint measures more difficult to adopt,[163] but they may additionally lose their attractiveness because of the implications for the passage of powers from Member States to the Community. The difficulty of such joint external action is illustrated by facts: while the Amsterdam and Lisbon reforms of the Treaties introduced explicit powers for the Community—now, the EU—to regulate third-country nationals internally,[164] both Treaties reserved most external powers in this regard to the national level[165] while the plenitude of optional clauses and undefined concepts in the directives and regulations on third-country nationals adopted under the AFSJ testify to the difficulty of reaching political accord even internally.[166] As a result, the internal-oriented bias of EU law may

[161] Post (n 148).

[162] ie only as regards international agreements, not for the rights that third-country nationals derive from market freedoms of Union citizens.

[163] For a detailed account of the complexities of reaching an agreement on immigration policy see G Papagianni, *Institutional and Policy Dynamics of EU Migration Law* (The Hague, Martinus Nijhoff Publishers, 2006).

[164] Title IV EC Amsterdam, Title V Chapter II Lisbon.

[165] Article 79(3) TFEU: external powers of the Union remain limited to readmission; see also limits under Protocol No 23 on External Relations of the Member States with Regard to the Crossing of External Borders. The Lisbon Treaty repealed Declaration No 18 on Article 73k(3)(a) of the Treaty establishing the European Community as regards immigration law. Member States that do not participate in the internal EU legislation are not bound by the external competence of the Union, see S Peers, *EU Justice and Home Affairs Law* (Oxford, Oxford University Press, 2006) 83. This is the case for Denmark, with which the Community had to conclude separate international treaties to fix its opt-out from the AFSJ: (2006) OJ L66/38 (responsibility for asylum applications); (2005) OJ L299/61 (civil and commercial jurisdiction); (2006) OJ L300/53 (service of documents). Under the Lisbon Treaty, the opt-outs of Denmark, the UK and Ireland are even wider than under the Amsterdam Treaty and cover the entire AFSJ, not only immigration law: compare Protocols 21 and 22 on the position of the UK and Ireland, and Denmark in respect of the AFSJ attached to the Lisbon Treaty with the respective protocols attached to the Treaty of Amsterdam. See also M Maes, MC Foblets and P De Bruycker (eds), *External Dimensions of EU Migration and Asylum Law and Policy* (Brussels, Bruylant, 2011); S Wolff and G Mounier, 'The External Dimension of JHA: A New Dimension of EU Diplomacy' in S Wolff, F Goudappel and J De Zwaan (eds), *Freedom. Security and Justice after Lisbon and Stockholm* (The Hague, TMC Asser Press, 2011); B Martenczuk and S Van Thiel (eds), *Justice, Liberty, Security: New Challenges for EU External Relations* (Brussels, ASP-VUB Press, 2010); A Kocharov, 'Governance of Migration in the EU: Home Affairs or Foreign Policy?' (2013) 15 *European Journal of Migration and Law*; P Garcia Andrade, 'The Legal Feasibility of the EU's External Action on Legal Migration: The Internal and the External Intertwined' (2013) 15 *European Journal of Migration and Law*.

[166] P De Bruycker, 'Legislative Harmonisation in European Immigration Policy' in R Cholewinski, R Perruchoud and E MacDonald (eds), *International Migration Law: Developing Paradigms and Key Challenges* (The Hague, TMC Asser Press, 2007); S Barbou Des Places and H Oger, 'Making the European Migration Regime: Decoding Member States' Legal Strategies' (2005) 6 *European Journal of Migration and Law*; K Groenendijk, 'Access of Third-country Nationals to Employment under the New EC Migration Law' in F Julien-Laferrière, H Labaye and Ö Edström (eds), *The European Immigration and Asylum Policy: Critical Assessment Five Years After the Amsterdam Treaty* (Brussels, Bruylant, 2005).

come at the price of *liberty from dependence* externally for both Member States and the Union.

6. THE RIGHTS–ADMISSION DICHOTOMY TO BALANCE *NEGATIVE* AND *POSITIVE LIBERTY*

Two relationships are at stake in mixed external agreements: the relationship between the Member States in the Community and the relationship between them and a third state. The obligation that Member States undertook between themselves in mixed external agreements is quite different from the obligations in the EC Treaty. To recognise the different nature of these two relationships, the Court drew a distinction between the *modus operandi* of Community law on the one hand and substantive provisions of the agreements on the other. Thus, direct effect of Community law and EC mixed external agreements as part thereof, was necessary in order to enforce the internal accord between Member States, and therefore did not depend on the asymmetry in obligations assumed by the Community vis-a-vis third states.[167] Conversely, the substance of rights created by the agreements reflects the extent of integration with third states. Substantive provisions of mixed external agreements could only be interpreted in line with similarly worded provisions of EC internal market law to the extent that the objectives of the agreement in question resembled the objectives of the EC Treaty—to the extent that the same *nature* of Union was envisaged.[168]

Abolition of obstacles to free movement played a pivotal role in defining the nature of Europe's Union. In combination with non-discrimination on the grounds of nationality, it ensured virtual representation of mobile Union citizens in their host polity. Reciprocity of commitment to virtual representation between polities defined Europe's deregulatory Union. To the extent that mixed external agreements do not provide for 'the abolition … of obstacles to freedom of movement for persons [and] services'[169] between the Member States and the third state, Member States retain their regulatory capacity over admission of third-country nationals to their territories and labour markets. Only once they are so admitted can the rights under the agreements arise.[170] Even where the agreements did

[167] Case C-469/93 *Chiquita Italia*, Case C-162/00 *Pokrzeptowicz-Meyer*, Case C-63/99 *Gloszczuk*, Case C-37/98 *Savas*: imbalance of obligations between the EU and a third state is no reason for not recognising direct effect.

[168] *Ex multis*: Case C-469/93 *Chiquita Italia*, Case C-37/98 *Savas*, Case C-262/96 *Surul*, Case C-416/96 *El Yassini*, Case C-63/99 *Gloszczuk* §36, Case C-257/99 *Barkoci and Malik* §37, Case C-235/99 *Kondova* §37.

[169] Article 3(c) EEC (1957).

[170] In legal terms, this was secured by the requirement, introduced by the Court, of belonging to the host Member State's labour force, which amounted to having a lawful residence and work permit; only in cases where the length of the work permit exceeded the length of the residence permit were the Member States obliged to extend residence rights of third-country nationals under the agreements, see Case C-416/96 *El Yassini*.

provide for the freedom of establishment for natural persons, this did not preclude 'a national system of prior control to check the exact nature of the activity envisaged by the applicant'.[171]

The Court thus distinguished between admission and rights: the former was a right only between Member States, while non-discrimination rights could extend to third-country nationals under EC external agreements. This introduced a dichotomy between the regulation of entry into the national territory and labour market (immigration for the purposes of economic activities) on the one hand and regulation of subsequent rights and status of third-country nationals on the other. This dichotomy followed the wording of the agreements (and, therefore, the accord reached between Member States) but also, and more importantly, the differences between the commitment of Member States in the Community (non-interference between national polities through reciprocal deregulation) and their commitment towards third states (elements of substantive rights without any limits on the political process).

In the national context, the resulting *admission–rights dichotomy* was criticised for its artificial nature:[172] taking into account the two-dimensional relationship between the polity and outsiders, both admission rules and subsequent rights of immigrants constitute tools for managing immigration flows. Migratory decisions will be affected both by the costs of gaining the initial entry and by subsequent costs and benefits that stem from rights in the host state. However, in the context of a Community of polities bound by reciprocal *non-interference*, this dichotomy acquires a structural function. From two-dimensional (nationals vs foreigners), the relationship becomes three-dimensional (nationals of one Member State—nationals of another Member State—nationals of a non-EU polity). This three-dimensional structure is reflected in enforcement of Community law. Between Member States, reciprocity is enforceable thanks to the jurisdiction of the ECJ; powers of the state can be abolished and rules between Member States instead enforced by individuals in national courts. When Community law regulates an internal interest—not in the sense of physical presence or nationality but in the sense of being bound by the system of EC law—enforcement of this law can follow the internal market model. This is the case with the rights of lawfully resident third-country workers under EC external agreements. With interests situated outside this mechanism of binding reciprocity—outside the EC legal order—enforcing *non-interference* is impossible and deregulation would reduce liberty of European polities—it would therefore be illegitimate. Instead of deregulation, regulation takes place. The admission–rights dichotomy thus corresponds to the regulation–deregulation option. By distinguishing between the interests that are lawful (authorised migration and the requirement of prior admission to the

[171] Case C-257/99 *Barkoci* & *Malik* §62, Case C-235/99 *Kondova* §61.

[172] AB Cox, 'Immigration Law's Organizing Principles' (2008) 157(2) *University of Pennsylvania Law Review* and M Ruhs and P Martin, 'Numbers vs. Rights: Trade-Offs and Guest Worker Programs' (2008) 42(1) *International Migration Review*.

national territory and labour market),[173] ie bound by the system of reciprocity in EC and national law, and the interests that are not so bound, the Court identified what type of liberty can be advanced through the abolition of powers of the state. More than the federal division of powers between the Member States and the EU, this draws a distinction between legitimacy of the Union based on *negative* and *positive liberty*.

The admission–rights dichotomy can be contrasted with the *purpose-of-immigration dichotomy* traditional in national immigration law. This type of dichotomy distinguishes between economic immigration (a power left to Member State competence) and all other immigration (a power shared between Member States and the Community). The logic of this dichotomy is the opposite of the internal market. If, in EC internal market law, individuals derive rights from their own action of moving between Member States and their choice defeats the regulatory powers of the state,[174] in immigration law, the rights of the individual are linked to the immigration status granted by the authorities of the host state according to the initial purpose of entry into its territory (student, worker, family member, etc). Switching between the statuses is difficult and must be authorised each time anew. In the internal market, rights of the individual enjoy deregulation, with the individual making migration choices; in immigration law, rights of the individual are subject to regulation and migration choices are made by the state.

The purpose-of-immigration dichotomy was introduced into EC law with the Treaty of Amsterdam, which, in Title IV EC Area of Freedom, Security and Justice[175] for the first time conferred powers on the Community to regulate third-country nationals.[176] These powers were conferred outside the internal market and will be discussed in detail in the next chapter. Of relevance here is that although the Treaty text provided for Community powers to regulate only non-economic migration while Member States preserved their exclusive power to regulate economic immigration by third-country nationals (dichotomy 2) or at least admission of economic migrants (dichotomy 1),[177] the combined effect of the two

[173] Case C-41/96 *El Yassini*; Case C-97/05 *Gattoussi*.

[174] Directive 2004/38/EC, Article 7(1), which codifies the earlier jurisprudence of the ECJ.

[175] Articles 61–63 EC Amsterdam.

[176] For an overview of the introduction of Title IV EC see K Hailbronner, 'European Immigration and Asylum Law under the Amsterdam Treaty' (1998) 35 *CML Rev*; J Niessen, 'Overlapping Interests and Conflicting Agendas: The Knocking into Shape of EU Immigration Policies' (2001) 3 *European Journal of Migration and Law*; J Apap, 'Shaping Europe's Migration Policy New Regimes for the Employment of Third Country Nationals: A Comparison of Strategies in Germany, Sweden, the Netherlands and the UK' (2002) 4 *European Journal of Migration and Law*; P De Bruycker (ed), *The Emergence of a European Immigration Policy* (Brussels, Bruylant, 2003); A Baldaccini and H Toner, 'From Amsterdam and Tampere to the Hague: An Overview of Five Years of EC Immigration and Asylum Law' in A Baldaccini, E Guild and H Toner (eds), *Whose Freedom, Security and Justice? EU Immigration and Asylum Law and Policy* (Oxford, Hart Publishing, 2007). On the preceding Treaty amendments as concerns third-country nationals, see Evans (n 29).

[177] Penultimate paragraph of Article 63 EC Amsterdam. This residual power of Member States is much reduced in the Lisbon Treaty—yet, the legislation analysed in this paragraph was adopted pursuant to the federal power balance set in Amsterdam.

dichotomies resulted in Community law regulating not only admission of non-economic immigrants, but also their access to the labour market. The *admission–rights dichotomy* introduced by the Court in order to solve the internal–external (deregulation–regulation) dilemma presented by external agreements clashed with the *purpose-of-immigration dichotomy* of EC immigration law. To the extent that the rights established under EC immigration law are sufficiently clear, precise and unconditional—and thus enjoy direct effect—they amount to a withdrawal of regulatory powers from the national political process.[178] EC immigration law adopted under this power accentuated the asymmetry of constraints on power between the Community and third states already present in mixed external agreements thanks to their direct effect in EC law on the one hand and the absence of mechanisms for enforcing reciprocity in the third contracting states on the other.

A good example of such asymmetry is the Association Agreement with Turkey. Unlike the mechanism with the EFTA states, which subjects interpretation of EFTA law in the third contracting state to a specially established court bound by an obligation of homogeneous interpretation in line with EU free movement law, no such court exists under the Association Agreement with Turkey. The implementation of the agreement and its law in Turkey depends entirely on Turkish national institutions and Turkish law. This lack of a reciprocity mechanism notwithstanding, a long line of ECJ case law established that the immigration-related rights contained in the Decisions of the EC-Turkey Association Council not only have direct effect in national legal orders but should be interpreted in line with similarly worded provisions of EC free movement law.[179] This case law was crystallised in *Payir*,[180] where the ECJ confirmed that the type of permit under which Member States admit Turkish nationals is irrelevant as long as the latter are lawfully employed for at least one year by the same employer. After this period, Article 6(1) of Decision 1/80 grants Turkish nationals a right to continue working for the same employer and, after four years of employment, a right to remain and change employers. Crucially, in *Payir* the Court established that the purpose for which the Turkish national was first admitted into the Member State had no relevance for the accrual of rights under the Decision. Turkish nationals admitted temporarily for part-time au pair work only, as well as Turkish students allowed to work part time, were equally covered by the Decision.[181] Considering that some provisions of EU law oblige Member States to admit third-country nationals to their territories and labour markets,[182] the combined effect of these provisions

[178] Case C-540/03 *Parliament v Council*, Case C-578/08 *Chakroun*.

[179] For discussion of this case law see Peers (n 165). Following the dichotomy logic, homogeneity of interpretation in the absence of an enforcement mechanism for the third state ends with the right to enter Member State territory, see Case C-221/11 *Demirkan*.

[180] Case C-294/06 *Payir*.

[181] Also Turkish refugees are covered: Case C-337/07 *Altun*.

[182] For instance, family members of Member State nationals under free movement law; family members of legally resident third-country nationals under Directive 2003/86/EC; third-country national researchers who fulfil the conditions of Directive 2005/71/EC; long-term resident third-country nationals from other Member States under Directive 2004/109/EC; students under Directive

and the rights under the EC-Turkey Association law result in a near-complete deregulation of immigration from Turkey to the EU without securing corresponding rights for Member State nationals in Turkey.[183]

The trade-off between internal interdependence and external independence—between enforcing *non-interference* between the peoples of Europe and their *liberty from dependence* externally—is not resolved: it is impossible to limit the national political process of one Member State vis-a-vis the others without simultaneously limiting all national political processes vis-a-vis the third contracting state.[184] Commitment of Member States in the EU is enforced even at the expense of their ability to further *positive liberty* externally. Deregulation as a constitutional choice among the peoples of Europe 'spills over' into their relations with external polities. Without a mechanism to enforce reciprocity vis-a-vis non-Community polities, this results in an overall loss in liberty of the peoples of Europe at all levels of power. On the face of it, Member States lose their powers to re-acquire them in the Community.[185] Yet, the latter are difficult to exercise: once a right is established in Treaty law, changing it requires unanimous ratification by all the peoples of Europe,[186] while for a policy area so politically sensitive where the diversity of policy preferences and interests across Member States is high, the accord is a difficult and slow target. Nothing similar to the national regulatory powers in immigration is created at the European level.[187] Deregulation takes place in practice though there is no loss of regulatory power in law.

Apparently, the goal of the admission–rights dichotomy is to keep Community law apolitical. The making of policy choices over contested political issues on which reasonable people may disagree (admission of third-country nationals)

2004/114/EC (Article 17 of this directive also obliges Member States to allow students to work at least 10 hours per week). Case C-491/13 *Ben Alaya*.

[183] In Case C-221/11 *Demirkan* the Court recognises that such liberalisation is not foreseen in the EC-Turkey Association law itself. The Lisbon Treaty reform introduced new Union objectives into the Treaties: to ensure 'efficient management of immigration flows' and to 'combat illegal immigration' by third-country nationals (Article 79 TFEU). To the extent that liberalisation is the opposite of regulation (see by analogy case C-376/98 *Tobacco Advertising* §83) and therefore management, it may be questioned how *Metock* and *Payir* can be reconciled with the Lisbon Treaty.

[184] Somek draws a similar conclusion from the study of broader non-discrimination law as regards markets vs solidarity: 'even if the Union had legal power to recreate a transnational equivalent to a national welfare state, the emergence of such a regime would be extremely unlikely owing to a net loss of social policy-making capacity suffered by the Member States when they are acting together', A Somek, *Engineering Equality: An Essay on European Anti-Discrimination Law* (Oxford, Oxford University Press, 2011) 7–8.

[185] Post (n 148).

[186] FW Scharpf, 'The Joint-Decision Trap: Lessons from German Federalism and European Integration' (1988) 66 *Public Administration* 239.

[187] National immigration schemes based on quotas have also been criticised for the inability to adjust the rules to the changing labour market and migration flows in a timely manner: A Constant and KF Zimmermann, 'Immigrant Performance and Selective Immigration Policy: A European Perspective' (2005) 195 *National Institute Economic Review* 105; G Orcalli, 'Constitutional Choice and European Immigration Policy' (2007) 18(1) *Constitutional Political Economy* 9. This ability is undermined further by the complexity and lengthiness of accord at the European level.

remains with the national polities and their political processes. This accords with the founding structure of the EC legal order, which limits national politics. In order to secure *non-interference* with each other's ability to pursue their own idea of *positive liberty*, the peoples of Europe limit their ability to pursue *positive liberty* not only vis-a-vis each other, but also in relation to the interests not bound by reciprocity in Union law. The result is radical and inward looking: it leads to a passive external policy for both Member States and the Community. The presumption is that the risk to Peace that would result from the interference between Member States is greater than the risk from the interference that could originate from outside the Community. The next chapter will show how the change in this underlying presumption causes a change in the structure of liberty advanced through Union law.

7. INTEGRATION THROUGH LAW OR INTEGRATION THROUGH POLITICS?

Regulation of the national political process emerges as a boundary and a hallmark of integration in Europe. On the one hand, each European polity retained its autonomy, in particular to regulate its own composition and therefore access to its national political process; on the other hand, no national polity can regulate the interests belonging to other European polities and minority interests created by EU free movement law. Reciprocal disempowerment of the national political processes ('albeit within limited fields')[188] is the best way to describe relations between the peoples of Europe. This happens either through commitment to a shared idea of *positive liberty* unanimously sealed in the Treaties (functional objectives and Treaty rights) or by reliance on mutual recognition (as regards decisions of the national political processes, eg rules on acquisition and loss of nationality)—a tool of partial deregulation pending a European policy choice.

Unlike any EC external agreement, integration between Member States in the Community involves regulation of their national political processes: powers of the Member States to interfere with each other are abolished in order to ensure reciprocal non-domination. This is the limit on the scope of migration rights under the mixed external agreements: to the extent that the 'object and purpose' of these agreements is to bind the political process between Member States, the substance of migration rights that they establish will coincide with EU free movement law.

This difference in the 'object and purpose' between the Treaty and mixed external agreements—a difference that stems from the role of the EEC and the EU in building Peace between Member States—leads to two possible lines of development. First, the power to regulate immigration by third-country nationals may remain with the national political process and the Court only enforces

[188] Case 32/84 *Van Gend en Loos* §3.

subsequently granted rights along the *Akrich-Barkoci & Malik* scenario. Policy choices—identification of *positive liberty* as regards immigration—continue to be made by each national polity; they are not subject to the European political process but are restrained by *non-interference* in Union law. Alternatively and second, enforcement of accord between Member States ventures so far as to withdraw all power to regulate immigration by third-country nationals from the national political process along the *Metock-Payir* line of cases, in which case the power to regulate third-country nationals shifts from Member States to the EU. In the latter scenario, the passage of powers from national to Community level is needed to preserve the capacity of European polities to identify and further their own *positive liberty* without dependence on the external interests not bound by reciprocity in Union law. To be legitimate, this would require identification of the idea of *positive liberty* jointly by all the peoples of the EU. This would transform the way integration takes place in Europe: from being based on *non-interference* through law, it now requires a political process to identify the shared commitment in a more expedient and fluid way than unanimous amendment of Union Treaties.

Both alternatives are problematic. In the *Akrich-Barkoci & Malik* scenario, even if policy choices are made exclusively on the national level, the European polities and their national political processes are interdependent because of the structure of EC legal order. Enforcement of and compliance with EC law takes place in the national legal order and eventually reflects the national idea of *positive liberty* as a union with the other peoples of Europe. In its operation, the EC legal order is not autonomous but, on the contrary, fully dependent for institutions and acceptance on each national polity.[189] It is for this reason that EC free movement law regulates the national political process not only in situations where it might interfere with the national political process of other Member States, but also in the situations that are purely internal to one national polity, as in *Zambrano*. Interest representation in the national political process must be such that *liberty from dependence* is ensured also internally within each national polity so that each people of Europe is able to develop its own idea of *positive liberty*. We will return to this in Chapter 5. The *Metock Payir* scenario is equally problematic, though this time for *liberty from dependence* externally. The next chapter shows how the need to advance independence vis-a-vis interests not bound by Union and national law leads to reconceptualising legitimacy of the Union and EU law.

[189] E Stein, 'Lawyers, Judges, and the Making of a Transnational Constitution' [1981] *American Journal of International Law* 75.

3

A Political Union: Positive Liberty

Figure 3.1: Ludwig Wittgenstein, *Philosophical Investigations* (1953)*

1. A NEW SOLUTION FOR AN OLD PROBLEM

In 1985, the Member States, with the exception of the UK and Ireland, signed the Schengen Convention whereby they agreed to abolish their internal borders.[1] This gave new life and force to the constitutional dilemma analysed in Chapter 2. The internal–external dilemma posed by the regulation of third-country nationals in mixed external agreements and by the derived rights in EC free movement law presented a trade-off between ensuring *non-interference* between the European polities internally versus their individual and joint capacity to pursue *positive liberty* externally. The abolition of internal borders, which institutes de facto mobility of all persons between Member States, including all third-country nationals, extends this dilemma to all regulation of third-country nationals. This chapter will show that the solution adopted in Union law—this time by the legislator and not the Court—presents an exact mirror image of the solution found under EU free movement law.

The abolition of internal borders between Member States creates new potential for cross-polity interference. Without checks at the internal borders, policy choices of one national polity affect the ability of other European polities to regulate immigration. Three problems for regulation of immigration by the national polities in Europe arise. First, the abolition of internal borders complicates combating illegal immigration. When immigration by third-country nationals is regulated by each European polity individually yet all polities share a borderless space,

[1] Convention implementing the Schengen Agreement of 14 June 1985 between the Governments of the States of the Benelux Economic Union, the Federal Republic of Germany and the French Republic on the gradual abolition of checks at their common borders (22/09/2000) OJ L239/19.

it is practically difficult to detect illegal immigrants, especially if they hold a valid residence permit for one of the Schengen Member States.[2] Although residence and employment of such migrants in the second state would be unlawful, in practice it is difficult to distinguish between a legal immigrant who merely exercises a right to travel in the Schengen area for a period of up to three months and a third-country national who makes use of this right to travel for de facto moving and settling in another Member State for a longer period—something that would require a separate authorisation from the new host Member State.[3] Second, regulating legal immigration also becomes problematic. The possibility of moving between Member States in the internal market could undermine the efforts of less attractive Member States (for instance due to the size and structure of their economy, languages, pre-existing immigrant communities, etc) to encourage legal immigration and the efforts of the more attractive Member States to select or restrict it. Third, there is a problem of burden sharing as regards the costs of processing asylum claims, of hosting refugees and of returning illegal immigrants. On the one hand, the abolition of internal borders opens up the possibility that asylum seekers who enter one Member State may thereafter choose where to claim asylum, leading to concerns that some Member States could be more attractive and thus become 'magnets' for asylum seekers while other Member States might be dissuaded from implementing effective border control, asylum policy and return. On the other hand, Member States on the EU's external borders are more exposed to 'unwanted' immigration flows as a result of their immutable characteristic (geography) and could therefore be facing larger costs of border controls, processing asylum claims and expulsion.

The interdependence created between Member States with the abolition of internal borders rendered it difficult for the European polities to 'manage migration flows'[4] individually. Reciprocal deregulation between Member States (abolition of internal borders) thus risked undermining their pursuit of their own *positive liberty*: the ability of each European polity to implement its own immigration policy. This interdependence—and potential *interference*—between the European polities with each other's *positive liberty* required protection of liberty in Union law. Legitimacy of the abolition of internal borders required Union action that would protect liberty.[5] As will be shown in this and the following chapters,

[2] Under Article 5 Schengen Convention and Article 1 Regulation 562/2006 Schengen Borders Code, third-country nationals lawfully present in one Schengen State can lawfully cross an internal border and stay in another Schengen State for a maximum of three months. However, in the absence of border checks and entry/exit stamps between the Schengen states, it might be difficult to identify overstayers as well as the other Schengen state through which migrants might transit (whether authorised or not).

[3] Under Article 21(d) Regulation 562/2006 Schengen Borders Code and Article 22 Schengen Convention, Member States may require third-country nationals who come into their territories to register their presence within three days of arrival.

[4] Article 79 TFEU.

[5] European Commission, *Communication on Migration* (04.05.2011) COM (2011) 248 final 4: 'poorly managed immigration can affect ... the trust of citizens in an area of free movement without internal borders'; European Council, *The Hague Programme* (13.12.2004) Council doc. 16054/04 3.

this action pertains to the constitutional soul of Europe much more than to the substance or level (EU or national) of policy choice. Beyond *negative* and *positive liberty*, the legitimacy of European policy choice must be sustained by rules of Union law that advance *liberty from dependence*.

Similar to the situation under the mixed external agreements, the interdependence that ensues from the abolition of internal borders and the potential for interference between Member States that results cannot be addressed through rights of the individual in Union law. It will be recalled from the previous chapter that in situations where the interests of Union citizens risked being under-represented in the national political process, directly effective rights in EU free movement law withdrew these interests from the regulatory reach of national politics. The concomitance of interest between the individual bearers of rights—Union citizens in cross-polity situations (to enforce their rights in Union law against the regulatory reach of their host polity)—and European polities (to have all Union polities respect the limit on the national political process imposed by the Treaties) secured reciprocal *non-interference* between polities in Union law. The interest of the individual with *locus standi* to enforce her rights in Union law coincided with the interest of at least one European polity. Crucial in this construct was that the individual acquired the *locus standi* enabling her to enforce an agreement between states.[6] Enforcement of Union Treaties by the individual rendered the power, size and the political process of polity irrelevant for the ability of each national polity to secure reciprocal *non-interference*. *Non-interference* between the national political processes was no longer a function of power politics between Member States. Action by the state, while possible through recourse to the CJEU, is not necessary to enforce *non-interference*. All European polities are equally protected from interference and thus equally able to advance their own *positive liberty*. The powers of the state vis-a-vis other states can be abolished.

No such mechanism to enforce reciprocal *non-interference* between polities in the Union is available when it comes to regulating third-country nationals. The members of European polities—Member State nationals, whose interests coincide with the interests of Europe's polities—are not subject to immigration law and therefore have no *locus standi* in matters of immigration.[7] The individuals who have legal standing are third-country nationals: it is they who are subject to immigration and asylum law. Their interests may well coincide with the goal of

[6] On the importance of the triangular relationship between the individual, the Union and the state in EU law, see E Guild, 'Discretion, Competence and Migration in the European Union' (1999) *European Journal of Migration and Law*; E Guild, *European Community Law from a Migrant's Perspective* (The Hague, Kluwer Law International, 2000). Vice versa, 'the incapacity of individuals to institute judicial or administrative proceedings against organizations renders them hostage to their nation states' considerations of high politics', A Peters, 'Membership in the Global Constitutional Community' in J Klabbers, A Peters and G Ulfstein (eds), *The Constitutionalization of International Law* (Oxford, Oxford University Press, 2009) 212.

[7] With the exception of any rights that third-country nationals derive from Union citizens and EU employers—see Chapter 2.

advancing liberty of European polities in Union law—but this will not always be the case. The same is true for criminal law, the other policy under the AFSJ: also there, the abolition of internal borders created interdependence between European polities while the interest of the individual will not always coincide with the interest of any European polity. This contraposition of the individual against the polity raises the importance of fundamental and citizens' rights: for citizens, to ensure that the majorities do not abuse the minorities in the political process; for non-citizens, because of the special value of human rights for the constitutional and international identity of each national polity.

Consider the fight against illegal immigration in a European polity A. Instead of enforcing expulsion from the EU as provided by Union law,[8] the members of polity A may decide (through their national political process) not to enforce the law in the expectation that the immigrant crosses the internal border into the neighbouring European polity B; the interest of members of polity B is to enforce EU law in polity A and expel the illegal immigrant; the interest of the illegal immigrant is to stay in the EU (and, preferably, in polity B); the interest of the members of polity A is to 'get rid' of the illegal immigrant with minimal costs, ie by circumventing Union law on expulsion (a cost for polity A) in the expectation that the immigrant, at her own cost, leaves polity A in order to move to polity B. While having *locus standi*, the immigrant will have no interest in enforcing Union law; members of polity B have an interest in enforcement but have no *locus standi*. Polity B will be affected by the political process in polity A (which thus decides to ignore Union law), yet the interest of persons in polity B will neither be represented in the political process of polity A nor enjoy adjudicative protection in Union law. Elimination of interference, actual and potential, between European polities with each other's capacity to pursue their own *positive liberty* (in this case, immigration policy) is not available for immigration policy. In the internal market, the risk of interference with cross-polity interests that could result from their under-representation in the national political process was counterbalanced by withdrawing these interests from the regulatory reach of politics with the help of directly effective rights. The absence of such a mechanism leads to a permanent loss of interest representation (a loss in *negative liberty* because the regulatory capacity of polity B is affected by polity A) and may result in domination between the polities (because members of polity B cannot vote in the national political process of polity A yet are affected by its policy choices) that would ensue from the abolition of internal borders. Interest representation or Voice is reduced not only for Member State nationals in cross-polity situations resulting from the exercise of free movement rights, but also for those polity members who remain within their national polities. Not even virtual representation is available, so that the presumption that by moving to another polity Union citizens implicitly accept and internalise the host polity's ideas about *positive liberty* is transformed into a much broader presumption that

[8] Directive 2008/115 Return, Case C-61/11 PPU *El Dridi*, Case C-329/11 *Achughbabian*.

by joining the Schengen space Union citizens renounce their independent capacity to identify and advance their own idea of *positive liberty*. On the one hand, the peoples of Europe thereby renounce their *liberty from dependence* on other polities while, on the other hand, Union citizens renounce the possibility of Exit from domination that was available under free movement in the internal market, where a Union citizen who did not accept her host polity's idea of *positive liberty* could Exit dependence on this polity by returning to her Member State of nationality. A similar dependence between the national polities on each other's ideas about *positive liberty* can be observed in the free movement of goods, where it is balanced by Union policies on competition and anti-dumping.[9] At the same time, Exit is foreclosed because the abolition of internal borders is part of Union law and as such is binding and difficult to amend.[10] The foreclosed Exit and reduced Voice that result from the abolition of internal borders undermine the social legitimacy of this deregulation in Union law.

Another example is competition for third-country workers with high human capital attributes.[11] While emphasising the divergence of national labour market needs, Member States agreed to 'increase the attractiveness of the European Union for highly qualified workers'[12] and simultaneously 'to establish a minimum level playing field within the Union'.[13] The 'level playing field' concerns elimination of competition between Member States,[14] which might result from national immigration schemes that (1) lower production costs by exploiting third-country workers and (2) favour 'wanted' third-country workers by granting them more rights compared to other Member States.[15] Different national entry and residence rights for third-country workers result in Member States competing between each

[9] See the discussion at the end of Chapter 5 and M Poiares Maduro, 'The Chameleon State. EU Law and the Blurring of the Private/Public Distinction in the Market' in R Nickel (ed), *Conflict of Laws and Laws of Conflict in Europe and Beyond* (Antwerp, Intersentia, 2010).

[10] This is so for the policy choice contained both in the Treaties and in secondary Union acts: the latter are more difficult to amend than national statutes. The Schengen system allows temporary closure of the internal borders in case of emergencies, including significant inflows of people, see Chapter II Regulation 562/2006 Schengen Borders Code.

[11] European Commission, *Policy Plan on Legal Migration* (2005) COM (2005) 669 final.

[12] European Council, *European Pact on Immigration and Asylum* (24.12.2008) Council doc. 13189/08, 5. European Commission, *Green Paper on an EU Approach to Managing Economic Migration* (2005) COM (2004) 811 final 4: 'the main world regions are already competing to attract migrants to meet the needs of their economies'. See also European Council, *The Hague Programme* (13.12.2004) Council doc. 16054/04 10: legal immigration is important for 'enhancing the knowledge-based economy in Europe, in advancing economic development, and thus contributing to the implementation of the Lisbon strategy'.

[13] Recital 19 Directive 2011/98/EU Single Permit.

[14] European Commission, *Communication on Immigration, Integration and Employment*, COM (2003) 336 final, 16; A Kocharov, 'Regulation that Defies Gravity. Policy, Economics and Law of Legal Immigration in Europe' (Autumn/Winter 2011) *European Journal of Legal Studies* 4:2.

[15] eg the UK points system, German green card, preferential treatment accorded to highly skilled immigrants in Sweden and the Netherlands. A Shachar, 'The Race for Talent: Highly-Skilled Migrants and Competitive Immigration Regimes' (2006) 81 *New York University Law Review* 148, 187; R Cholewinski, *The Legal Status of Migrants Admitted for Employment* (Council of Europe Publishing, 2004) 44; S Mahroum, 'Europe and the Immigration of Highly Skilled Labour' (2001) 39(5) *International Migration*.

other instead of joining forces as a single destination against traditional immigration countries like the US. For instance, the Proposal for the Blue Card Directive states that in a situation where each Member State has different national entry and residence conditions for highly qualified workers, national systems are bound to be in competition, weakening the attractiveness of the EU as a whole and leading to 'distortions in immigrants' choices'; this, according to the Commission, triggers the need for a common EU admission system.[16] The Commission presented this objective as a deregulation issue, whereby 'the obstacles encountered ... in relation to the complexity and diversity of [national] rules' could act as a deterrent in the capacity of the EU to attract third-country workers and business,[17] thus ignoring the constitutional role of deregulation in the internal market. The ability of one European polity to pursue its own immigration policy will be affected by the policy pursued elsewhere in the Union—yet, despite this potential interference between the polities, polity members only have Voice within their respective national polities.

A key difference in terms of enforcement between EU law on legal migration under the AFSJ and the rights of third-country workers under the mixed external agreements analysed in Chapter 2 is that the former provides for a minimum level of rights, while the latter provides for the maximum level (equal treatment). Minimal rights of third-country nationals do not remove cross-polity interference; on the contrary, they expressly allow each national polity to compete with the others on the level of rights it offers third-country migrants. Although the explicit reservation of Member State parallel powers in immigration in the penultimate paragraph of ex-Article 63 EC was removed in Lisbon, EU directives on immigration allow Member States to keep their national permits in parallel with Union law.[18]

The solution adopted in EU immigration and asylum law under the AFSJ involves both Exit and Voice. On the one hand, an effort is made to preserve partial Exit. This is achieved through numerous optional clauses in secondary Union law,[19] by setting in Union law only minimum standards,[20] by preserving Member

[16] Proposal for the Blue Card Directive, COM (2007) 637 final 7. When introducing the Blue Card Proposal, Commissioner Frattini alleged that while the US attracts 55% of all skilled migrants worldwide, the EU attracts only one-eleventh of that number, see European Commission SPEECH/07/526, Lisbon, 13.09.2007.

[17] Explanatory memorandum to the proposal for a directive on Intra-Corporate Transferees, COM (2010) 378 final 2. Similar reasoning is found in the explanatory memorandum to the Blue Card Proposal, COM (2007) 637 final 2.

[18] See Article 13 Directive 2003/109/EC Long-Term Residents, Article 3(4) Directive 2009/50/EU Blue Card, Article 4 Directive 2014/36/EU Seasonal Workers, Article 2(3) Directive 2014/66/EU Intra-Corporate Transferees. The latter directive restricts the scope of residual national powers compared to the previous directives: 'This Directive shall be without prejudice to the right of Member States to issue residence permits, other than the intra-corporate transferee permit covered by this Directive, for any purpose of employment for *third-country nationals who fall outside the scope of this Directive.*' (emphasis added).

[19] The so-called 'may' clauses, eg Articles 4(3), 5(1)(a), 5(2), 7(2), 9(2), 9(3), 9(4), 11(2)–(5), 14(2)–(5), 15, 16(2), 16(4), 18(4), 20(2), 21(2), 22(1), 22(3), 22(4) Directive 2003/109/EC Long-Term Residents.

[20] eg Council Directive 2004/83/EC of 29 April 2004 on *minimum* standards for the qualification and status of third-country nationals or stateless persons as refugees or as persons who otherwise need

State powers to regulate the admission of economic immigrants,[21] to issue residence and work permits,[22] and to set immigration quotas.[23] Cross-polity interference is minimised through restrictions on mobility of third-country nationals between Member States.[24] On the other hand, the impossibility of eliminating cross-polity interference entirely is remedied through express Union powers to regulate third-country nationals.[25] These aim to replace the loss in *positive liberty* accruing to each national polity with an alternative idea of *positive liberty* identified and pursued in the EU. The possibility of interference by the national polities in each other's policies and policy choices undermines the Voice of polity members in the national political processes. The ensuing dependence of each national polity on other polities in the EU will be remedied by the creation of a European policy if—and only if—*liberty from dependence* and Voice are secured in the process of making policy choices at the Union level.

2. EMANCIPATION OF POLITICS AND THE EUROPEAN POLITICAL SPACE

By the time Community powers to regulate third-country nationals were introduced into the EC Treaty with the Amsterdam Treaty reform, policy rigidity associated with functional Treaty objectives was viewed as detrimental for the development of a common policy. Prior to the Amsterdam Treaty, regulation of immigration by third-country nationals remained at the national level and was only coordinated between Member States through non-binding tools;[26] it did

international protection and the content of the protection granted (30.9.2004) OJ L304 12; Recital 19 Directive 2011/98/EU Single Permit; Article 4(2) Directive 2014/66/EU Intra-Corporate Transferees.

[21] Article 79(5) TFEU: 'This Article shall not affect the right of Member States to determine volumes of admission of third-country nationals coming from third countries to their territory in order to seek work, whether employed or self-employed'.

[22] Article 8 Directive 2009/50/EU Blue Card, Article 14(3) Directive 2003/109/EC Long-Term Residents, Article 6 Directive 2014/66/EU Intra-Corporate Transferees, Articles 2(2) and 8(3) Directive 2014/36/EU Seasonal Workers.

[23] Including for lawfully resident third-country nationals who move between Member States: Article 14(4) Directive 2003/109/EC Long-Term Residents, Articles 6 and 18(7) Directive 2009/50/EU Blue Card.

[24] Despite the abolition of internal borders, this is achieved in law through the requirement for third-country nationals to reapply for residence permits when they move between Member States (Directive 2003/109/EC Long-Term Residents, Directive 2009/50/EU Blue Card, Directive 2004/114 Students, Directive 2005/71 Research, Directive 2014/66/EU Intra-Corporate Transferees), the rules on return of unauthorised migrants including return to the Member State which authorised their entry and residence on its territory (Directive 2008/115 Return), the Dublin rules on asylum applications and the Member States responsible for asylum seekers (Regulation 604/2013 Dublin III).

[25] Title V Chapter 2 TFEU.

[26] Article K(1)3 TEU-Maastricht; Council Resolution of 20 June 1994 on limitation on admission of third-country nationals to the territory of the Member States for employment (19/09/1996) OJ C274, 3–6; Council Resolution of 30 November 1994 relating to the limitations on the admission of third-country nationals to the territory of the Member States for the purpose of pursuing activities as self-employed persons (19/09/1996) OJ C274, 7–9; the situation was different for borders, as the Schengen Convention was a binding treaty in international law.

not form part of the mainstream Community law (the so-called Community pillar) and was not restrained by any functional objectives to frame policy choice. The absence of functional objectives facilitated accord between Member States, although the non-binding nature of this accord led to low efficiency of thus established rules. To remedy the latter shortcoming, it was decided to insert the legal basis previously contained in the Maastricht intergovernmental pillar into the EC Treaty, thus enabling the enactment of binding law. The legal basis for regulating third-country nationals migrated between the pillars together with its shopping-list structure.[27] Community law adopted under the new competence now had to comply with the overarching objectives of Article 2 EC—but this was the only (and very broad) limitation of policy choice. The legal basis itself contained no functional objectives. In effect, the 'intergovernmental agreement in the Treaties has created a European competence, but left the definition of substantive policy choices to directives and regulations adopted in joint-decision processes involving the Commission, the Council and, increasingly, the Parliament'.[28] Without functional objectives to determine policy, the powers of the European Community to regulate immigration under the AFSJ were 'singularly less specific'[29] compared, for example, to free movement law.

The Lisbon Treaty emancipated politics further. It omitted Article 2 EC, leaving Union policies without any overarching objectives.[30] The Union is instead founded on values: respect for human dignity and human rights, freedom, democracy, equality, the rule of law, pluralism, non-discrimination, tolerance, justice, solidarity and equality between women and men.[31] Values differ from functional objectives in terms of the breadth of policy choice they concede: values do not prescribe any balance of interests to pursue through policy, they do not constitute a shared idea of 'ideal life' but instead guide how this idea is to be determined. Values

[27] Article K.1 Maastricht contained only a legal base. This shopping-list structure was transferred directly to the EC Treaty in Amsterdam, see Articles 62 and 63 EC Amsterdam.

[28] F Scharpf, 'Legitimate Diversity: The New Challenge of European Integration', *Les Cahiers européens de Sciences Po*, no 01 (Paris, Centre d'études européennes, Sciences Po, 2002) 6.

[29] E Guild and H Staples, *Labor Migration in the European Union*, in P De Bruycker (ed), *The Emergence of a European Migration Policy* (Brussels, Bruylant, 2003) 214.

[30] Some former objectives of the Community have been renamed 'requirements' and placed in Title II TFEU (Provisions Having General Application): the promotion of a high level of employment, the guarantee of adequate social protection, the fight against social exclusion, and a high level of education, training and protection of human health (Article 9 TFEU); environmental protection (Article 11 TFEU); consumer protection (Article 12 TFEU). Other objectives were moved to Article 3(3) TEU dedicated explicitly to the internal market: sustainable development based on balanced economic growth and price stability, a highly competitive social market economy, aiming at full employment and social progress, and a high level of protection and improvement of the quality of the environment; scientific and technological advance; combating social exclusion and discrimination, promotion of social justice and protection, equality between women and men, solidarity between generations and protection of the rights of the child; promotion of economic, social and territorial cohesion, and solidarity among Member States; respect for its rich cultural and linguistic diversity, safeguarding and enhancing Europe's cultural heritage.

[31] Article 2 TEU: this must be a transposition of former Article 6 EU, which spoke of 'principles' on which the EU was founded.

thus define the identity of the polity (the principles that shape its political process) while functional objectives define policy choice (a specific balance of interests). Some European policies remain founded on functional objectives contained in policy-specific articles of the Treaty (the so-called legal bases for Union acts).[32] For instance, the free movement provisions in the internal market, and free movement rights of Union citizens, retained their functional flavour of prescriptive choice: no matter how broad these powers are, neither the Member States nor the Union can (1) restrict free movement of Union citizens and (2) regulate purely internal situations. However, for Union policies whose legal bases omit functional objectives, and to the extent that they do, the policy choices are now entirely open for a decision at some later stage. This does not simply raise the role of the political process but emancipates politics from the chains of predetermined choice. In Union policies not defined by functional Treaty objectives and directly effective Treaty rights, the political process can finally serve its purpose to represent and balance competing interests and competing ideas about ideal life.

Immigration under the AFSJ is one such policy of open choice.[33] Unlike their predecessors in the Amsterdam Treaty, Articles 77–79 TFEU foresee a *common* Union policy on third-country nationals, specifically adding fields for Union action.[34] Although these powers are shared between the Union and the Member States, the broadened legal bases allow transfer of more powers to the Union than prior to the Treaty of Lisbon.[35] Even the express reservation of national powers to regulate access to economic activities by third-country nationals in Article 79(5) TFEU was circumvented de facto through point (2)(b) of the same article.[36] Differently from the internal market, the distribution of competences between

[32] See also Article 2(6) TFEU.

[33] A Kocharov, 'Subsidiarity after Lisbon: Federalism without a Purpose?' in L Azoulai, L Boucon and FX Millet (eds), *Deconstructing EU Federalism through Competences*, EUI Working Paper LAW 2012/06; D Thym, 'EU Migration Policy and Its Constitutional Rationale: A Cosmopolitan Outlook' (2013) 50 *CML Rev*.

[34] Article 79(2)(a) TFEU allows the Union to adopt not only 'standards on procedures' for the issue of residence permits as ex-Article 63(3)(a) EC, but also to regulate other matters related to the issue of permits, ie conditions for their acquisition. Article 79(2)(b) TFEU allows the introduction of conditions for freedom of movement for third-country nationals within the Union. Article 79(4) TFEU contains a supportive Union competence to adopt measures that would 'provide incentives and support for the action of Member States' aimed at integration of legally resident third-country nationals, wording that excludes harmonisation. Concerning the freedom to travel within the Schengen space, Article 77(2)(c) TFEU abolished the three-month cut-off period, replacing it with a 'short period' to be defined, again, in secondary law. All this expands potential powers of the EU without creating Treaty rights with direct effect.

[35] Member States remain competent to regulate immigration to the extent that these powers have not been exercised by the Union, see Protocol 25 Lisbon: 'With reference to Article 2 of the Treaty on the Functioning of the European Union on shared competence, when the Union has taken action in a certain area, the scope of this exercise of competence only covers those elements governed by the Union act in question and therefore does not cover the whole area'.

[36] Article 79(2)(b) TFEU establishes Union competence in 'the definition of the rights of third-country nationals residing legally in a Member State'; it was used in Directive 2005/71 Research, Directive 2004/114/EC Students, Directive 2003/86/EC Family Reunification establish a right of admission and a right to engage in work; Directive 2003/109/EC Long-Term Residents established a right to work.

the Union and Member States in the area of immigration law is not defined by the exercise of economic activity but on the basis of the immigration status that the individual receives from the national immigration authorities upon entering the state (eg family member, student, Blue Card holder or worker). This nearly fictional construction of competences has allowed the Union, since the Amsterdam Treaty, to regulate access to work by third-country nationals whose official reason for admission into Member State territory is other than economic activities, ie the vast majority of immigrants. One may wonder whether this 'legal illusion' annihilates the *effet utile* of the express reservation in Article 79(5) TFEU.

The same occurred as regards the express reservation of Member State powers in Article 153 TFEU.Under Article 153 TFEU, the Union can only exercise powers in the field of social security by unanimity of Member States (point 1), while Union powers over wages is excluded (point 5). Nevertheless, Article 5(3) Directive 2009/50/EC Blue Card and Article 5(4)(b) Directive 2014/66/EU Intra-Corporate Transferees regulate wages, while the social security provisions governing third-country nationals were adopted in Union law under the legal base that requires QMV—all under the immigration legal base in Article 79 TFEU. Thus, a constitutional choice is made: for the regulation of social security and wages of Union citizens, national polities remain the agora for majority rule, while the regulation of wages and social security of third-country nationals can be done by majority in the EU. Article 21(3) TFEU also provides for the adoption of social security and social protection measures, but only for Union citizens, when these are necessary to ensure free movement; also these measures are to be adopted by unanimity.

Residual competences of the Union were also broadened. Article 352 TEC, the Lisbon successor to Article 308 EC, opened this legal base to all Union measures that attain 'one of the objectives set out in the Treaties' as opposed to mere functioning of the internal market or to only one Treaty.[37]

At the same time, no rights are contained in immigration legal bases under the AFSJ, leaving broad amplitude of policy choice. The breadth of potential action by the Union raises the importance of securing *non-dependence* of national polities that could result from the shift in the making of policy choices from the national political process to the EU. If such a shift is accompanied by an overall decrease in accountability, this could lead to the domination of polity by the vested minority interests (including national governments) internal to it. Where the counter-minoritarian guarantees associated with making policy choices at Union level are lower than those available in the national political process, national governments might be tempted to engage in the 'empty' exercise of Union powers, for instance by adopting EU directives that do not contain any specific policy choice (eg multiple optional clauses and 'may' provisions that can accommodate any national policy). This way, a government may continue to regulate as before, yet circumventing accountability in the national political process.

[37] A Rosas and L Armati, *EU Constitutional Law. An Introduction* (Oxford, Oxford University Press, 2010) 21.

Nor is policy choice contained by objectives that define Union powers in the legal base. Article 77 TFEU confers on the Union competence in the field of visas and border controls; this power should ensure 'absence of any controls on persons … when crossing internal borders'. Article 78 TFEU is the legal base for regulating asylum; the common asylum policy should offer 'appropriate status to any third-country national requiring international protection and ensur[e] compliance with the principle of non-refoulement'. Article 79(1) TFEU contains Union powers to regulate immigration:

> The Union shall develop a common immigration policy aimed at ensuring, at all stages, the efficient management of migration flows, fair treatment of third-country nationals residing legally in Member States, and the prevention of, and enhanced measures to combat, illegal immigration and trafficking in human beings.

Nothing is omitted—these are *all* the objectives.[38] How is the Union to exercise these powers and in which direction will immigration policy turn? The Treaty gives no answer. The policy may be restrictive; it may be permissive; it may even comprise purely internal situations.[39] Only the fight against illegal migration is sufficiently precise to define a policy: the Union may not facilitate illegal migration and trafficking in human beings. Nor may the Union break 'the Geneva Convention of 28 July 1951 and the Protocol of 31 January 1967 relating to the status of refugees, and other relevant treaties'[40]—similar to values, this is an affirmation of those features of constitutional identity that bring together Union polities and legitimate the Union in international law, as opposed to defining policy choices that would establish a specific balance of interests.[41] 'Management of migration flows' and 'fair' treatment of third-country nationals could cover all and *any* policy choice.

[38] Indeed, Articles 78(2) and 79(2) TFEU do not even speak of 'objectives' but of 'purposes'.

[39] The latter is now expressly included in Article 79(2)b TFEU, which gives the Union powers to define 'the rights of third-country nationals residing legally in *a* Member State' without requiring any mobility between states, whether within the EU or between Member States and third countries. Prior to the entry into force of the Lisbon Treaty, the Community adopted Directive 2003/86/EC Family Reunification, which defines rights of third-country nationals also in purely internal situations despite a quite different wording in Article 63(3)(a) EC: 'The Council … shall … adopt: measures on immigration policy within the following areas: (a) conditions of entry and residence, and standards on procedures for the issue by Member States of long-term visas and residence permits, including those for the purpose of family reunion'—without any mention of the rights once admitted.

[40] Article 78(1) TFEU.

[41] Similar affirmations regarding the constitutive elements that Union polities share are found in the Charter and the ECHR, as well as Title II TEU *Provisions on Democratic Principles*. For Alexy, these are constitutional principles (as opposed to rights or even policy objectives), see R Alexy, *A Theory of Constitutional Rights* (Oxford, Oxford University Press, 2002) 47. On the difference between functional objectives and broader constitutional principles in EU law, see also A Von Bogdandy, 'Founding Principles of EU Law: A Theoretical and Doctrinal Sketch' (2010) 16(2) *European Law Journal*. Both regulation of entry and rights will have an impact on migration flow and therefore constitute 'management' of migration; this makes it difficult to justify the divorce of entry (Member State competence) from rights (EU competence), see AB Cox, 'Immigration Law's Organizing Principles' (2008) 157(2) *University of Pennsylvania Law Review* and M Ruhs and P Martin, 'Numbers vs. Rights: Trade-Offs and Guest Worker Programs' (2008) 42(1) *International Migration Review*. More on this in Chapter 4.

Nor are these powers directed by their link to the internal market. Introduced to balance the interdependence caused by the abolition of internal borders,[42] the power to regulate third-country nationals under the AFSJ in Article 3(1)(d) EC followed the competence over the internal market (point 1(c) of the same article) and both were subject to the (mainly economic) goals of Article 2 EC. Article 61(a) EC—the first article of the immigration Title of the EC Treaty—made reference to Community measures on asylum, the free travel area, and crossing of external borders (Articles 62(2) and (3) and 63(1)(a) and (2)(a) EC respectively) in conjunction with the 'measures aimed at ensuring the free movement of persons in accordance with Article 14'. Article 14 EC provided for the progressive establishment of the internal market as an area without internal borders and with free movement of persons. Although the rest of the immigration articles contained no functional objectives,[43] they were compensated by the goals of Article 2 EC[44] and the chronological order in Article 3 EC: the internal market retained its central role as a means to secure Peace, the AFSJ auxiliary to it. The Lisbon Treaty broke this connection. Immigration remains linked to the abolition of internal borders but abolition of internal borders no longer serves the internal market. Instead, it is a separate policy that precedes the internal market in the Treaty text:

1. The Union's aim is to promote *peace*, its values and the well-being *of its peoples*.
2. The Union shall offer its *citizens* an *area of freedom, security and justice* without internal frontiers, in which the free movement of persons is ensured in conjunction with appropriate measures with respect to external border controls, asylum, immigration and the prevention and combating of crime.
3. The Union shall establish an *internal market*.[45]

This gives new prominence to the AFSJ[46] and changes the orientation of the Union as a whole. Not merely an internal market characterised by a precise balance of

[42] For an opinion that EU immigration law constitutes a 'flanking' measure to free movement of persons see also P Boeles, M Den Heijer, G Lodder and K Wouters (eds), *European Migration Law* (Cambridge, Intersentia, 2009) 135.

[43] Point (b) of Article 61 EC provided for the adoption of measures on legal immigration and on 'safeguarding the rights of third-country nationals in accordance with Article 63 EC'—free movement was no longer mentioned, nor were there any other objectives. Articles 62 and 63 EC, which contained competence in immigration policy, did not provide any objectives either, only a legal base.

[44] A Von Bogdandy and J Bast, 'The Federal Order of Competences' in A von Bogdandy and J Bast (eds), *Principles of European Constitutional Law* (London, Hart/CH Beck/Nomos, 2010) 287–88.

[45] Article 3 TEU, emphasis added. Compare to ex-Article 2 EC: '*The Community shall have as its task*, by establishing a common market and an economic and monetary union and *by implementing common policies or activities referred to in Articles 3* and 4, to promote throughout the Community a harmonious, balanced and sustainable development of economic activities …'; Article 3 (1) EC: 'For the purposes set out in Article 2, the activities of the Community shall include …: (c) an internal market characterized by the abolition, as between Member States, of obstacles to the free movement of goods, persons, services and capital; (d) *measures concerning the entry and movement of persons as provided for in Title IV*; …'.

[46] Several authors noted that the new structure of the Treaties after Lisbon is bound to affect interpretation of Union powers and content of secondary law. See P Craig, *The Lisbon Treaty* (Oxford, Oxford University Press, 2010) 337; S Peers, 'EU Immigration and Asylum Competence and Decision-Making in the Treaty of Lisbon' (2008) 10 *European Journal of Migration and Law*.

interests fixed in the Treaties through functional objectives, the Union now constitutes an area of freedom, security and justice[47] for the benefit of its citizens.[48] A 'spill-over' of the internal market in the past, the AFSJ is an independent goal and measure of European integration now. Certainly, this is not a revolution that happened overnight from 30 November to 1 December 2009 with the entry into force of the Lisbon Treaty but a gradual evolution that has been in the making since the Single European Act.[49] The Lisbon Treaty finalised this process. Not only is there a shift in focus from one policy (internal market) to another (the AFSJ) and a more holistic approach to the Union's reach as a result (the nexus between Union citizenship and the AFSJ)[50] but also and more importantly, the openness of policy choice accompanying this shift. Withdrawn from the negotiation between the polities before Lisbon thanks to functional Treaty objectives and Treaty rights, the vision of 'ideal life' to be built in Europe is now open to negotiation and debate. Without Treaty rights and functional objectives, regulation of immigration under the AFSJ allows and requires that the idea of *positive liberty* to be pursued in Union law be identified subsequent to Treaty ratification—in the *European* political space. There is now *de jure* a space for politics in the Union.

This is a change in the constitutional role of Union law. Under the internal market and mixed external agreements, a specific policy choice identified in primary law through functional objectives and directly effective rights negated the very purpose of the political process. The policy was chosen unanimously by all European polities and fixed in the Treaty or international agreement itself; amendment of policy choices also had to be unanimous. In contrast, under the AFSJ and with the Lisbon Treaty, policy choices in immigration and asylum are open for co-decision with the EP and under majority rule in the Council.[51] This shifts not only conferred functional powers to implement policy choices made by each European polity when it ratified the Treaties—as it was for shared powers under Community law—but potentially also the very arena in which the policy choice is made. Instead of the national political processes being the agora for interest representation that leads to a certain balance of interests, a specific policy choice, a vision of

[47] Article 67(1) TFEU.

[48] According to Article 20(2) TFEU, it is Union citizens who 'shall enjoy rights and be subject to the duties provided for in the Treaties'. A Rosas and L Armati, *EU Constitutional Law* (Oxford, Hart Publishing, 2012) 182–83.

[49] For an overview of the history of the AFSJ see Boeles et al (n 42) 32–32; S Peers, *EU Justice and Home Affairs Law* (Oxford, Oxford University Press, 2011) ch 2.

[50] According to Article 3(2) TEU, the AFSJ is to 'offer its citizens an area … without internal frontiers, in which the free movement of persons is ensured in conjunction with appropriate measures with respect to external border controls, asylum, immigration and the prevention and combating of crime'.

[51] The Amsterdam Treaty provided for the exercise of this competence by unanimity in the Council, with a gradual passage to QMV (Articles 62, 63 and 67 EC); the Lisbon Treaty introduced the ordinary legislative procedure (co-decision and QMV) for all immigration law under the AFSJ (Articles 77(2) and 78(2) TFEU). How this majoritarian political process works in practice, eg whether mutual concessions and bargaining take place in the Council, is another issue—in fact, ensuring that this majoritarian political process is deliberative and does not lead to dependence is a key constitutional function of EU law.

shared *positive liberty*, these can now result from representation and balancing of interests at the *European* (no longer national) level, where majorities are identified by reference to more than one European polity (and, ideally, to all of them).[52] For those policies where Union powers are defined by functional Treaty objectives, a change in the decision-making procedure in the Council and the EP does not have such implications: the policy choice is made in the Treaties and is not open for subsequent change. Yet, for powers not limited by Treaty objectives, a space for the political process at the Union level is now open. To the extent that functional Treaty objectives no longer limit the exercise of Union powers, EU law becomes 'more about framing the search for meaning in a political community than the revelation of a meaning that has been previously set into constitutional rules'.[53] The *constitutional* role of Union law is to provide rules for the political process in which such a meaning or policy choice that embodies a shared European idea of *positive liberty* can be legitimately (re)negotiated in Europe. Such rules for the political process would raise legitimacy by safeguarding liberty in the enactment of secondary Union law.

3. EMERGENCE OF A EUROPEAN POLITICAL PROCESS

Regulation Not Deregulation

Once the identification and pursuit of *positive liberty* by each national polity without interference between them is impossible,[54] three scenarios for the regulation of third-country nationals in Union law emerge. The difference between the three scenarios lies in who can decide (identify and pursue) *positive liberty*. This decision-making capacity may be vested in (1) the individual polity member, (2) the individual third-country national (not a member of any European polity), or (3) the European political process. These will now be discussed in turn.

Under the *Metock* model discussed in Chapter 2, the bearers of Treaty rights are Member State nationals, members of European polities bound by reciprocity; Treaty rights of Union citizens withdraw their interest (their capacity to identify and pursue their own *positive liberty*) from the political process on both national and European levels. The power to make and pursue policy choices is shifted not

[52] Currently, the UK, Ireland and Denmark enjoy opt-outs from the AFSJ under Protocols Nos 21 and 22 Lisbon; for a detailed analysis see F Tekin, *Differentiated Integration at Work. The Institutionalisation and Implementation of Opt-Outs from European Integration in the Area of Freedom, Security and Justice* (Baden-Baden, Nomos, 2012). Differentiated integration is also present in other areas of Union law, eg the euro. For an interesting analysis of both in conjunction with legitimacy of the EU see BMJ Szewczyk, 'European Citizenship and National Democracy: Contemporary Sources of Legitimacy of the European Union' (2011) 17 *Columbia Journal of European Law*.

[53] M Poiares Maduro, 'In Search of A Meaning and Not in Search of The Meaning: Judicial Review and the Constitution in Times of Pluralism' [2013] *Wisconsin Law Review* 543.

[54] The *Akrich* scenario discussed in Chapter 2.

upwards from Member States to the Union but downwards from the polity to its individual members. This downward shift does not imply a net loss of *positive liberty* but a change in the function of polity, in what part of *positive liberty* is determined in the course of the political process. What is lost by polity members in their capacity to determine *positive liberty* jointly is gained by each of them individually. This changes the role of polity in the making of policy choices[55] but does not affect the overall balance of liberty. Political process on this aspect of *positive liberty* (migration) disintegrates, but the system of reciprocity between individuals in the polity and between polities in the Union remains in place. This model endures for Union citizens in parallel to EU immigration and asylum law under the AFSJ.

When it comes to third-country nationals, deregulation of the capacity of national polities to determine and pursue *positive liberty* leads to a shift in this capacity from the national polity and political process to the individual third-country national, whose interest is thus withdrawn from the political process on both national and European levels. This would happen in particular were the Treaties to contain directly effective rights for third-country nationals such as if free movement rights were extended to third-country nationals. The more difficult it is to change the scope and substance of such rights through the political process (such as by amending EU Treaties), the more the capacity of each European polity to pursue *positive liberty* as regards immigration is lost not on a reciprocal basis between the polities bound by Union law but to a member of an external polity not bound in reciprocal terms. The loss by European polities of their capacity to determine their own *positive liberty* would not be compensated by other aspects of liberty inasmuch as third-country polities and their members are not bound by non-domination as *non-interference* similar to that which results between Member States in the Union thanks to the binding nature of reciprocity in EU legal order. (De)regulation of any aspects of immigration policy at EU level does not ensure *non-interference* with the idea(s) of *positive liberty* of the peoples of Europe.

The irrelevance of the internal market model—characterised by a shift in the identification of *positive liberty* from the polities but to the individual, with *non-interference* between the polities enforced by individuals thanks to directly effective rights—for third-country nationals under the AFSJ emerged already in the first proposals.[56] In 2001, the Commission drafted two directives modelled on the

[55] Another question is whether such a shift should result from a decision by the Court or by the people. See *ex multis*, C Hübner Mendes, *Constitutional Courts and Deliberative Democracy* (Oxford, Oxford University Press, 2014); N Komesar, *Imperfect Alternatives; Choosing Institutions in Law, Economics, and Public Policy* (Chicago, IL, University of Chicago Press, 1994); A Barak, *The Judge in a Democracy* (Princeton, NJ, Princeton University Press; A Vermeule, *Law and the Limits of Reason* (Oxford, Oxford University Press, 2008).

[56] This has also been observed on the Union citizenship side of free movement in the EU: JHH Weiler, *The Constitution of Europe: 'Do the New Clothes Have an Emperor?' and other essays on European integration* (Cambridge, Cambridge University Press, 1999) 326: the same logic of the 'European Common External Tariff towards the rest of the world', ie 'internal free movement and residence requiring a common European "membership" policy—has been rejected'.

free movement of persons in the internal market.[57] The rationale of both proposals was to link rights of the individual to the actual exercise of economic activities. Following the internal market model, belonging to the national labour force would trigger the rights of the individual (a third-country national) in Union law thus limiting the national political process. Indeed, if what were created were a common market, it would hardly make sense to distinguish between the production factors on the basis of their passport as long as they belonged to the labour force of one of the Member States.[58] From this perspective, it appeared reasonable to use the free movement model.

These suggestions to extend the internal market to legally resident third-country workers under the AFSJ found no support in the Council. The first proposal was withdrawn four years after its introduction[59] while the second proposal was amended in all that resembled free movement law.[60] Subsequent directives instituted additional legal barriers for third-country nationals moving between Member States.[61] Although the Lisbon Treaty removed the explicit authorisation of parallel national immigration schemes from the Treaty,[62] such reservation remained in force through EU immigration directives.[63] The power of European polities to identify and pursue their *positive liberty* was not abolished. Rights of third-country nationals continue to be determined in the political process. Extending free movement rights to third-country nationals would, on the contrary, preclude all political process.

The resulting formula for Union powers currently in the Treaty follows this pattern of constitutional choice. The clear-cut separation between the AFSJ and

[57] Proposal for a directive on the conditions of entry and residence of third-country nationals for the purpose of paid employment and self-employed economic activities (11.7.2001) COM (2001) 386 final, see S Peers and N Rogers (eds), *EU Immigration and Asylum Law* (The Hague, Martinus Nijhof, 2006) ch 21. Proposal for a directive on the status of third-country nationals who are long-term residents (13.3.2001) COM (2001) 127 final; see S Boelaert-Suominen, 'Non-EU Nationals and Council Directive 2003/109/EC on the Status of Third-Country Nationals Who Are Long-Term Residents: Five Paces Forward and Possibly Three Paces Back' (2005) 42 *CML Rev*.

[58] Case C-41/96 *El Yassini*; Case C-97/05 *Gattoussi*; Case C-268/99 *Jany*.

[59] In 2005, see B Ryan, 'The EU and Labor Migration: Regulating Admission or Treatment?' in A Baldaccini, E Guild and H Toner (eds), *Whose Freedom, Security and Justice?* (Oxford, Hart Publishing, 2007).

[60] S Peers, 'Implementing Equality? The Directive on Long-Term Resident Third-Country Nationals' (2004) 29 *European Law Review*; Boelaert-Suominen (n 57).

[61] This is so even for lawfully resident third-country nationals: A Skordas, 'Immigration and the Market: the Long-Term Residents Directive' (2006) 13 *Columbia Journal of European Law*; A Kocharov, 'What Intra-Community Mobility for Third-Country Workers?' (2008) 6 *European Law Review*; S Iglesias Sanches, 'Free Movement of Third-Country Nationals in the European Union?' (2009) 15(6) *European Law Journal*.

[62] Penultimate paragraph of Article 62 EC: 'Measures adopted by the Council pursuant to [legal immigration, illegal immigration and mobility of legally resident third-country nationals between Member States] shall not prevent any Member State from maintaining or introducing in the areas concerned national provisions which are compatible with this Treaty and with international agreements'.

[63] Article 8 Directive 2009/50/EU Blue Card, Article 14(3) Directive 2003/109/EC Long-Term Residents, Article 6 Directive 2014/66/EU Intra-Corporate Transferees, Articles 2(2) and 8(3) Directive 2014/36/EU Seasonal Workers.

the internal market has already been mentioned. The immigration Articles of the AFSJ contain no directly effective rights. Limiting the capacity of European polities to determine their own *positive liberty* by shifting this capacity to the third-country national individual is not the choice made in the Treaties. Rather, the opposite. While the Treaties leave the choice as regards immigration policy open by omitting functional objectives, one specific choice is excluded. Article 79(1) TFEU specifies that the Union is to develop a 'common immigration policy' that would ensure 'efficient management of migration flows', the opposite of deregulation and abolition of power of the state. Management of migration flows by the Union or its Member States implies regulation of immigration, not deregulation with a right that the individual may enforce against the polity (as it is in the internal market).[64] The rationale for regulating third-country nationals under the AFSJ is the mirror image of the internal market: deregulation between the polities is not envisaged. Deregulation between Member States as concerns immigration, even were it to take place, would have to rely exclusively on enforcement by the states (because the interest of the individual with *locus standi* will not always coincide with the balance of interest struck in Union law)—the opposite of the European model for integration between national polities.[65]

Regulation of third-country nationals follows another model of liberty. The impossibility of ensuring *non-interference* between the national polities without reliance on power politics between Member States requires that the identification and pursuit of *positive liberty* in the Union be shifted from the national polities to the EU. Although national polities lose their individual *positive liberty*, they regain it together in Europe.

Majority Not Unanimity

Not fixing a specific policy choice in the Treaties through functional objectives and directly effective rights is the first step to the European *positive liberty*. Yet, this step is insufficient for creating Europe's constitutional soul. Union law will only have a constitutional function if *positive liberty* is shaped at Union level through a majoritarian political process rather than unanimity or consensus. Under unanimity or consensus, the national polities in Europe remain the agora for policy choice. But if identification of the European idea of *positive liberty* takes place under majority rule then Union law will have a constitutional role.

[64] This is not to say that there are no limits on the regulatory powers of the Union and Member States that result from international law, in particular as regards regulation of asylum and refugees under Article 78 TFEU or the right to private and family life Article 79 TFEU, as well as the limits resulting from the general provisions of the Treaties and the EU Charter of Fundamental Rights. In particular, international law imposes obligations on the regulatory capacity of polities, thus limiting their policy choices. See Section 2 in this chapter.

[65] See Section 1 in this chapter.

Under the Treaty of Lisbon, the identification of European *positive liberty* goes through several stages. First, the Lisbon Treaty codified the pre-existing practice of having the objectives of immigration policy set by the European Council in its Conclusions.[66] Although not endorsed with legislative powers, the European Council is now an official institution of the Union, responsible for providing it 'with the necessary impetus for its development' and defining 'the general political directions and priorities thereof',[67] in particular 'the strategic guidelines for legislative and operational planning within the area of freedom, security and justice'.[68] These decisions are taken in the European Council by consensus.[69]

Second, based on Conclusions of the European Council, the Commission refines policy objectives. However, the ability of the Commission to (re)formulate Union objectives has been significantly reduced in Lisbon. Prior to the Lisbon Treaty, the Commission could suggest its own policy objectives for immigration under the AFSJ, thus creating a sort of trialogue with the Council and the European Council, supplemented by stakeholder consultations and impact assessments. With the leading role of the European Council as objective setter secured in the Lisbon Treaty, the Commission may no longer conduct dialogue with the Council on objectives but only define the objectives set by the European Council without changing them entirely.[70] Policy objectives thus refined are found in consultation documents of the Commission and, at a later stage, explanatory memoranda and impact assessments[71] accompanying proposals for legislative acts; in the areas of shared competences such as immigration under the AFSJ, the Commission is obliged to 'consult widely' before issuing legislative proposals; it is obliged to include in draft legislative acts 'a detailed statement making it possible to appraise compliance with the principles of subsidiarity and proportionality',[72] which inevitably includes policy objectives.

Third, the objectives formulated by the Commission form part of recitals to legislative proposals that may or may not be accepted by the Council and the European Parliament during the legislative process.[73] For most policies of the Union,

[66] Article 15 TEU regarding Union policies generally, Article 68 TFEU specifically for common immigration policy, Article 22 TEU for the Union's external action and Article 26 TEU for the CFSP; compare to ex-Art 250 EC, which provided that the Commission would set the agenda for the Community with no provision for the agenda-setting role of the European Council.

[67] Article 15(1) TEU.

[68] Article 68 TFEU.

[69] Article 15(4) TEU.

[70] P Ponzano, C Hermanin and D Corona, *The Power of Initiative of the European Commission: A Progressive Erosion?* (Notre Europe, 2012).

[71] For the 'Integrated Impact Assessment' procedure introduced in 2002, see H Toner, 'Impact Assessments: A Useful Tool for "Better Lawmaking" in EU Migration Policy?' in Baldaccini, Guild and Toner (eds) (n 59).

[72] Article 2 Protocol 2 Lisbon.

[73] When EU secondary acts lack clearly stated objectives, the effects that these acts produce have been treated as their objectives by the Court, see Case C-300/89 *Titanium Dioxide*; Joined Cases C-317/04 and C-318/04 *PNR*.

including immigration under the AFSJ,[74] secondary legislation is adopted by the QMV in the Council and simple majority in the EP (co-legislation or 'ordinary' legislative procedure). Since the Council and the Parliament may amend both the substantive provisions of acts and their objectives, majoritarian legislative procedure plays a decisive role in setting objectives. Although QMV rules concern the legislative procedure in the Council as opposed to the political agreement between heads of state and government in the European Council, in practice the ability of Member States to block ensuing secondary law in the Council is likely to improve their bargaining power in the European Council. National governments with 'heavier' votes in the Council will have more influence over the 'consensus' in the European Council, too. In particular, three large Member States that represent 35 per cent of Union population together with any fourth Member State may block the adoption of secondary EU law,[75] leaving small Member States little leverage.

What emerges is a stepwise procedure for making Europe's policy choices. Although formally the rule is consensus of all European polities in the European Council, majoritarian legislative procedure translates into majoritarian policy choice. This is so both under the rules of Union law and in practice. National ideas of *positive liberty* feed into majoritarian policy choice at the Union level both through the EP and the Council (where weighted voting reflects polity populations). The EP co-legislates by a majority of its members (MEPs), who are elected separately in each national polity. The fact that EP elections take place simultaneously across Member States does not change this fact; indeed, even despite the frail efforts to stage 'European' EP debates in the course of the 2014 campaign, these were held separately in each national polity while the arguments advanced by the candidates varied markedly from one polity to the next. For instance, Martin Schulz campaigned in Italy not as a German but as a European while his campaign in Germany had an explicit 'vote German' slogan.[76] MEPs' ideas about *positive liberty* are likely to follow their constituencies, ie national polities. Conflicts between the peoples of Europe over policy choices (ideas about *positive liberty)* are especially likely for immigration policy because many aspects of this policy pertain to those interests of each national polity that are defined by its immutable characteristics such as geography, language or the size of the labour market. Member State governments recognised this explicitly.[77] At the same time, the number of MEPs elected in each national polity reflects each national polity's population, while

[74] All immigration law under the Lisbon Treaty is adopted following the ordinary legislative procedure: Article 77(2) TFEU and Articles 16 and 17 TEU.

[75] Article 16(4) TEU: 'As from 1 November 2014, a qualified majority shall be defined as at least 55% of the members of the Council, comprising at least fifteen of them and representing Member States comprising at least 65% of the population of the Union. A blocking minority must include at least four Council members, failing which the qualified majority shall be deemed attained'.

[76] *EU Observer* (23.05.2014) 'Vote for Schulz to ensure a German commission president, says ad'.

[77] *European Pact on Immigration and Asylum* (24.12.2008) Council doc 13189/08, 4–5; *The Stockholm Programme—An open and secure Europe serving and protecting citizens* (3.3.2010) Council doc 5731/10, 99.

the voting in the Council is weighted by the same criterion. Thus, more powerful and less powerful polities are created, with a potentially permanent interest cleavage between them. This could resurrect power politics, lead to 'asymmetrically negotiated outcomes'[78] and domination between the peoples of Europe, instead of creating a European political space where all interests find a Voice and ability to influence policy choice, so that it would be perceived by all polities as their 'own'. There is now a *European* political process and a constitutional role for Union law.

4. CONSTITUTIONAL ELEMENTS OF POST-LISBON LAW

The Liberal and Republican Models of Legitimation in Europe

Two models for making policy choices emerge from the Treaties. On the one hand, before the Treaty of Lisbon, Community powers were defined by functional Treaty objectives that were approved by every national polity. The balance of interests for Community policies was fixed through functional Treaty objectives and directly effective rights that can only be changed by unanimity of all national polities in the process of Treaty amendment. Under this model, discussed in the previous chapter, national polities remain the agora for identification of *positive liberty* and for legitimation of policy choices; Union law ensures reciprocal *non-interference* by the national polities in their respective capacities to identify and pursue *positive liberty*. On the other hand, a political process at the Union level is enabled for Union powers that are not directed by functional Treaty objectives and Treaty rights. Under this post-Lisbon model, policy choices are made not in and by each national polity but by the majority identified with reference to all the polities of the EU. What is pursued is not the policy choice of each national polity identified in its political process but the idea of *positive liberty* shaped by all polities in the European political space.

These two different roles for Europe—one where *positive liberty* is shaped by European polities jointly, the other where EU law secures the capacity of each national polity to identify and pursue its own idea of *positive liberty*—correspond to two traditions of legitimating discourse, which can be summarised as the republican and the liberal:

> Whereas the former emphasizes the common good of the polity and the collective self-determination of its citizens, the latter highlights the protection of individual rights and the need to base the exercise of governing powers on the consent of those who are affected.[79]

[78] J Habermas, 'Why Europe Needs a Constitution' (2001) 11 *New Left Review* 11.

[79] FW Scharpf, *Legitimacy Intermediation in the Multilevel European Polity* (October 2012) Max Planck Institute for the Study of Societies, Cologne, MPIfG Discussion Paper 12/6 3 who notes: 'In the literature, these labels are not used consistently, and contemporary discussions of democratic legitimacy tend to combine arguments derived from both traditions. I hope to show, however, that it is theoretically and pragmatically useful to identify the distinct logics of these discourses'.

The split between the liberal and the republican is not clear cut and policies may exhibit both. Bellamy, for example, distinguishes between, on the one hand, political constitutionalism based on counter-minoritarian guarantees and the political process as the source of policy choice and, on the other hand, legal constitutionalism based on counter-majoritarian guarantees and judicial enforcement of individuals' rights, noting that 'There are elements of both legal and political constitutionalism in most constitutions'.[80] More specifically for the European Union, Majone discerns federations from confederations based on whether the Union places greater emphasis on liberties of the individual or on liberties of its constituent polities.[81] This dual structure of liberty in the EU reflects the 'hermaphrodite'[82] nature of Europe's legitimacy, linked to liberty of both national polities and their individual members.

Consent through output legitimacy is the basis for liberal legitimation (the *non-interference* model of EU constitutional law): Union law is accepted as long as it secures for each national polity and its polity members the attainment of their own idea of *positive liberty* without interference by other polities. This model is insufficient where elimination of interference between the polities is impossible, such as discussed in Section 1 of this chapter. For such policies, republican legitimation is needed. Republican legitimation is based on Loyalty, so that a loss in one aspect of one's own *positive liberty* (a specific policy choice) is compensated by another aspect of one's own *positive liberty* (the value placed on the continued relationship with the other). The relevance of the republican model of legitimisation in Union law increased with the Treaty of Lisbon: majoritarian decision making requires this form of legitimation, while the omission of functional objectives and directly effective rights from the legal bases in the Treaty enables it.

The liberal and republican models appear split along the different mechanisms of enforcement. Liberal legitimacy in Europe is based on reciprocity of *non-interference* between national polities enforced by the individual in national courts. Thanks to this unique mechanism of enforcement, the ability to benefit from *non-interference* is no longer a function of power politics between states, rendering the peoples of Europe equal in Union law. This mechanism of enforcement eliminates the possibility that smaller or otherwise less powerful polities permanently lose their *liberty from dependence* to larger or more powerful European polities. Crucial for this egalitarian mechanism of enforcement is that the individuals empowered to enforce Union law act as a proxy for the European interest (non-domination attained through deregulation).

This power-neutral mechanism of enforcing reciprocity between the national polities is structurally impossible for policies that regulate the interests that are external to the system of reciprocity established in law. An interest is external not

[80] R Bellamy, *Political Constitutionalism: A Republican Defence of the Constitutionality of Democracy* (Cambridge, Cambridge University Press, 2007) 5.

[81] G Majone, *Dilemmas of European Integration* (Oxford, Oxford University Press, 2005).

[82] An expression borrowed from G Amato, 'Foreword' in HJ Blanke and S Mangiameli (eds), *The Treaty on European Union, A Commentary* (Berlin, Springer, 2013).

in the sense of membership in any European polity or physical presence in Europe but in the sense of not being bound by 'certain elements of the social contract'[83] established in law. Instead of being a proxy for Union interest, the European idea of *positive liberty* identified under the AFSJ often comes in contrast with the interest it aims to contain. For policies that regulate interests external to the system of reciprocity in Union law,[84] a problem of enforcement of Union law arises both against the national polities and against the regulated interest. This renders deregulation between Member States nugatory of liberty: abolishing the regulatory power of the state (the ability of each national polity to pursue its own *positive liberty* through regulation) is not compensated by the gain in *non-interference* by other polities. For polities and persons bound by reciprocity in Union law, there is no one with *locus standi* interested in enforcing reciprocity of deregulation. For polities and persons not bound by Union law, deregulation only facilitates interference with the interest of Union polities. This, in turn, diminishes overall liberty and Loyalty in the EU.

Due to this difference in the mechanism of enforcement, empowerment of external interests in Union law does not advance *negative liberty*. The power to make policy choices would shift neither upwards to the Union nor downwards to the individual polity members but to the individuals and polities who are outside the system of Union law (and thus not bound by the reciprocity that the EU legal order creates). The nature of the regulated interest as external to the system of reciprocity in national and Union law means not only that deregulation is impossible but that the exercise of power by the state is needed to further European *positive liberty*. The balance between the three aspects of liberty can be preserved by shifting the pursuit of *positive liberty* and the making of policy choices up to the EU.

This explains the bulking of policies on third-country nationals (both legal and illegal immigration)[85] together with the provisions on criminal cooperation under the AFSJ. Reciprocal deregulation in Union law does not advance liberty of EU polities. Freedom of movement in the internal market (deregulation with a downward shift in policy choice from the national polities to individual polity members) is mirrored in the three systems of forced migration established under the AFSJ (regulation with an upward shift in policy choice from the national polities individually to their joint decision in the EU): the Common European Asylum System,

[83] M Poiares Maduro, 'Europe's Democratic Deficit Lies in Its Member States' in Foundation for European Progressive Studies, Italiani Europei, Fondation Jean-Jaurès, Friedrich Ebert Stiftung, *Renaissance for Europe—A Democratic Union of Peace, Prosperity and Progress* (2013).

[84] Compare with Chapter 2, Section 3 and Case C-221/11 *Demirkan* discussed therein.

[85] Legal immigration is there due to the choice, on the one hand, to abolish the internal borders, while, on the other hand, not to have a common EU admission policy. This means that all mobility of third-country nationals into the national territory needs to fall under national competence, ie both first admission to the EU and subsequent movement between Member States. Extending freedom of movement to third-country nationals would undermine the ability of each national polity to regulate first admission. As a result, third-country nationals fall under EU free travel rules and yet require a separate national permit to move within the EU for periods exceeding three months: the line between what is legal and what is not is crossed just as easily as the abolished internal borders.

return of illegal immigrants, and the European Arrest Warrant. First, the Common European Asylum System (CEAS) is based on the Dublin Convention,[86] which was incorporated into EU secondary law.[87] The main rule of the CEAS is that applications for asylum must be made and examined in only one Member State—the state responsible for the asylum seeker and, once recognised, for the refugee. There are therefore EU law criteria for assigning responsibility for asylum seekers between Member States,[88] common minimum standards for examination of asylum applications[89] and the treatment of asylum seekers and refugees.[90] Asylum seekers who move within the EU are transferred back to the responsible Member State and there are rules on allocating the costs associated with such transfers.[91] Second, the European measures on return of illegal immigrants consist of (1) EU secondary law[92] and (2) readmission agreements between the Union on the one side and individual third countries on the other.[93] Member States agree, in EU secondary law, to make every effort to return illegal immigrants[94] and allocate responsibility for this return among themselves,[95] while readmission agreements with third states should facilitate the removal of illegal immigrants from the territory of the EU.[96] Third, Council Framework Decision[97] 2002/584/JHA on the European Arrest Warrant (EAW)[98] is the cornerstone of EU's judicial cooperation in criminal matters[99] and replaces 'the multilateral system of extradition between Member States with a system of surrender'[100] of persons indicted or sentenced for any of the 32 types

[86] Convention determining the State responsible for examining applications for asylum lodged in one of the Member States of the European Communities (19.8.1997) OJ C254/01.

[87] Regulation 343/2003 Dublin II, Regulation 604/2013 Dublin III.

[88] Regulation 604/2013 Dublin III, Regulation 2725/2000 Eurodac.

[89] Directive 2004/83/EC Qualification and Directive 2005/85/EC Procedure.

[90] Directive 2003/9/EC Reception.

[91] Case C-179/11 *Cimade*.

[92] Directive 2008/115 Return, Directive 2001/40 Mutual Recognition Expulsion, Decision 2004/573/EC Joint Removal Flights, Decision 2004/191/EC Financial Imbalances Mutual Recognition of Expulsion, Directive 2002/90 Facilitation Illegal Migration, Directive 2003/110 Transit Removal by Air, Directive 2004/81 Victims of Trafficking, Directive 2009/52 Employer Sanctions.

[93] For a full inventory of Readmission Agreements see *Inventory of the Agreements Linked to Readmission*, European University Institute, Robert Schuman Center for Advanced Studies, http://rsc.eui.eu/RDP/research/analyses/ra/.

[94] Directive 2008/115 Return, Case C-61/11 PPU *El Dridi*.

[95] Directive 2001/40 Mutual Recognition Expulsion, Directive 2003/110 transit removal by air, Decision 2004/573/EC Joint Removal Flights, Decision 2004/191/EC Financial Imbalances Mutual Recognition of Expulsion. See also Decision 2002/946/JHA Penal Framework Illegal Migration and Directive 2002/90 Facilitation Illegal Migration for the interface between illegal immigration and criminal law.

[96] This is fundamental for the ability of the Member States to deport illegal immigrants because under international law, the destination state must accept the transfer of the individual to its territory, see Case C-357/09 PPU *Kadzoev*.

[97] As a legal instrument, a framework decision is similar to a directive, see Article 34(2)(b) EU Amsterdam: 'Framework decisions shall be binding upon the Member States as to the result to be achieved but shall leave to the national authorities the choice of form and methods. They shall not entail direct effect'. See also Case C-105/03 *Pupino*.

[98] Amended by Council Framework Decision 2009/299/JHA.

[99] Established under Article 82 TFEU.

[100] Case C-168/13 PPU *Jeremy F*, §34; Case C-396/11 *Radu*, §33; Case C-399/11 *Melloni*, §36.

of offence listed therein; for these offences, the Framework Decision abolishes the principle of double criminality and obliges national judicial authorities to recognise arrest warrants issued by their colleagues in other Member States.[101]

A word of caution is needed here. It is not being claimed that the internal market is a wholly liberal policy while the AFSJ is wholly republican. Although the internal market tends to be based on liberal legitimation while the AFSJ tends to rely on republican legitimation, legal bases do not follow the legitimacy models strictly so that often a policy choice will contain a mixture of both models. For instance, regulation of third-country workers under the mixed internal agreements is legitimised under the republican model when the policy choice is made in the national political process of each European polity separately; however, it is enforced between the Member States along the internal market, ie liberal model. In this tendency to rely on the liberal or republican models, the different parts of EU migration law may be construed as a continuum: free movement follows the liberal model, followed by third-country workers under the mixed external agreements, legal migration under the AFSJ, asylum, illegal migration law and, finally, the EAW, which largely follows the republican model.

Composite European Political Process

Although in the national political processes the two models of legitimation routinely coexist,[102] in the European Union they appear mutually exclusive at least in one respect. To the extent that the liberal model seeks to preserve the national political process while the republican model seeks to replace it, the two models are incompatible in their conception of the EU. The liberal model makes redundant the national political process for enforcing *negative liberty*; this strengthens legitimacy of the national political process by furthering the capacity of each national polity to identify and pursue its own *positive liberty* independently from its ability to enforce *non-interference* vis-a-vis other European polities. The liberal model seeks to further self-determination of each national polity by obliterating power politics between Member States. On the other hand, the republican model seeks to create a *European* political process in the course of which a shared idea of *positive liberty* would be developed. To the extent that European political process substitutes and replaces the national political process, the republican model of legitimation cannot coexist with the liberal model in Europe's constitutional construct.

An obvious way to structure the European political process is by analogy with federal states.[103] Much of EU constitutional reform thus focused on creating the

[101] On the principle of mutual recognition in EU criminal law see Peers (n 49) ch 9.

[102] Scharpf, (n 79) 13.

[103] For a critique of this arrangement see S Cassese, 'Is there really a "Democratic Deficit"?' in S Cassese and G della Cananea (eds), *Institutional Reforms in the European Union: Memorandum for the Convention* (EuropEos, 2002).

institutions and procedures for a variant of European democracy, whereby the Voice of individual citizens feeds directly into the process of European policy choice in an attempt to create an independent source of legitimacy for Union powers.[104] Empowering the European Parliament, citizens' initiatives, the duty of the Commission to consult stakeholders, and the *Spitzenkandidaten* arrangement create a direct link between policy preferences of Union citizens and policies of the EU; they constitute components of a European democracy.[105] Linking the preferences of Union citizens directly to European policy choice withdraws from the national polities the faculty to identify and pursue their own *positive liberty*. National political processes are rendered redundant for developing and pursuing policy choice, exactly opposite to the liberal model. Whereas the liberal model preserves and empowers national political processes, the republican model structured as a European democracy disempowers and substitutes them. Structuring the European political process as a European democracy modelled on a (federal) state is incompatible with the liberal model of legitimation of Europe.

A European democracy presents further problems. Linking citizens' Voice to European policies through the EP elections would shift polity level from Member States to the EU. This ignores the importance and structure of Loyalty for the legitimacy of majoritarian choice. Loyalty exists when one aspect of one's own *positive liberty*—the value placed on continued union with the other(s)—compensates for the loss that results from majority rule in another aspect of *positive liberty*—the value placed on a particular policy choice. Self-perception of citizens as a polity is crucial for Loyalty to exist. Shifting direct democracy from Member States to the Union requires self-perception of Union citizens as a single unified group for the purpose of identification of shared *positive liberty*. Only then will the value of *positive liberty* as a union with the others compensate for being outvoted on preferred policy choices. Without self-perception of Union citizens as a polity, majoritarian policy choices made in the European democracy will not be accepted. In the absence of Loyalty, the decline in Voice resulting from the upward shift in polity (combined with a decline in Voice due to EU enlargement) will lead to Exit: neither the process nor the output of the European democracy will be legitimate in the eyes of Union citizens.

Given the fundamental role of the self-perception of polity for legitimacy and the absence of such self-perception by the peoples of Europe, majoritarian identification of shared *positive liberty* in Europe cannot be achieved directly

[104] M Poiares Maduro, 'O superavit democrático europeu' (2001) XXXVI (158–59) *Análise Social* 121.

[105] For a criticism of the attempts to politicise EP elections see S Bartolini, 'Should the Union Be "Politicised"? Prospects and Risks' in S Hix and S Bartolini, *Politics: The Right or the Wrong Sort of Medicine for the EU?* Policy Paper No. 19 (Paris, Notre Europe, 2006); FW Scharpf, *Political Legitimacy in a Non-optimal Currency Area* (2013) MPIfG Discussion Paper 13/15; A Kocharov, 'In the Image of State: Constitutional Complexities of Engineering a European Democracy' in F Fabbrini, E Hirsch Ballin and H Somsen (eds), *What Form of Government for the European Union and the Eurozone?* (Oxford, Hart Publishing, 2015).

by Union citizens in the course of European democracy. It must go through national polities. Without self-perception of Union citizens as a united political community, majoritarian policy choice in Europe can only rely on national Loyalty. The need to rely on national Loyalty implies that political accountability can only take place through the national political process, while process legitimacy is composed of both European and national levels. This would contrast with a European democracy where the Voice of individual citizens bypasses national polities to elaborate *positive liberty* through Voice at Union level, undermining national political process and the Loyalty it creates. A European democracy that substitutes itself for the national political process is bound to undermine its legitimacy.[106] Only by going through the national political processes, can national Loyalty bridge the absence of European polity and legitimate majoritarian choice in the Union.

The need to rely on national Loyalty for the legitimacy of European policy choice requires a composite European political process.[107] First, each polity through its national political process identifies its own *positive liberty*, composed of (1) preferred policy choices and (2) the value placed on continuity of the Union. Second, this idea of *positive liberty* is negotiated between the peoples of Europe so that individual polities may adjust their ideas of *positive liberty* in order to elaborate a shared vision of ideal life. Acceptance of majoritarian policy choice in Europe takes place within each national polity—the agora where Loyalty allows for a decrease in Voice. Only within the national polities can a feeling of ownership be created through 'shared participation in the authorship and reproduction' of the idea of *positive liberty*. This—and this way only— is how the republican and the liberal models coexist in Union law. Both the liberal and republican models preserve and enhance national polities—and ensure non-Exit from the EU. Together, they form a constitutional framework for interaction between the peoples of Europe and eliminate power politics between Member States.

Permanent and Temporary Exit to Europe

Composite European political process already takes place in Europe today. The lack of enthusiasm of Union citizens for the European polity and their 'empowerment' in Union law evidences a rejection of polity shift. A minuscule fraction

[106] M Poiares Maduro, 'Introduction' in M Poiares Maduro, B De Witte and M Kumm (organisers), *The Democratic Governance of the Euro* (2012) European University Institute, RSCAS working paper 2012/08 1: 'The EU should not be constructed as a challenge to national democracy but, instead, as offering democracy and social justice where States can no longer offer them'.

[107] R Bellamy, 'A European Republic of Sovereign States: Sovereignty, Republicanism and the European Union' (2016) June, *European Journal of Political Theory* 17, calls it 'a double form of delegation'; on the necessity to rely on the national polities and political processes see also R Bellamy, '"An Ever Closer Union Among the Peoples of Europe": Republican Intergovernmentalism and Demoicratic Representation within the EU' (2013) 35(5) *Journal of European Integration*.

of Union citizens make use of their right to reside in another Member State and many of those who do move only temporarily in order to enhance their career prospects upon return.[108] Voter turnout in EP elections is in permanent and steady decline;[109] Union citizens use Europe to vote against their national governments rather than on the substance of European issues.[110] A similar use of Europe for self-empowerment was noted also for national courts: lower national courts refer requests for preliminary rulings directly to the CJEU instead of following up the national court hierarchy.[111] This pattern is explained by national Loyalty and a distinction between permanent and temporary Exit.

European elections could represent two types of Exit to Europe. A *permanent* Exit from the national political process occurs where citizens use their vote in Europe to express policy preferences or an idea of *positive liberty* on the policy at stake in the vote; national political processes lose their relevance for identification of *positive liberty*—instead, this idea is identified in the course of a European democracy; the polity is shifted from national to Union level. A *temporary* Exit from the national political process occurs where the vote cast in European elections is used to signal dissatisfaction with the incumbent national government; the vote is not about identification of *positive liberty* at Union level (it is not about Union policies) but about the pursuit of *positive liberty* at the national level (how well the government furthers the interests of its polity). Without removing the government from power through the national political process (*permanent* Exit), *temporary* Exit aids the incumbent government by delivering both the message and a possibility to act on it. *Permanent* Exit rejects the national political process; *temporary* Exit preserves and enhances it. This opportunity of temporary Exit from the national to the European is used by the individuals and national institutions for self-empowerment within the national polity in both adjudicative and political spheres. The challenge of republican Europe is to avoid temporary Exit for self-empowerment instead being used by the governments to overpower the individual and the polity.

Treaty reforms focused on increasing the participation or Voice of Union citizens at the *European* level fail insofar as they seek to induce a polity shift in favour of Europe. Without a self-perception of European peoples as a single polity, shifting the reference group for majoritarian identification of *positive liberty* from the national level to the EU amounts to domination that suppresses identity—and, for this reason alone, it cannot be perceived as legitimate in the

[108] A Favell, *Eurostars and Eurocities. Free Movement and Mobility in an Integrating Europe* (Oxford, Blackwell Publishing, 2008); A Favell and E Recchi, 'Social Mobility and Spatial Mobility' in A Favell and V Guiraudon (eds), *Sociology of the European Union* (London, Palgrave, 2011).

[109] H Mahony, 'EU Election Turnout at Record Low After All', *EU Observer* (6.8.2014).

[110] S Piedrafita and V Renman, *The 'Personalisation' of the European Elections: A Half-hearted Attempt to Increase Turnout and Democratic Legitimacy?* (April 2014) EPIN Paper No. 37 3: 'elections to the EP to second-order elections largely focused on domestic rather than European issues'.

[111] This possibility of temporary Exit is unique to EU legal order: compare for instance to the ECHR, where all levels of the national jurisdiction need to be exhausted before recourse to the ECtHR.

Western political culture.[112] However, the creation of Voice at Union level succeeds in another crucial way. Far from being 'second-order elections',[113] European elections and referenda allow citizens to (re)gain Voice in the national political process. The possibility to sanction national governments through Voice in Europe corrects shortcomings in interest representation in the course of the national political process, and thus advances *liberty from dependence* within each national polity.[114] National polities and national political processes not only retain their standing as the agora for identification of *positive liberty*, but their legitimacy is enhanced through the possibility of *temporary* Exit. Availability of *temporary* Exit increases Loyalty within national polities and allows reducing Voice as the decision making is transferred to Europe. By creating a venue for *temporary* Exit, Union law furthers national Loyalty and the perception, within each national polity, of the importance of continuing Europe's Union.

The European and national political processes are interdependent and constitute a single system of legitimacy. One cannot exist without the other. In its identification and pursuit of *positive liberty*, the national political process relies on *non-dependence* ensured in Union law.[115] The opposite is also true. Without self-perception of Union citizens as a single polity, majoritarian policy choice in Europe does not have its own source of legitimacy that would be independent from the national polities. By creating a temporary Exit from the national political process, Union law reinforces legitimacy of the national political process, which in turn enhances legitimacy of European majoritarian choice. Under the current constitutional construct of Union Treaties and given the self-perception of Union citizens as first of all members of national polities, Union law can be legitimate only if it strengthens national polities.

Peace, Peoples and Pluralism in Europe's Constitutional Construct

National polities in post-WWII Europe rely on liberty secured in Union law. The interdependence between liberty and legitimacy is expressed in Union Treaties

[112] VA Schmidt, 'Identity and Legitimacy in the European Union: Is more Politics the Answer?' in S Lucarelli, F Cerutti and V Schmidt (eds), *Debating Political Identity and Legitimacy in the European Union* (London, Routledge, 2011).

[113] K Reif and H Schmitt, 'Nine Second-order Elections' (1980) 8(3) *European Journal of Political Research*; F Jacobs, 'European Parliament Elections in Times of Crisis' (2014) 1 *Intereconomics* 7: 'A related risk often referred to by political scientists is that voters may perceive these as "second-order elections" in which national governments are not directly at stake and that this will either lead to indifference and abstention or else provide an ideal opportunity to register a protest vote against incumbent governments and establishment parties'.

[114] In addition to securing *liberty from dependence* within each national polity through EU free movement law, see Chapter 2.

[115] D Halberstam, 'Systems Pluralism and Institutional Pluralism in Constitutional Law: National, Supranational and Global Governance' in M Avbelj and J Komarek (eds), *Constitutional Pluralism in the European Union and Beyond* (Oxford, Hart Publishing, 2012) 100: 'European governance can be seen as an extension of the Member State's own constitutional project of limited collective self-governance'.

in three different yet interconnected concepts. First, and for the first time with Lisbon, the primordial importance of Peace is recognised not merely in the Preamble and the articles on external action but in the main text of the Treaty: 'The Union's aim is to promote peace'.[116] Peace is decisive for Loyalty because it is the value most shared by Union citizens.[117] Second, the Treaties make explicit that Peace begins with the national polities: 'The Union's aim is to promote peace … of its peoples',[118] and 'the peoples of Europe' are thus united in 'an ever closer union'.[119] The multiple references to Europe's 'peopleS' imply that the European idea of Peace requires preservation of a plurality of distinct European peoples, not the creation of a single 'European people' through operation of Union law. Third, and again for the first time with Lisbon, Pluralism is introduced in Treaty text alongside democracy, equality, non-discrimination and the rule of law.[120] Pluralism is followed by Europe's commitment to the 'equality of Member States before the Treaties' and to the respect for Member States' national identities, constitutional and political.[121] Equality of Union citizens is ensured in their role as members of their national polities and in their relations with the EU.[122] Therefore, Pluralism refers to the plurality of national polities, national constitutions and national political processes that the national constitutions establish. Together, Peace, Peoples and Pluralism protect the peoples of Europe not simply as cultural groups but in their political function, each with its political process to identify its own *positive liberty* without interference by and dependence on others. The idea is that each European polity can identify and pursue its own idea of *positive liberty* aided by the operation of Union law. This is the deeper role of Union law in securing Peace: inability to pursue one's own *positive liberty* may result in aggression and war.[123]

The two models of legitimation in Europe—the liberal and the republican—correspond to the two models for Peace. Although achieved differently under the

[116] Article 3(1) TEU.

[117] Eurobarometer 2003, *Citizenship and the Sense of Belonging*, 8; according to the same survey, democracy was the value that best represented Member States.

[118] Article 3(1) TEU; this does not exclude the aim of the Union to promote Peace in the world, Article 3(5) TEU.

[119] Preamble TEU.

[120] Article 2 EU.

[121] Article 4 EU.

[122] Union citizens shall 'receive equal attention' from EU institutions pursuant to Article 9 TEU and an 'opportunity to make known and publicly exchange their views in all areas of Union action' pursuant to Article 11(1) TEU; Article 20(2) TFEU and others bestow on Union citizens rights and duties; national polities retain the liberty to define their membership: Article 20(1) TFEU preserves national citizenship while Article 25 TFEU preserves the role of the national political process in determining the rights of Union citizens: 'the Council, acting unanimously in accordance with a special legislative procedure and after obtaining the consent of the European Parliament, may adopt provisions to strengthen or to add to the rights listed in Article 20(2) [TFEU]. These provisions shall enter into force after their approval by the Member States in accordance with their respective constitutional requirements'.

[123] J Dollard, NE Miller, LW Doob, OH Mowrer and RR Sears, *Frustration and Aggression* (Newhaven, CT, Yale University Press, 1939).

liberal and republican models, Peace as non-domination of polities in the Union is the foundation for both. National polities and national political processes remain intact and are enhanced under both models.

Under the liberal model, Peace is a messianic promise that can be attained by ensuring *non-interference* between polities in the EU. This is achieved through reciprocal deregulation buttressed by a mechanism of enforcement based on directly effective rights that enjoy primacy and binding uniform interpretation, and on the concomitance of interest between the European polities and individuals with *locus standi*. By empowering lower levels within the state (individuals and national courts), Union law constrains the power of the national political processes to regulate (and, therefore, interfere with) interests from other polities. This eradicates power politics—and exhausts Peace as messianic legitimacy. Once the desired degree of *non-interference* between the polities is achieved, messianic legitimacy of Peace is depleted. But the liberal model equally finds its limit where reciprocity of deregulation ends short of securing Peace as *non-interference*.

There are two examples. First, external agreements involve polities that are not bound by the mechanism of reciprocity secured in Union law; the impossibility of enforcing *non-interference* vis-a-vis a third polity translates into a trade-off between, on the one hand, *non-interference* between polities in the Union and, on the other hand, the ability of each European polity to pursue its own *positive liberty* vis-a-vis an outside polity. This is the dilemma examined in Chapter 2. Second, the individual with *locus standi* may also be outside the system of binding reciprocity secured by law. Illegal immigration and criminal law are in this sense similar, drawing a sharp contrast with legal immigration and asylum. In the former two cases the individual concerned is situated outside the law, so the interests of the individual may but will not necessarily coincide with the interest of the polity. These individuals Exit from or are otherwise outside the system of reciprocity established through law (constitutional function) so that their interests cannot act as a proxy for the shared idea of *positive liberty* embodied in law (policy function). On the contrary, the interests of the individual who is within the law, whether a criminal suspect or a legally resident third-country national, will by definition coincide with the interests of the polity that adopted the law, posing a question of whether it is at all justified, from the constitutional and systemic perspective (as opposed to the policy-making perspective) to shift these policy areas from the liberal to the republican model in the EU.

Between the national polities in the Union, this means that the agreement between them cannot always rely on 'grassroots' enforcement by the individual thanks to directly effective rights. In both examples, the impossibility of abolishing state powers for enforcing reciprocity of obligations between national polities requires another model for Peace.

Under the republican model, Peace becomes an ongoing process of negotiating *positive liberty*, no longer an end result. This offers a source of legitimacy for the Union that can only end with its dissolution. Instead of solving their differences through conflict, the national polities solve them through politics regulated in Union law. In policies where *non-interference* as reciprocal deregulation is impossible, national polities can retain their *positive liberty* only jointly in the EU. In such situations, non-domination must be secured not by preventing conflict between national polities but by solving it in Union law. Power politics is eliminated not by disempowering the national political processes 'albeit within limited fields'[124] but by rules on their interaction. In the course of this interaction—in the European political process—national ideas about *positive liberty* are bound to conflict, not every polity can be appeased. Peace under the republican model gives a deeper constitutional function to Union law.[125]

5. PLURALISM UNDER UNION LAW

Both liberal and republican models of legitimation centre on the idea of *positive liberty* elaborated in the national political process. Under the liberal model, EU law enables elaboration of *positive liberty* in each national political process by eliminating interference, both actual and potential, between European polities. The capacity of Union law to secure *non-interference* between the national polities determines legitimacy; neither the substance of each polity's *positive liberty* nor the legitimacy of each national political process directly affect legitimacy of the Union.[126] The lack of interaction between the national political processes makes the liberal model of legitimation agnostic to the idea of *positive liberty* developed within each national polity. This explains not only why internal situations fall outside the scope of Union law under the liberal model of legitimation, but also which situations are considered internal. Democracy, rule of law, respect for human rights and protection of minorities are an integral part of the Copenhagen criteria that must be fulfilled by each candidate Member State before joining the EU.[127] They set a standard for the national constitutional systems that regulate the national political process and thus validate it on the international scene. While the fulfilment of these criteria is a precondition for joining the EU—an act whose legitimacy must be accepted by each national polity but also by the actors external to the Union—the continuity of their fulfilment after accession is monitored less strictly.[128] Nor is this necessary under a purely liberal model. Once

[124] Case 32/84 *Van Gend en Loos* §3.

[125] For a similar idea although not linked to Peace, see N Walker, *After finalité? The Future of the European Constitutional Idea*, EUI Working Paper LAW No. 2007/16.

[126] For the time being and for the sake of clarity, the argument raised in Chapter 2—that reliance of Union law on the national polities and institutions requires internal legitimacy of each national polity—is set aside. We will return to them in Chapter 5 and the Conclusion.

[127] European Council in Copenhagen 21–22 June 1993 Conclusions of the Presidency SN 180/1/93 REV 1, p 13.

[128] The Nice Treaty introduced what is now Article 7 TEU, which provides for suspension of Member States' right in the event of 'a clear risk of a serious breach by a Member State' of the 'values of respect for human dignity, freedom, democracy, equality, the rule of law and respect for human rights, including the rights of persons belonging to minorities'.

a polity joins the Union (the legitimacy of the joining step being important), the good functioning of the national political process is an internal matter of each national polity and does not affect legitimacy of Union law. Thanks to the *non-interference* secured in Union law, each national political process is insulated from the others—and so are the norms of national constitutional law. Constitutional pluralism describes this fact:

> No state's constitution is as such validated by that of any other, nor is it validated by Community law. For each state, the internal validity of Community law in the sense mandated by the 'supremacy' doctrine results from the state's amendment of constitutional and sub-constitutional law to the extent required to give direct effect and applicability to Community law. On the other hand, the Community's legal order is neither conditional upon the validity of any particular state's constitution, nor upon the sum of the conditions that the states might impose, for that would be no Community at all. It would amount to no more than a bundle of overlapping laws to the extent that each state chose to acknowledge 'Community' laws and obligations. So relations between states inter se and between states and Community are interactive rather than hierarchical. The legal systems of member-states and their common legal system of EC law are distinct but interacting systems of law, and hierarchical relationships of validity within criteria of validity proper to distinct systems do not add up to any sort of all-purpose superiority of one system over another. It follows also that the interpretative power of the highest decision-making authorities of the different systems must be, as to each system, ultimate. It is for the CJEU to interpret in the last resort and in a finally authoritative way the norms of Community law. But equally, it must be for the highest constitutional tribunal of each member-state to interpret its constitutional and other norms, and hence to interpret the interaction of the validity of EC law with higher level norms of validity in the given state system.[129]

With *non-interference* between the national polities secured in Union law, even the most radical normative equality of competing claims to final authority between the national constitutions and EU law 'is not logically embarrassing, because strictly the answers are from the point of view of different systems'.[130] Under the liberal model of legitimation, the national and EU constitutional systems remain separate because policy choices are made in each national political process. Thus, constitutional pluralism is only possible when EU law is adopted under the unanimity or consensus of all national polities.

With the introduction of QMV and absent the mechanism to ensure *non-interference* between the polities, normative dependence between the constitutional orders arises. Republican legitimation becomes necessary, the situation is reversed. Under the republican model, national Loyalty and legitimacy of the ideas about *positive liberty* elaborated in the national political process feed into the European political process. This gives new prominence to one's own *positive liberty*: elaboration of one's own *positive liberty* within each national

[129] N MacCormick, *Questioning Sovereignty: Law, State, and Nation in the European Commonwealth* (Oxford, Oxford University Press, 1999) 117–18.

[130] ibid 119.

polity is no longer an internal matter. Legitimacy of the Union requires that each national polity develop and further its own idea of *positive liberty*, and that this process and the ensuing idea are perceived as legitimate by its polity members. The extent to which national constitutional law generates and preserves legitimacy of the national political process thus directly affects legitimacy of the Union and its policies. The substance of the national idea of *positive liberty* becomes fundamental for Europe's legitimacy because in order to compensate for the loss in one aspect of one's own *positive liberty* that ensues from majoritarian policy choice in Europe, another aspect of one's own *positive liberty* must be present: the value placed on continuity of the Union. This value needs to be internalised by each national polity as an integral part of its own *positive liberty*. Loyalty to the national polity and the sense of ownership of the national idea of *positive liberty* will then prevent Exit from the Union. But to maintain national Loyalty and the sense of ownership, *liberty from dependence* (Voice) for individual polity members must be ensured in the national political process. This is so because

> nations are not real entities at all, but elements ultimately of individual consciousness. For any country or nation, each of us has her or his own conception of it, and our sense of identification is not with some objective 'out-there' entity, but rather with our own idea of the nation ... there must be as many Englands as there are English people, and these are not all the same thing. Rather, there is at best a partially overlapping consensus of England-ideas from the point of view of those who self-identify as English, and then also, perhaps, from the point of view of self-defined outsiders. England as a nation is not something that justifies the overlapping consensus, but an idea that emerges from it, to the extent that any consensus does in fact emerge.[131]

The idea of *positive liberty* elaborated in the national political process reflects one's own identity and shapes the sense of ownership, belonging and Loyalty to the polity. Constitutional law is pivotal for developing and maintaining this idea. As a set of norms, constitutional law is designed 'to bring about certainty of expectation, especially in anticipation of [the] unavoidable disappointment'[132] that results to minority from majority rule. By regulating interest representation in the political process, constitutional law creates an expectation that this 'disappointment', the loss in Voice, will not be permanent, that there are no permanent losers—it blocks the cognitive function of learning from disappointment. This is achieved through the republican and liberal functions present in national constitutional law. On the one hand, equal participation secures Voice for all polity members; on the other hand, equal respect is secured for those polity members whose interests are connected to immutable characteristics such as race, birth, age or disability—this is achieved through constitutional rights that withdraw these interests from the regulatory reach of the political process. Together, equal participation and

131 ibid 172, citing AP Cohen, 'Personal Nationalism: a Scottish View of some Rites, Rights, and Wrongs' (1996) 23 *American Ethnologist* and 'Peripheral Vision: Nationalism, National Identity and the Objective Correlative in Scotland' in AP Cohen (ed), *Discriminating Relations: Anthropological Essays on Boundary, Identity and Authenticity* (London, Routledge, 1999) 186–218.

132 N Luhmann, *Law as a Social System* (Oxford, Oxford University Press, 2004) 164.

equal respect—the participatory and the deliberative elements of democracy—the counter-minoritarian and counter-majoritarian functions of constitutional law—secure *liberty from dependence* and legitimacy of majoritarian policy choice. Even when majority rule results in disappointment for the outvoted minority, this disappointment is restricted to only one aspect of *positive liberty* (the policy choice on which the minority was outvoted); the expectation of equal Voice and respect preclude learning from disappointment; Exit from the national political process does not take place. Disappointment with a specific policy choice falls short of systemic frustration and does not breed aggression or Exit from the reciprocal obligations of Peace in law.

Without *non-interference* secured in Union law, national constitutional orders are no longer separate but form part of a single system of norms created by constitutional communication produced in each constitutional order. Policy choices made within one constitutional order affect the choices made in another constitutional order and both feed into the European political process. Failure of the national constitutional order to ensure interest representation or Voice of polity members in one national political process (*liberty from domination*) undermines legitimacy of *positive liberty* elaborated in its course, curtails legitimacy of Union policies, and undermines legitimacy of other political processes across the Union. The same is true for certainty of expectation created by constitutional law: communication created in one national constitutional order affects the certainty of expectation in another. The meaning of communication depends on the context, experience and identity of its receiver.[133] Where the political experience across Member States differs, the same constitutional communication may result in different (certainty of) expectation across national polities. This may destabilise the Union, reduce national Loyalty and prompt Exit.

In order to convey a meaning by means of language, participants in the communication process need to share grammar rules and experiences of reality.[134] To convey a certainty of expectation and protect against disappointment by means of law, members of polities that integrate through law need to share rules on interest representation and protection (constitutional law that regulates the political process) so that their experience of the political process is shared.[135] The mechanism of interest representation in the national political process—the rules of national

[133] L Wittgenstein, *Philosophical Investigations* (Oxford, Basil Blackwell Ltd, 1958).

[134] D Patterson, 'Methodology and Theoretical Disagreement' in U Neergaard, R Nielsen and L Roseberry (eds), *European Legal Method Paradoxes and Revitalization* (Copenhagen, DJOF Publishing, 2011) 232.

[135] D Halberstam, 'Constitutional Heterarchy: The Centrality of Conflict in the European Union and the United States' in J Dunoff and J Trachtman (eds), *Ruling the World? Constitutionalism, International Law, and Global Governance* (Cambridge, Cambridge University Press, 2009) 326–55; M Poiares Maduro, 'Contrapunctual Law: Europe's Constitutional Pluralism in Action' in N Walker (ed), *Sovereignty in Transition* (Oxford, Hart Publishing, 2003) 501–37; J Komárek, 'The Institutional Dimension of Constitutional Pluralism' in M Avbelj and J Komárek (eds), *Constitutional Pluralism in the European Union and Beyond* (Oxford, Hart Publishing, 2012) 231–47.

constitutional law—are no longer an internal matter of each European polity.[136] For Union policies under the republican model of legitimation, integration through law, to be legitimate (ie without Exit of polity members from the national political process and of polities from the Union), requires stabilising certainty of expectation through the establishment of 'a political culture that can be shared by all European citizens'.[137] National political cultures—if not national constitutional identities—need to converge in order to secure legitimacy of European policy choice. Policy and constitutional interdependence between the national polities in the EU raised the 'imperative that each Member State take account of [other Member States'] interests when designing and implementing its immigration, integration and asylum policies',[138] basing its own policy choice 'on the principles of transparency and democratic control' and the 'common standards on the integrity of authorities'.[139]

Ensuring uniformity in political experience across the national polities is the constitutional function of Union law under the republican model of legitimation and Peace. The more Union policies are decided by European majority and the less Union law secures *non-interference*, the more the rules of the national political process fall within the scope of Union law. The more absent Loyalty at Union level, the more important citizens' Voice is in the national political process for the legitimacy of the EU. Community legal order (but not its policies, which followed functional objectives ratified unanimously by all European polities in the Treaties) derived legitimacy from the capacity to assure each polity *liberty from interference.* To the extent that securing *non-interference* in Union law is impossible (in particular, for regulating the actors and phenomena situated outside EU and national law), the EU (both its legal order and policies) relies for legitimacy on the national political processes that compose and interact in the European political space. For Union policies legitimated under the republican model, the constitutional function of Union law is to secure *liberty from dependence* both between and within the national political processes. Legitimacy of the composite European political process requires pluralism under Union law:[140]

> [F]ree will can be a reality where one's own choices are respected as choices of another under conditions of reciprocity … Substantive justifications are necessarily secondary.

[136] M Poiares Maduro, 'Rendre plus visible le sentiment d'appartenance à un espace européen' in J Jappert and S Landa (eds), *Favoriser l'émergence d'une identité européenne grâce au sport: réalité ou utopie?* (Think tank Sport et Citoyenneté, 2013) 41: 'De plus en plus, notre espace politique et social européen n'est plus un espace purement national'.

[137] Habermas (n 78) 16: 'the empirical circumstances necessary for an extension of that process of identity formation beyond national boundaries … are: the emergence of a European civil society; the construction of a European-wide public sphere; and the shaping of a political culture that can be shared by all European citizens'. See also: J Habermas, *Democracy, Solidarity and the European Crisis*, Lecture delivered on 26 April 2013 in Leuven: 'a shared political perspective'.

[138] *European Pact on Immigration and Asylum* (24.09.2008) Council doc 13440/08, 3.

[139] Presidency Conclusions, Tampere European Council 15 and 16 October 1999, SI (1999) 800, point 7.

[140] By analogy with 'pluralism under international law', see MacCormick (n 129) 118: 'According to pluralism under international law, the obligations of international law set conditions upon the valid-

> What matters, instead, is a normative structure that governs the conditions under which people have to yield to determinations made by others. Without such a structure, which requires respect for choices within the constraints established by some ordre public, there would be no law.[141]

The difference in the enforcement mechanism between the liberal and republican models translates into a difference in the scope of Union constitutional law. Both models secure non-domination by abolishing power politics between Member States. Under the liberal model, EU law derived legitimacy from securing *non-interference* between the polities, which was enforced by the individual in a cross-polity situation thanks to directly effective rights; under the republican model, legitimacy of Union law depends on securing equal Voice and concern in the political process, both national and European. Under the liberal model, the abolition of power politics between Member States was possible thanks to the setting of policy choice in the Treaties; under the republican model, the substance of policy choice is not only irrelevant for enforcing non-domination between the polities but fixing it in the Treaties reduces liberty, both individual and collective, of polities in the Union. Under the republican model, the idea of *positive liberty* results from the political process, is not a restraint on it; the making of policy choices is thus shifted from primary to secondary Union law; interest representation in the political process advances legitimacy while mobility of Union citizens between the polities withdraws their situation from the scope of Union law inasmuch as Member State nationals cannot participate in the national political process of other Member States. From regulating the status and rights of the individual under the liberal model, EU constitutional law under the republican model must refocus on regulating the political process both in Member States and in the EU.

ity of state and of Community constitutions and interpretations thereof, and hence impose a framework on the interactive but not hierarchical relations between systems'. Similarly, for Tomuschat, 'the core principles of international law assume a foundational, rather than a merely supplementary, function for the state and its constitution', see A Von Bogdandy, 'Constitutionalism in International Law: Comment on a Proposal from Germany' (2006) 47(1) *Harvard International Law Journal* 228, citing C Tomuschat, 'Der Verfassungsstaat im Geflecht der internationalen Beziehungen' (1978) 36 *Veröffentlichungen der Vereinigung der deutschen Staatsrechtslehrer* 7, 51–53.

[141] A Somek, 'Monism—A Tale of the Undead' in Avbelj and Komárek (eds) (n 135) 372.

4

Conflict in Union Law

So that we ought not to attain this greatest unity even if we could, for it would be the destruction of the state.
Aristotle, *The Politics*, Book II Chapter 2

1. CONFLICT AS THE OBJECT OF UNION LAW

DEPARTURE FROM FUNCTIONAL Treaty objectives created a European political space and introduced conflict as the object of Union law. Two models of legitimising Union law and power emerged from the analysis in Chapter 3. Both models rely on Peace as non-domination for legitimacy of Union law. Under the liberal model, EU law secures non-domination as *non-interference* between European polities into each other's capacity to identify its own idea of *positive liberty*; the idea of *positive liberty* to be pursued in the Union is identified by each European polity and ratified unanimously by them all in the Treaties. Under the republican model, EU law secures non-domination by creating and enhancing capacity to elaborate an idea of shared *positive liberty* that goes beyond a unanimous agreement between European polities. Legitimacy results not from securing *non-interference* with the idea of *positive liberty* of each national polity but from the capacity to develop new ideas of *positive liberty* shared and pursued by all the polities of the EU. The process of negotiating and identifying shared objectives—the European political process composed of national political processes as discussed in Chapter 3—lends legitimacy of the national political process to European policy choice. Under the liberal model, policy choices are both made and legitimated in the national political process; under the republican model, policy choices are *legitimated* in the national political process but they are *made* in the *European* political space. The main difference between the liberal and republican models lies in the making of policy choices. Under the liberal model, they are made in the national polities; under the republican model, in the EU.

The two modes of legitimation correspond to two types of conflict: the conflicts to avoid and the conflicts to solve, both by recourse to Union law.[1] The conflicts to avoid are characterised by static interest cleavages between the polities in the EU,

[1] For a view that advocates a reconceptualisation of EU public law to embrace social conflicts see M Dani, 'Rehabilitating Social Conflicts in European Public Law' (2012) 18(5) *European Law Journal.*

which can be prevented through static policy choice. Here belong situations with diametrically opposed interests across the polities, such as market protectionism[2] or the management of external borders.[3] The immutable nature of these interest cleavages creates a permanent risk of domination between the peoples of Europe, which can be balanced in Union law through immutable rules of *non-interference* set in primary law (Union Treaties and mixed external agreements) with the help of functional objectives and directly effective rights, both legitimised in each national polity. Reciprocity of *non-interference* is secured through the role of the CJEU and the mechanism of enforcement based on the concomitance of interest between the individual with *locus standi* and the European idea of *positive liberty*. This enables abolition of power politics between Member States (deregulation of free movement in the internal market) because it is no longer necessary to secure non-domination between the polities. In case of conflict, *non-interference* between European polities prevails not only over each polity's *positive liberty* vis-a-vis other Union polities, but also over their ability to assert *positive liberty* externally, vis-a-vis non-Union polities. When Union law follows the liberal model, the republican model of legitimation is precluded to the extent that functional objectives and directly effective rights are contained in primary law: policy choice is withdrawn from politics.

The conflicts to solve do not involve static interest cleavages but conflicting ideas about 'ideal life'; they cannot be solved with any one policy choice for it would only perpetuate the conflict. On the contrary, they are ongoing conflicts to renegotiate continuously under Union law. Here belong situations where the interest of each polity is bound to change with the circumstances and time, for instance the policy on legal immigration or product safety standards. The foundation for the idea of *positive liberty* in each polity will be the same: labour immigration policy to match its labour market needs, and product quality standards that ensure health and safety of consumers. In other words, no society wants to have unsafe products on its shelves or immigration policy that results in mass unemployment and social unrest—yet, beyond these meta principles, reasonable people may disagree on the exact policy preferences in each set of circumstances and moment in time. In addressing such conflicts, Union Treaties refocus away from static policy choice (functional objectives and directly enforceable rights) that aims to eliminate static interest cleavages to managing dynamic conflicts of ideas through EU rules for making policy choices. Under the republican model, legitimacy of the Union and its law is no longer linked to specific policy choices but to the process of making policy choices. The republican model is unavoidable insofar as the mechanism to enforce reciprocity without reliance on the power of

[2] For instance, the first situation discussed in Chapter 2, Section 1, as well as state aids and (potential) protectionism of home producers/products such as in Case 120/78 *Cassis de Dijon*.

[3] For instance, the situation with the Dublin system and return of illegal immigrants discussed in Chapter 3, Section 1.

the state is unavailable because the interest of the individual regulated in law—the individual with *locus standi*—does not coincide with the European idea of *positive liberty*. This is the structural feature of all activities banned by law, such as unauthorised immigration or crime:[4] the individual who has *locus standi* does not have an interest in enforcing the law, hence state powers must be preserved. Reciprocity of obligations between European polities cannot rely on grassroots enforcement, powers of the state cannot be abolished, *non-interference* without state powers is unenforceable. Legitimating policy choices in such policy areas under the liberal model based on *non-interference* would reintroduce power politics into the relations between Member States; Union law would not make Peace any more real than any rule of international law.

For policies where the legal bases allow either liberal or republican legitimation (in terms of openness of policy choice and the mechanism to enforce reciprocal *non-interference*), identifying and distinguishing between the two types of conflict becomes central for furthering liberty of the peoples of Europe, legitimacy of EU law and Loyalty in the Union. Permanent interest cleavages between the European polities can be resolved through *non-interference* secured in primary law (EU Treaties and international agreements). The interests endangered by conflict are permanently withdrawn from the political process by protecting them in Union law. This is the liberal model. Cross-polity conflicts between ideas of *positive liberty* cannot be resolved permanently in the Treaties: unlike immutable interests, ideas are subject to change. This type of conflict requires continuous negotiating and re-elaborating, under the rules of Union law, of a new idea of *positive liberty* that can be internalised by all.[5] The European idea of *positive liberty* emerges from this process in the form of secondary Union law (regulations, directives, framework decisions). This is the republican model.

This chapter traces the reorientation of Union legislative process and the relevant principles of Union law from conflicts of interests to conflicts of ideas. Elements of the republican model emerge in the conception and division of powers. The principles of subsidiarity and proportionality are central to this: their role and application changes together with the nature of conflict. While implicitly recognised by the institutional practice and in case law of the Court, the new role of Union law in regulating republican conflicts requires a shift from policy choice as an instrument of constitutional conflict solving towards rules and principles of Union law for continuous (re)negotiation of policy choice.

[4] There is also the issue of illegal versus unwanted immigration: asylum seekers and refugees are perfectly legal but they are unwanted inasmuch as their reception is not part of a polity's idea of positive liberty identified in its national political process (and quite independently from obligations in international law). Republican legitimation would be needed for all 'unwanted' immigration in the EU.

[5] R Bellamy, *Political Constitutionalism. A Republican Defence of the Constitutionality of Democracy* (Cambridge, Cambridge University Press, 2007) 205: 'citizens are more likely to submit to an authority in which they regard themselves as having a part—however small that may be'.

2. LEGITIMACY OF POLICY CHOICES

Under both liberal and republican models, the existence of cross-polity conflict is a necessary precondition for legitimating Union law. Conflict implies the existence of interdependence between the European polities in terms of their internal (as perceived by their own polity members) and/or external (as perceived by other polities) liberty and legitimacy. Without interdependence, there can be no conflict. Not only should the interests and ideas differ across polities but they must be able to interfere with one another. The existence of interdependence, when a polity cannot pursue its own *positive liberty* without reliance on other polities, is the first step in legitimating the shift in the agora for the making of policy choices from the national political process to the European political space. This is the essence of the EU law principle of subsidiarity:[6]

> [I]n areas which do not fall within its exclusive competence, the Union shall act only if and in so far as the objectives of the proposed action cannot be sufficiently achieved by the Member States, either at central level or at regional and local level, but can rather, by reason of the scale or effects of the proposed action, be better achieved at Union level.[7]

By giving preference to a lower level of government, subsidiarity recognises the value of Loyalty or self-identification between people in groups. The Loyalty bond between people increases with the decrease of membership in the group. Thus, the principle seeks to advance legitimacy as *liberty from dependence* on the central authority and as diversity of ideas about *positive liberty* pursued in different groups. This is not an individualistic principle inasmuch as it implies the value of groups. Rather, it is a principle that advances legitimacy in the making and implementation of *shared* policy choice. As such, subsidiarity works both in favour of and against the power of smaller groups: it is a balancing principle, where the legitimacy of smaller groups is balanced against their conflict-solving ability. The inability of a smaller group to solve conflicts undermines liberty of the group

[6] See generally: A Estrella, *The EU Principle of Subsidiarity and Its Critique* (Oxford, Oxford University Press, 2002); T Tridimas, 'The Rule of Reason and its Relation to Proportionality and Subsidiarity' in A Schrauwen (ed), *Rule of Reason. Rethinking another Classic of European Legal Doctrine* (Groningen, Europa Law Publishing, 2005); P Craig, *EU Administrative Law* (Oxford, Oxford University Press, 2006) ch 12; M Cartabia, N Lupo and A Simoncini (eds), *Democracy and Subsidiarity in the EU* (Bologna, Il Mulino, 2013); C Kirchner, 'Competence Catalogues and the Principle of Subsidiarity in a European Constitution' (1997) 8 *Constitutional Political Economy*; M Kumm, 'Constitutionalising Subsidiarity in Integrated Markets: The Case of Tobacco Regulation in the European Union' (2006) 12(4) *European Law Journal*; N MacCormick, 'Democracy, Subsidiarity, and Citizenship in the "European Commonwealth"' (1997) 16 *Law and Philosophy*; A Mills, 'Federalism in the European Union and the United States: Subsidiarity, Private Law, and the Conflict of Laws' (2010) 32(2) *University of Pennsylvania Journal of International Law*; JE Fleming and JT Levy (eds), *Federalism and Subsidiarity* (New York, New York University Press, 2014); AG Toth, 'Is Subsidiarity Justiciable?' (1994) 19(3) *European Law Review*; NW Barber, 'The Limited Modesty of Subsidiarity' (2005) 11(3) *European Law Journal*; A Goucha Soares, 'Pre-Emption, Conflicts of Powers and Subsidiarity' (1998) 23(2) *European Law Review*; G de Burca, *Reappraising Subsidiarity's Significance after Amsterdam* (2000) Harvard Jean Monnet Working Paper 7/99.

[7] Article 5(3) TEU.

and results in domination or interference, so that if a larger group can solve this conflict, the power can legitimately shift to this extended group.

Without conflict and interdependence, reducing regulatory autonomy of each European polity through action at Union level would undermine rather than serve legitimacy. A smaller group may legitimately lose policy-making power in favour of a larger group only to the extent this advances its liberty by addressing the potential conflict. This idea is reflected in the EU law principle of proportionality:[8] 'Under the principle of proportionality, the content and form of Union action shall not exceed what is necessary to achieve the objectives of the Treaties'.[9]

In the context of functional conferred powers of the Union, subsidiarity and proportionality complement each other in advancing all the three aspects of liberty. Together, the two principles determine not merely the division of powers between the Union and Member States but legitimacy of policy choices made on the national level and in the EU. This chapter argues that in the absence of functional Treaty objectives to direct policy choice, subsidiarity and proportionality lose their role for the federal division of powers and instead acquire a new role where subsidiarity advances legitimacy by identifying the type of conflict to be resolved in Union law. This way, when two different models of legitimacy are available—the liberal model based on *negative liberty* and the republican model based on *positive liberty*—subsidiarity advances legitimacy by helping arbitrate between the two models.

Two elements of Union Treaties accommodate the emerging republican model and allow subsidiarity and proportionality to further legitimacy. The first element is the distinction between Treaty and Union objectives in the definition of principles of Union law. The second element is the new subsidiarity review procedure under Protocol No 2 Lisbon. They will be discussed in turn.

The Source of Objectives

Despite the emergence of shared Union powers not limited by functional objectives in Treaty text, many constitutional principles of Union law remain founded on objectives. Yet, these are not the same objectives but rather objectives of three different types. First, there are references to the *objectives set out in the Treaties generally*, mainly in provisions that confer powers on the Union: in Article 352 TFEU (implied powers), Article 5(2) and (4) TEU (conferral of powers and proportionality), Article 13(2) TEU (powers of Union institutions),[10] Article 23

[8] M Klatt and M Meister, *The Constitutional Structure of Proportionality* (Oxford, Oxford University Press, 2012); N. Emiliou, *The Principle of Proportionality in European Law* (London, Kluwer Law International, 1996); E Ellis (ed), *The Principle of Proportionality in the Laws of Europe* (Oxford, Hart Publishing, 1999).

[9] Article 5(4) TEU.

[10] Although Article 13(1) TEU states more generally that the Union's 'institutional framework' shall promote objectives of the Union generally and ensure inter alia 'continuity' of Union's policies and actions—in striking disregard of the realities of the republican model, where changeability of policy choice is an inherent feature of the political process.

TEU (CFSP), Article 216(1) TFEU (external powers). Second, some legal bases refer to *specific Treaty objectives*: Articles 120 and 145 TFEU refer to the objectives of Article 3 TEU, while Article 205 TFEU refers to the objectives of Chapter I Title V TEU. Third, there are references, many of them in provisions that limit Member State powers, to the *objectives of the Union*, not only those in Treaty text: Article 20(1) TEU (enhanced cooperation), Article 1 TFEU (declares that Member States confer competences on the Union in order 'to attain objectives they have in common'), Article 3(6) TFEU, last paragraph Article 4(3) TFEU (the duty of sincere cooperation for Member States, refers to 'Union's objectives'),[11] Article 5(3) TFEU (the principle of subsidiarity refers not to Treaty objectives but to 'the objectives of the proposed action'), Articles 13(1), 7, 65(4) and 311 TFEU and Article 52(1) Fundamental Rights Charter. This structure reflects the system whereby the exercise of Union powers is limited by the Treaties,[12] while the exercise of Member State powers is limited by both the Treaties and further commitments undertaken by the peoples of Europe subsequently in the EU.

Apparently insignificant until the Treaty of Lisbon, the distinction between Treaty and Union objectives acquires a new meaning in the liberal/republican context. From its inception and until the Lisbon Treaty, subsidiarity was understood as a two-tier test[13] both parts of which must be fulfilled: (1) the Member States acting individually must be unable to achieve the objective and (2) the objective must be attainable by Member States acting together in the Union. For shared powers defined by functional Treaty objectives, subsidiarity pertains to the exercise of powers by the Union once policy choices are made. The question is whether 'the Union shall act'.[14] It might thus appear that under the republican model subsidiarity does not address the relevant question: who should *make* policy choices? This is where the distinction between Union and Treaty objectives plays an important role. Subsidiarity institutes a nexus between the inability of Member States, acting individually, to achieve a *Union objective*,[15] the ability of the Union to achieve this objective, and the exercise of power by the EU. Once compliance with subsidiarity

[11] Case C-61/11 PPU *El Dridi* §56: the CJEU confirmed that Article 4(3) TEU binds Member States also as regards objectives of EU directives under the AFSJ.

[12] Including the tasks of Union institutions, see Case C-370/12 *Pringle*.

[13] A Von Bogdandy and J Bast, 'The Federal Order of Competences' in A von Bogdandy and J Bast (eds), *Principles of European Constitutional Law* (London, Hart/CH Beck/Nomos, 2010) 303. It has been pointed out that the first part of the test (Member States cannot achieve an objective) and the word 'better' in the second part of the test (can 'be better achieved at Union level') imply that the two parts of the test are mutually exclusive, see R Schütze, 'Subsidiarity after Lisbon: Reinforcing the Safeguards of Federalism?' (2009) 68(3) *Cambridge Law Journal*.

[14] Article 5(3) TEU.

[15] Article 5(3) TEU; or the objective of the proposed legislative act, see point 5, Protocol No 30 on the application of the principles of subsidiarity and proportionality annexed to the Treaty of Amsterdam (10.11.1997) OJ C340, 105. After the Lisbon Treaty, it is no longer possible to say that 'Functional delimitation of the powers attributed to the Union is therefore essential from a subsidiarity point of view.' See M Desomer and K Lenaerts, 'Bricks for a Constitutional Treaty of the European Union: Values, Objectives and Means' (2002) 27(4) *European Law Review* 387.

is established, Article 5(4) TFEU provides that Union action should be limited to what is necessary to achieve *Treaty objectives*.[16]

The grounding of subsidiarity in objectives *of the Union* and not only Treaty objectives indicates that the focus is not merely on the division of powers but on the problem or *conflict* to be resolved. Powers are exercised to address specific conflicts and it is these that subsidiarity brings to light. The focus on conflicts enables subsidiarity to go further than solely answering the question of who should act. Subsidiarity review acquires multiple functions: to identify if there is a conflict, if there is interdependence, and perhaps even what type of conflict it is. Structural conflicts of interests are avoided through *non-interference*; fluid conflicts of ideas are managed through a process of developing a shared idea of *positive liberty*. For policies that could fall under either the liberal or the republican model, subsidiarity review could supplement identification of the legal base (liberal or republican) that is the most conducive to liberty, legitimacy and Loyalty. By contrast, the focus of proportionality on *Treaty objectives* indicates that for Union policies not defined by functional Treaty objectives proportionality should be examined by reference to Peace—the main Treaty objective left.[17] This expands the potential role of proportionality from limiting power to structuring the political process, for instance through advancing the accountability of power. Instead of answering the question of whether EU interference with a polity's regulatory powers is proportionate (a question that only makes sense under the liberal model), proportionality could assist in identifying the level of regulation (national or Union) that offers the most appropriate representation and protection of all the relevant interests. Even when the result of subsidiarity review weighs towards republican legitimation, shortcomings in the safeguards for interest representation at Union level, as compared to the national political process, could militate against Union-level policy choice.[18] This would in particular be the case where shifting policy choices from the national political process to the Union circumvents accountability of those who make policy choices.[19]

[16] Article 5(4) TFEU: 'Under the principle of proportionality, the content and form of Union action shall not exceed what is necessary to achieve the objectives of the Treaties'. Article 3(6) TEU: 'The Union shall pursue its objectives by appropriate means commensurate with the competences which are conferred upon it in the Treaties'. Prior to the Lisbon Treaty, Article 5 EC referred to 'the objectives of this Treaty', while 'the objectives of the measure' were the focus of point 7, Protocol No 30 on the application of the principles of subsidiarity and proportionality annexed to the Treaty of Amsterdam (10.11.1997) OJ C340, 105.

[17] See Chapter 3, Section 4, 'Peace, Peoples and Pluralism in Europe's Constitutional Construct'.

[18] M Poiares Maduro, 'In Search of A Meaning and Not in Search of The Meaning: Judicial Review and the Constitution in Times of Pluralism' [2013] *Wisconsin Law Rev* 560: 'This requires courts to develop criteria for institutional comparison and judicial deference on the basis of the constitution and, particularly, its ideal of a rational, free, intersubjective, and inclusive deliberation'.

[19] On how European integration undermines sovereignty by silencing national democracy and empowering the executive (who can Exit accountability in the national political process by shifting policy choices to the EU), see DM Curtin, *Postnational Democracy* (The Hague, Kluwer Law International, 1997) 41–48; P Mair, *Popular Democracy and the European Union Polity* (2005) European Governance Papers (EUROGOV) No C-05-03.

Subsidiarity Review Procedure

The second element that attunes the structure of EU legitimacy to the emerging republican model is the subsidiarity review procedure, revolutionised under Protocol 2 Lisbon.[20] Although Article 5(3) TEU, similarly to its predecessor Article 5 EC, institutes a presumption in favour of lower-level action,[21] the substance of the new procedure reversed this presumption:

> Any national Parliament or any chamber of a national Parliament may, within eight weeks from the date of transmission of a draft legislative act ... send to the Presidents of the European Parliament, the Council and the Commission a reasoned opinion stating why it considers that the draft in question does not comply with the principle of subsidiarity.[22]

The presumption in favour of Union acts must now be rebutted. Although the Protocol requires the Commission to 'consult widely', issue a 'detailed statement' on subsidiarity and engage with other institutions in subsidiarity review,[23] in practice challenging the arguments of the Commission in favour of Union action is no easy task. Only when a majority of national parliaments take the position that the proposal does not comply with the principle of subsidiarity must the proposal be reviewed.[24] However, the Commission does not have to amend or withdraw the draft proposal but merely restate the argument (not necessarily a different argument) as to why it complies with subsidiarity anew. An action for infringement of subsidiarity may then be brought in the CJEU by 'Member States, or notified by them ... on behalf of their national Parliament[s]'.[25] However, to date, the Court has never annulled EU secondary law for a failure to comply with

[20] On the new procedure and the principles of subsidiarity post-Lisbon see: A Vergés Bausili, *Rethinking the Methods of Dividing and Exercising Powers in the EU: Reforming Subsidiarity and National Parliaments* (2002) NYU School of Law, Jean Monnet Working Paper 9/02; D Edward, 'Subsidiarity as a Legal Concept' in P Cardonnel, A Rosas and N Wahl, *Constitutionalizing the EU Judicial System* (Oxford, Hart Publishing, 2012); A Cygan, '"Collective" Subsidiarity Monitoring by National Parliaments after Lisbon: The Operation of the Early Warning Mechanism' and T van den Brink, 'The Substance of Subsidiarity: The Interpretation and Meaning of the Principle after Lisbon' in M Trybus and L Rubini (eds), *The Treaty of Lisbon and the Future of European Law and Policy* (Cheltenham, Edward Elgar, 2012); VM Muniz-Fraticelli, *The Structure of Pluralism* (Oxford, Oxford University Press, 2014) ch 3; A Biondi, 'Subsidiarity in the Courtroom' in A Biondi, P Eeckhout and S Ripley (eds), *EU Law After Lisbon* (Oxford, Oxford University Press, 2012); T Raunio, *Destined for Irrelevance? Subsidiarity Control by National Parliaments* (19/11/2010) Elcano Royal Institute Madrid—Spain Working Paper 36/2010; P Kiiver, *The Early Warning System for the Principle of Subsidiarity: Constitutional Theory and Empirical Reality* (London, Routledge, 2012); A von Staden, 'The Democratic Legitimacy of Judicial Review Beyond the State: Normative Subsidiarity and Judicial Standards of Review' (2012) 10(4) *International Journal of Constitutional Law*.

[21] See also second paragraph of Article 1 TEU.

[22] Article 6 Protocol 2 Lisbon.

[23] Articles 2 and 5–8 Protocol No 2 Lisbon.

[24] Article 7(3) Protocol 2 Lisbon.

[25] Article 8 Protocol No 2 Lisbon. The Lisbon Treaty removed the limit on the jurisdiction of the CJEU as regards EU immigration policy contained in ex-Article 68 EC.

subsidiarity.[26] Furthermore, an opportunity to challenge compliance with subsidiarity exists only for new legislation and not the Recast versions thereof.[27] Although Protocol 2 Lisbon makes no distinction between proposals for new and Recast legislation,[28] the practice has been not to subject the latter to subsidiarity review by national parliaments. Once the Union exercises its shared powers, subsequent amendments of secondary acts are not subject to subsidiarity review.

Finally, despite the name of the Protocol, 'on subsidiarity and proportionality', proportionality is excluded from the review procedure by national parliaments. Proportionality is grounded in Treaty objectives. Without functional objectives in the legal base, the main Treaty objective left for proportionality review is teleological understanding of Peace as non-domination of polities in the Union. This, however, is not an analysis that pertains to the federal division of powers addressed by the Protocol and the review procedure. When reviewed against functional Treaty objectives, proportionality furthers legitimacy in terms of the federal division of powers—a role fulfilled by both legislature and courts; reviewed against the main Treaty objective of Peace, proportionality furthers legitimacy through constitutional review that ensures interest representation in the political process—a role that is better fulfilled by courts. Exclusion of proportionality from the review procedure under the Protocol—a procedure tailored for the legislative stage—is consistent with the republican model and the absence of functional objectives in Treaty text. When legitimacy is based on *positive liberty* as opposed to *non-interference*, limiting the powers to identify and further *positive liberty* no longer makes sense.[29]

3. DECIDING WHO DECIDES (IN) UNION LAW

Conflicts of ideas and conflicts of interests clearly emerge from the subsidiarity and proportionality justifications found in the recitals of secondary Union law. Below is a list of objectives that are supposed to legitimate EU secondary acts in immigration and asylum law under the AFSJ. Conflicts of ideas (that command

[26] Some authors note that the Court 'effectively equates the test of subsidiarity with the test of competence thus removing all independent legal value from the former', see Tridimas (n 6).

[27] Such as when a directive was adopted, and later another directive is proposed to replace it, eg Proposal for a directive of the European Parliament and of the Council on the conditions of entry and residence of third-country nationals for the purposes of research, studies, pupil exchange, remunerated and unremunerated training, voluntary service and au pairing (recast) COM (2013)0151—C7-0080/2013—2013/0081 (COD) Although the Treaties do not preclude subsidiarity review of Recast Proposals, they are not subject to subsidiarity review by the national parliaments: this could also indicate that subsidiarity is not about policy choice but the nature of the problem/conflict to be resolved.

[28] Article 3 Protocol 2 Lisbon: 'For the purposes of this Protocol, "draft legislative acts" shall mean proposals from the Commission, initiatives from a group of Member States, initiatives from the European Parliament, requests from the Court of Justice, recommendations from the European Central Bank and requests from the European Investment Bank for the adoption of a legislative act'.

[29] See Section 4 below.

republican legitimation) are highlighted in *italics*, while conflicts of interests (that command liberal legitimation) are underlined.

Legal immigration:

- the determination of a *harmonised* legal framework at Community level concerning the *conditions of entry and residence* of third-country nationals for the purpose of paid employment and self-employed economic activities and of the procedures for the issue by Member States of the relevant permits;[30]
- the determination of terms for *granting and withdrawing* long-term resident *status* and the *rights* pertaining thereto and terms for the exercise of rights of residence by long-term residents in other Member States;[31]
- to determine the *conditions of admission* of third-country nationals for the purposes of study, pupil exchange, unremunerated training or voluntary service;[32]
- the introduction of a special *admission procedure* and the adoption of *conditions of entry and residence* applicable to third-country nationals for stays of more than three months in the Member States for the purposes of conducting a research project under a hosting agreement with a research organisation;[33]
- the introduction of a special *admission procedure* and the adoption of *conditions of entry and residence* for more than three months applicable to third-country nationals in the Member States for the purposes of highly qualified employment, and their family members;[34]
- the laying down of a single *application procedure* for issuing a single *permit* for third-country nationals to work in the territory of a Member State and a *common set of rights* for third-country workers legally residing in a Member State;[35]
- the introduction of a special *admission procedure*, the adoption of *conditions on entry and stay* for the purpose of seasonal work by third-country nationals and the *definition of their rights* as seasonal workers;[36]
- a special *admission procedure* and the adoption of *conditions of entry and residence* for the purpose of intra-corporate transfers of third-country nationals.[37]

[30] Recital 14, Proposal for a Council Directive on the conditions of entry and residence of third-country nationals for the purpose of paid employment and self-employed economic activities, COM (2001) 386 final, withdrawn in 2003. Recital 6 mentioned the objective of reinforcing competitiveness of the Community to recruit third-country workers globally though without reference to subsidiarity and proportionality—apparently this was not perceived as the (only) objective legitimising Union action.

[31] Recital 24 Directive 2003/109/EC.

[32] Recital 24 Directive 2004/114/EC.

[33] Recital 23 Directive 2005/71/EC.

[34] Recital 25 Directive 2009/50/EC.

[35] Recital 30 Directive 2011/98/EU.

[36] Recital 51 Directive 2014/36/EU.

[37] Recital 44 Directive 2014/66/EU.

Asylum:

- to establish *minimum standards* for giving *temporary protection* in the event of a mass influx of displaced persons and measures promoting a balance of efforts between the Member States in receiving and bearing the consequences of receiving such persons;[38]
- to establish minimum standards on the reception of asylum seekers in Member States;[39]
- the *establishment of a right* to family reunification for third-country nationals to be exercised in accordance with common rules;[40]
- the establishment of criteria and mechanisms for determining the Member State responsible for examining an asylum application lodged in one of the Member States by a third-country national;[41]
- to establish *minimum standards* for the granting of *international protection* to third-country nationals and stateless persons by Member States and the *content of the protection* granted;[42]
- to establish *minimum standards* on *procedures* in Member States for granting and withdrawing refugee status.[43]

Illegal immigration:

- cooperation between Member States on expulsion of third-country nationals;[44]
- *introducing a residence permit* for the third-country nationals concerned who cooperate in the fight against trafficking in human beings;[45]
- to establish common rules concerning return, removal, use of coercive measures, detention and entry bans;[46]
- to *counteract illegal immigration* by acting against the employment pull factor;[47]
- financial burden sharing for cooperation between Member States;[48]
- other directives[49] and decisions[50] on illegal immigration do not contain references to subsidiarity.

Only five of the 20 recitals (underlined) explicitly mention cross-polity conflicts of interests. In most cases (italics), the objectives listed are not suitable for the liberal formula of subsidiarity and proportionality review: they do not explain why

38 Recital 23 Directive 2001/55/EC.
39 Recital 18 Directive 2003/9/EC.
40 Recital 16 Directive 2003/86/EC.
41 Recital 16 Regulation 343/2003.
42 Recital 37 Directive 2004/83/EC.
43 Recital 31 Directive 2005/85/EC.
44 Recital 5 Directive 2001/40/EC.
45 Recital 20 Directive 2004/81/EC.
46 Recital 20 Directive 2008/115/EC.
47 Recital 36 Directive 2009/52/EC.
48 Recital 4 Decision 2004/191/EC.
49 Directive 2002/90/EC, Directive 2003/110/EC.
50 Decision 96/749/JHA, Decision 2002/946/JHA.

suddenly Union action is needed where previously Member States regulated with ease. Under the liberal model, subsidiarity review answers the question of what level of power is the most suitable to advance policy choice. However, if establishing common rules were *the* problem to address in Union law then clearly only a supranational measure would be suitable for introducing such rules. No subsidiarity review is needed:

> Since Member States alone (without co-ordination or a central institution) can never achieve the best balance in terms of uniformity, it is not legitimate to review the exercise of regulatory powers accorded to them under the Treaty by means of a uniformity test.[51]

Harmonisation is even more meaningless when not all Member States participate and those who do are allowed to maintain their national systems alongside common rules.[52] Were harmonisation or common rules to determine the federal balance of powers, Union competence would become exclusive[53] leaving both principles without *effet utile*. Without a conflict of interests, liberal legitimation is impossible. Only a permanent conflict of interests between polities can legitimate a limit on their political processes that ensues from Union law: such a limit, to be proportionate, must itself be limited to ensuring *non-interference* between the polities. However, if these recitals merely list the areas where there may be conflicts of ideas, then a case for republican legitimation can be made, provided that there is also interdependence. Under the republican model, subsidiarity answers the question of what polity, national or European, should be taken for the purpose of majoritarian policy choice. Without functional objectives for Union action set out in Treaty text, this is *the* question that necessarily precedes both the making of policy choices and the decision about which level of power is the most suitable to advance it.

Identifying interdependence is how the institutions (perhaps subconsciously) approached subsidiarity review of EU immigration law under the AFSJ. The following analysis will review the legislative process in the field of legal immigration. This policy is chosen for two reasons. First, it is a policy that could be legitimated under either liberal or republican models. Binding deregulation between the European polities could be enforced for legal immigration thanks to the concomitance of the European interest (regulating rights of legal immigrants) with the interest of the individual with *locus standi* (third-country nationals who benefit from these rights), similar to what took place under the mixed external agreements, making the republican model unnecessary. At the same time, there is a risk of cross-polity interference (the 'level playing field' argument) that suggests the republican model.

[51] M Poiares Maduro, *We the Court* (Oxford, Hart Publishing, 1998) 171.

[52] *Ex multis* Article 13 Directive 2003/109/EC; UK, Ireland and Denmark opted out of EU measures on legal immigration altogether.

[53] Case C-376/98 *Tobacco Advertising*; GA Bermann, 'Proportionality and Subsidiarity' in C Barnard and J Scott (eds), *The Law of the Single European Market: Unpacking the Premises* (Oxford, Hart Publishing, 2002) 86.

We can therefore expect arguments based on both conflicts of interests and conflicts of ideas—and see how the institutions manoeuvre between the two. Second, much of legal immigration law was subject to subsidiarity review by national parliaments with the ensuing documents available on the IPEX website.[54] This is different for illegal immigration and asylum law, the first generation of which was adopted prior to the Lisbon Treaty and therefore did not benefit from the subsidiarity review procedure under Protocol 2 Lisbon, resulting in too few documents for a meaningful assessment.

Four directives were adopted after the Treaty of Lisbon: Directive 2009/50 Blue Card, Directive 2011/98 Single Permit, Directive 2014/36 Seasonal Workers, Directive 2014/66 Intra-Corporate Transferees. Analysis of the subsidiarity reasoning for these directives and the secondary EU law on legal immigration that preceded them reveals three interconnected strings of reasoning:

1. establishment of a common policy—internal market;
2. abolition of internal borders—fight against illegal migration;
3. fair treatment of third-country nationals—international competitiveness.

The first string of reasoning was born from the fiasco of the first Commission proposal, which aimed at 'the determination of a harmonised legal framework at Community level concerning the conditions of entry and residence' of third-country workers.[55] The Council opined that provisions concerning access to and conditions of employment of third-country nationals who reside legally in the territory of the EC could be adopted only on the basis of Article 137(1)(g) EC (currently Article 153(1)(g) TFEU) inasmuch as they did not imply a right for such persons to circulate freely within the Community.[56] Arguing *a contrario*, for a directive to be adopted under the AFSJ competence on legal immigration, there must be an element of mobility of third-country nationals between Member States.[57] On examination of this proposal, the EP followed the CJEU[58] and the Council to conclude that the absence of a 'Community element' infringed the federal balance of powers:

> The differences noted by the Commission between the Member States' rules [in the area of immigration policy] do not in themselves prove any need for harmonisation. Only the Member States can guarantee the flexibility geared to the national, regional and sectoral requirements of the labour market. [A]pproximation of legislation would be necessary

[54] The platform for EU Interparliamentary Exchange: www.ipex.eu.

[55] Recital 14, Proposal for a Council Directive on the conditions of entry and residence of third-country nationals for the purpose of paid employment and self-employed economic activities, COM (2001) 386 final.

[56] Opinion of the Council legal service (12.11.2002) doc 14150/02.

[57] This is perhaps a transposition of CJEU case law on the internal market, where the presence of a provision on mobility between Member States may play a crucial role in determining existence of Union competence: compare case C-376/98 *Tobacco Advertising* with case C-377/98 *Biotech Directive*.

[58] Case C-376/98 *Tobacco Advertising*.

only if any third-country national admitted to a Member State were permitted to work in any Member State.[59]

The parallel proposal for a directive on long-residents, in addition to integration[60] and a call for the 'determination' of status,[61] contained the objective of establishing the 'terms for the exercise of rights of residence in other Member States' which would 'contribute to the effective attainment of an internal market' and 'constitute a major factor of mobility on the Union's employment market'.[62] The Parliament, however, ignored the transnational element, merely stating that subsidiarity 'need not be brought into play here, since by definition common measures need only be adopted at Community level'.[63]

The EP retained this position in subsequent proposals, failing to examine competences or subsidiarity. One of the most clear examples is Directive 2003/86/EC Family Reunification, where the situation was not much different from the first (2001) Proposal: the directive justifies subsidiarity by an abstract call for 'common rules';[64] cross-polity aspects and mobility within the EU are absent, while its main objective is the 'integration of third-country nationals in the Member State'[65]—a purely internal situation not covered by Article 63 EC.[66] This despite a clear obligation on all EU institutions to review proposals for compliance with the principle of subsidiarity.[67]

The introduction of subsidiarity review by national parliaments significantly improved the quality of reasoning. Subsidiarity review of legal immigration law by national parliaments began with the Seasonal Workers and Intra-Corporate Transferees Proposals[68]—the two directives that address the status and rights of third-country workers demanded in the specific sectors of the national labour markets. The Italian, Spanish and Portuguese Parliaments agreed with the Commission that the demand for some types of workers was shared across Member States, a fact sufficient, according to these Parliaments, to confirm the necessity

[59] Report of the European Parliament on the Commission proposal for adoption of a Council directive on the conditions of entry and residence of third-country nationals for the purpose of paid employment and self-employed economic activities (23 January 2003) A5-0010/2003 final, 39.

[60] Recitals 4 and 12 Directive 2003/109/EC.

[61] Recital 24 Directive 2003/109/EC.

[62] Recitals 24 and 18 Directive 2003/109/EC.

[63] Report of the European Parliament (30.11.2001) A5-0436/2001 final.

[64] Recital 16 Directive 2003/86/EC.

[65] Recital 4 Directive 2003/86/EC.

[66] Report of the European Parliament (24.03.2003) A5-0086/2003 final.

[67] Article 1 Protocol 2 Lisbon.

[68] Proposal for a Directive of the European Parliament and of the Council on the conditions of entry and residence of third-country nationals for the purposes of seasonal employment (13.07.2010) COM (2010) 379 final and Proposal for a Directive of the European Parliament and of the Council on conditions of entry and residence of third-country nationals in the framework of an intra-corporate transfer (13.07.2010) COM (2010) 378 final—now Directives 2014/36 and 2014/66. Directive 2011/98, also adopted after the entry into force of the Treaty of Lisbon, was not reviewed by the national parliaments, presumably because the proposal for this directive was launched and discussed in 2007 or over two years before the entry into force of the Lisbon Treaty and its Protocol No 2.

of Union law.[69] The German, Latvian and Lithuanian Parliaments engaged in substantive review of the proposals without finding any subsidiarity concerns.[70] One parliament declared, without discussing subsidiarity further, that failing to act under Article 79 TFEU 'would contradict provisions and objectives of the Treaty'.[71] However, France, Austria and the UK pointed to the insufficiency of the Commission's reasoning and data on which it was based;[72] these national parliaments noted the inconsistency between, on the one hand, the statements of the Council acknowledging differences between the national labour markets,[73] recognised also in Article 79(5) TFEU, and, on the other hand, the assumption of the Commission that some categories of workers are equally in demand across Member States.[74] The latter argument hints at a potential conflict between national polities that could arise from competition for workers, while the former implies, conversely, that there is no conflict to solve in Union law. Provisions on mobility between Member States of third-country workers contained in the proposals were ignored—this would have been a clearly internal market argument based on the liberal model.

The second string of reasoning relates to the argument that the opening of venues for legal migration is somehow linked to the fight against illegal migration. The Austrian, Dutch, Polish and UK Parliaments questioned the suitability of a directive on legal immigration for solving the problem of illegal immigration.[75]

69 As regards the proposal for a directive on seasonal workers, see Cortes Generales 14 de octubre de 2010.—Serie A Núm 355, pp 2–3; Camera dei Deputati, documento finale approvato dalla commissione (doc XVIII, n 31) 25.11.2010; Written Opinion COM (2010)379 Assembleia da República, European Affairs Committee, 27.09.2010 available on www.ipex.eu. Regarding the proposal for a directive on intra-corporate transferees the Italian Senate stated that it belongs to the body of law regulating illegal migration, without reasons for this conclusion; see Senato della Reppublica, resoluzione approvata dalla commissione lavoro e previdenza sociale sull'atto comunitario N. COM (2010) 378 definitivo sottoposto al parere motivato sulla sussidiarietà (doc XVIII, n 53).

70 See, on the Seasonal Workers Proposal, German Bundesrat: Empfehlung 13.09.2010 Drucksache 442/1/10 and Beschluss 24.09.2010 Drucksache 442/10; Latvian Saema: Opinion of the Saeima European Affairs Committee on the subsidiarity and proportionality check for the final wording of the proposal for Directive of the European Parliament and of the Council COM (2010) 379, 14.10.2010; Lithuanian Saimas: Committee of European Affairs Conclusion regarding compliance with the principles of subsidiarity and proportionality of the proposal to adopt the directive on the conditions of entry and residence of third-country nationals for the purposes of seasonal employment, 08.10.2010.

71 Opinion of the Latvian Saeima European Affairs Committee on the subsidiarity and proportionality check for the final wording of the proposal for Directive of the European Parliament and of the Council COM (2010) 379 on the conditions of entry and residence of third-country nationals for the purposes of seasonal employment, 14.10.2010.

72 Subsidiarity review of the Seasonal Workers Proposal: Points 6–7, Reasoned opinion of the EU Committee of the Austrian Federal Council on Commission proposal COM (2010) 379 final; Meeting of the French Senate, 13 October 2010 Justice et affaires intérieures; Opinion of the UK House of Commons, European Scrutiny Committee, 13.10.2010, available at www.publications.parliament.uk/pa/cm201011/cmselect/cmeuleg/428-iii/428iii12.htm.

73 European Pact on Immigration and Asylum (24.12.2008) Council doc 13189/08, pp 4–5.

74 See, eg, Explanatory Memoranda to the proposals for the Blue Card Directive, COM (2007) 637 final, and Seasonal Workers Directive, COM (2010) 379 final.

75 On the Seasonal Workers Proposal: Reasoned opinion of the EU Committee of the Austrian Federal Council on the Commission proposal COM (2010) 379 final; UK House of Commons, European Scrutiny Committee, Reasoned opinion (13.10.2010) concerning the Commission proposal

In its reply to this concern, the Commission acknowledged that the proposal addressed illegal migration only indirectly, reiterating that 'the Schengen area without internal borders requires common minimum rules in order to reduce the risk of overstaying and irregular entries that may be caused by lax and diverse rules on the admission of seasonal workers'.[76] This argument seems to relate more to the return of unauthorised immigrants than to legal immigration rules: indeed, as we have seen, for structural reasons, Union acts on illegal immigration cannot be legitimated under the *non-interference*/liberal model.

The Commission also advanced an argument of external policy that 'remov[ing] obstacles to legal migration' would strengthen 'the commitment of third countries to tackling irregular migration'.[77] The UK House of Commons noted that it was impossible for the Union to offer immigration concessions in negotiation with third states due to the lack of competence over the admission of third-country workers under Article 79(5) TFEU.[78] Both the national parliaments and the Commission failed to appreciate the inadequacy of an internal directive that regulates all third-country nationals independently of nationality as a bargaining tool in negotiations with third states, which look to obtain special concessions for their own nationals only.

The third string of reasoning concerns the necessity to 'establish a level playing field within the EU'[79] in terms of 'fair treatment'[80] of third-country nationals. The objective of 'fair treatment' does not comply with subsidiarity and proportionality per se: although a minimum set of rights may prove beneficial to individual third-country nationals, this alone cannot justify withdrawing policy choice from the national political process.[81] The mere fact that a measure is perceived as overall beneficial *for third-country nationals* cannot justify the transfer of powers further

COM (2010) 379 final; UK House of Lords (26.10.2010) Subsidiarity assessment: admission of third country nationals as seasonal workers, Council of the EU 15526/10, Interinstitutional File 2010/0210 (COD); Letter 23452 of 14 October 2010 from the Dutch House of Representatives to the Vice-President of the European Commission; Opinion of the Senate of the Republic of Poland of 21 October 2010.

[76] Commission Reply to Opinions Concerning Subsidiarity Received from National Parliaments on the Proposal for a Directive on the Conditions of Entry and Residence of Third-Country Nationals for the Purposes of Seasonal Employment COM (2010) 379, especially point IV.B. Admission rules are already regulated in Article 21 Regulation 810/2009/EC (the Schengen Borders Code).

[77] Explanatory memorandum to the Proposal for a Directive of the European Parliament and of the Council on the conditions of entry and residence of third-country nationals for the purposes of seasonal employment (13.7.2010) COM (2010) 379 final, 6.

[78] The UK House of Commons European Scrutiny Committee (26.10.2010) Seasonal Workers and Intra-corporate Transfers, available at www.publications.parliament.uk/pa/cm201011/cmselect/cmeuleg/428-iii/428iii12.htm.

[79] Proposal for a Council Directive on a single application procedure for a single permit for third-country nationals to reside and work in the territory of a Member State and on a common set of rights for third-country workers legally residing in a Member State, COM (2007) 638 final.

[80] *Tampere Conclusions*. The Lisbon Treaty introduced the reference to 'fair treatment' of third-country workers into the legal base; while it is open to debate what level of treatment would amount to 'fair', presumably it is not the same as 'equal'.

[81] In case C-540/03 *European Parliament v Council*, the parties implicitly accepted and the CJEU did not review the validity of this objective for legitimating the passage of powers.

away from *Union citizens* (accountability) and the transfer of policy choice from the national political process to the European political space (a de facto shift in polity for the purposes of QMV). Although criticising the low level of rights guaranteed to third-country nationals, the overwhelming majority of national parliaments seem to recognise rights protection per se as a valid argument capable of justifying the transfer of powers. For the directives on legal immigration, only the UK House of Commons considered these arguments.[82] Acknowledging Union competence where it is exceeded for measures that are perceived as beneficial undermines the credibility of the European institutions should they wish to adopt EU acts that are considered burdensome. In order to ground Union law in legitimacy, whether liberal or republican, identification of interdependence is also needed.

EU provisions on 'fair treatment' address interdependence between Member States in two ways. They *eliminate competition between Member States*[83] in terms of (1) lowering production costs by exploiting third-country workers and, vice versa, (2) attracting the best third-country workers by offering them more rights. Despite a strong republican potential, this string has been framed strikingly in internal market terms.

Elimination of competition between Member States refers to two situations. First, differences in rights between third-country workers and Union citizens could result not only in 'unfair' competition between the two[84] but also 'unfair' competition between Member States' manufacturers who could reduce costs by employing third-country workers.[85] If one Member State provides for equal rights for third-country workers while another does not, this would allow the latter state's manufacturers to compete on lower production costs by employing workers with fewer rights. On the one hand, it does not qualify as an internal market problem characterised by permanent cross-polity interest cleavages because it can be expected that in each national polity there would be an equal interest in avoiding dumping from third-country workers: 'If the interests regulated by a national measure are equal in the different Member States, then there is no suspicion of over-representation of national interests or under-representation of the interests of nationals of other Member-States'.[86] Virtual representation of cross-polity interests takes place.[87] On the other hand, it could qualify under the republican model if interdependence between Member States was such that the incompatibilities between the national standards of 'fair treatment' caused a drop in each polity's *positive*

[82] Opinion of the UK House of Commons, European Scrutiny Committee (13.10.2010) on the Seasonal and Intra-Corporate Worker Proposals.

[83] European Commission, *Communication on immigration, integration and employment*, COM (2003) 336 final, 16.

[84] Commission reply to the opinions concerning subsidiarity received from national parliaments on the proposal for a directive on the conditions of entry and residence of third-country nationals for the purposes of seasonal employment COM (2010) 379.

[85] Meeting of the French Senate, Justice et affaires intérieures (13.10.2010).

[86] Poiares Maduro (n 51) 174.

[87] A Somek, *The Cosmopolitan Constitution* (Oxford, Oxford University Press, 2014) 27.

liberty and thus a need to develop a shared idea of *positive liberty* in the EU. The link to cross-polity competition between manufacturers is not only unnecessary in this regard but becomes tenuous. The only solution to address the risk of dumping in working conditions in connection with third-country workers is to ensure them *equal* treatment as a directly effective right, while *fair* (as opposed to *equal*) treatment established by means of a directive (and thus with no direct horizontal effect) does not allow for effective redress by third-country workers against their employers. Many national parliaments pointed to the need to secure full equality[88] though the underlying structural problem was not addressed.

Second, elimination of competition between Member States *internally* should be distinguished from joining forces *externally* to compete with the traditional countries of immigration for 'wanted' immigrant workers.[89] For instance, the impact assessment accompanying the proposal for a directive on employed and self-employed third-country nationals cited the 'possibility to accede to 27 labour markets' as 'an incentive for [highly qualified workers] in their decision of entering the EU economy' which could 'only be granted through Community action' going as far as 'a common understanding on the admission'—only to conclude seven pages later that 'creating a residence card valid throughout the Union would not be consistent with the principles of subsidiarity and proportionality'—without specifying the reason for this conclusion.[90] The Commission presents this objective as a deregulation issue, whereby 'the obstacles encountered … in relation to the complexity and diversity of [national] rules' could act as a deterrent in the capacity of the EU to attract third-country workers and business.[91] Different national entry and residence conditions cause competition between Member States for 'wanted'

[88] On the Seasonal Workers Proposal, see opinions from Austria (Reasoned opinion of the EU Committee of the Austrian Federal Council on the Commission proposal COM (2010) 379 final), France (French Senate, Réunion de la commission des affaires européennes (16.10.2010) Examen de la proposition de directive E 5515 (emploi saisonnier des ressortissants de pays tiers)), and Germany (Bundesrat: Empfehlung (13.09.2010) Drucksache 442/1/10); a similar conclusion on the Blue Card Directive from the Finnish Parliament, Statsrådets skrivelse till Riksdagen om ett förslag till rådets direktiv om villkor för tredjelandsmedborgares inresa och vistelse för högkvalificerad anställning, 27 December 2007.

[89] *The Hague Programme* (13.12.2004) Council doc 16054/04, 10; *European Pact on Immigration and Asylum* (24.12.2008) Council doc. 13189/08, p. 5; *Green Paper on an EU Approach to Managing Economic Migration* (2005) COM (2004) 811 final, 4; *Policy Plan on Legal Migration* (2005) COM (2005) 669 final; European Commission SPEECH/07/526 by Commissioner Frattini, Lisbon, 13.09.2007; Explanatory Memorandum to the Proposal for a Council Directive on the conditions of entry and residence of third-country nationals for the purposes of highly qualified employment (23.10.2007) COM (2007) 637 final, pp 2 and 7; Recital 6 Directive 2005/114/EC; Recital 17 Directive 2005/71/EC; Recital 7 Directive 2010/50/EC; Recital 6, Proposal for a Council Directive on the conditions of entry and residence of third-country nationals for the purpose of paid employment and self-employed economic activities, COM (2001) 386 final; Recital 7 Directive 2010/50/EC.

[90] Commission Staff Working Document SEC(2007) 1403, pp 20 and 27.

[91] Explanatory memorandum to the proposal for a directive on Intra-Corporate Transferees, COM (2010) 378 final, 2. Similar reasoning is found in the explanatory memorandum to the Blue Card Proposal, COM (2007) 637 final, 2.

third-country workers, which, according to the Commission, triggers the need for a common EU admission system.[92] The logic is similar to EU action in the field of external relations, specifically in the context of worker provisions in mixed external agreements, when third-country nationals were regulated in EC law without necessarily any conflict potential between Member States.[93] The need to ensure that the Community acts as a single entity on the international arena is a strong supranational element that calls for joint action even in situations otherwise internal to one Member State. This is perhaps the strongest argument in favour of Union action under the republican model, however limited it may be by a lack of Union competence.[94]

Neither national governments[95] nor national parliaments[96] raised subsidiarity issues on this external objective per se. However, two parliaments found contradictions between seeking to raise the rights of third-country nationals on the one hand and avoiding competition between Member States for third-country workers on the other, since competition will likely lead to more rights for these workers.[97] These two problems are mutually exclusive, placing in doubt an instrument that aims to achieve both. Competition between national immigration systems also loops back to the opposite concern, that of becoming a magnet for 'unwanted' third-country nationals who were admitted by other Member States; this is effectively the second string of reasoning linked to the abolition of internal borders, where *non-interference* is unenforceable and republican legitimation is the only option.

[92] Blue Card Proposal, COM (2007) 637 final, 7.

[93] On the contrary, there was a unanimous agreement between the national polities in Europe; Case 12/86 *Demirel*; Case C-246/07 *Commission v Sweden*.

[94] Article 79(5) TFEU reserves to Member States their exclusive powers over admission of third-country workers. Some national parliaments note that while attracting skilled workers is a major issue, EU immigration law offers little added value in this regard: *Statsrådets skrivelse till Riksdagen om ett förslag till rådets direktiv om villkor för tredjelandsmedborgares inresa och vistelse för högkvalifice rad anställning*, attachment Arbetsministeriets promemoria (Finland, 27.12.2007). For the argument that competition between immigration destinations is beneficial for attracting the highly skilled, see A Shachar, 'The Race for Talent: Highly-Skilled Migrants and Competitive Immigration Regimes' (2006) 18 *New York University Law Review* 156–57.

[95] Except for a few reservations raised by some Member States in relation to social security matters, see Council Working Party on Migration and Expulsion (08.05.2008) doc 8249/08, interinstitutional file 2007/0228 (CNS).

[96] Eg Asembleia da República, Comissão de Assuntos Europeus (12.10.2010) Parecer COM (2010) 378 Final; Asembleia da República, Comissão de Trabalho, Segurança Social e Administracão Pública, Relatório (28.09.2010) Proposta de Directiva do Parlamento Europeu e do Conselho relativa às condições de entrada e residência de nacionais de países terceiros no quadro de transferências dentro das empresas, Comissao de trabalho, seguranca social e administracaop pública, Asembleia da República.

[97] UK House of Commons, European Scrutiny Committee, Reasoned Opinion (13.10.2010) concerning the Commission proposal COM (2010) 379 final; UK House of Commons, European Scrutiny Committee hearing 13.10.2010, record available at www.publications.parliament.uk/pa/cm201011/cmselect/cmeuleg/428-iii/428iii12.htm (07.09.2011); Letter 32452 from the Dutch House of Representatives to the Vice-President of the European Commission (14.10.2010).

4. DEMISE OF THE VERTICAL BALANCE OF POWERS

Subsidiarity as a tool for limiting Union powers in immigration policy is unconvincing and there are structural reasons for this. Under the liberal model, Union law derives legitimacy from its ability to protect national ideas of *positive liberty* from interference by others—hence the presumption in favour of national action. Only such limits on the national ideas of *positive liberty* that are necessary to ensure reciprocal *non-interference* are legitimate. In the context of the conferral of powers in Article 5 TEU and following the literal wording of the Lisbon and Amsterdam Protocols—all drafted with the liberal model in mind—subsidiarity and proportionality present themselves as power-allocating principles that enter into play *after* a policy choice is made.[98] Subsidiarity and proportionality ensure that Union law only limits the national political process when this is necessary to protect it from interference by others. Subsidiarity therefore seeks out permanent structural conflicts arising from cross-polity interest cleavages. Where there is a risk of such conflicts, the Union is not only allowed to act but reciprocal limits in EU law on the national political processes (deregulation attained by empowering the individual through rights) are necessary to protect the liberty of each national polity. The permanent and structural nature of this type of conflict implies that the need for Union law does not cease: no subsidiarity review of proposals for Recast law is needed.

Without functional Treaty objectives, this understanding is reversed. If subsidiarity ensures that powers of the Union are limited to those necessary to further a shared idea of *positive liberty* as identified outside the Treaties—yet, this idea is itself open to (re)negotiation and change (exactly because it is not contained in the Treaties)—then the vertical limits on Union powers no longer make sense. On the contrary, limiting Union powers may undermine legitimacy for legitimacy now derives not from the ability to limit the political process but from the ability to further it. The problems addressed under the republican model are not static cleavages but conflicts between the constantly changing ideas about *positive liberty*. What needs to be solved are political conflicts that involve different and incompatible ideas about 'ideal life', on which reasonable people may disagree:

> Though the question of competences is often presented as an issue of simply determining who is more efficient or effective in exercising certain competences, in reality, it often hides profound different conceptions of the polity and the common good it should pursue … Underlying the discussions on competences are, therefore, different conceptions of the European political community and the nature of the political and civic links between its citizens.[99]

[98] Subsidiarity was conceived also as a policy development tool, see G De Burca, 'The Quest for Legitimacy in the European Union' (1996) 5 *MLR*. Importantly, subsidiarity could be used both to expatriate and repatriate powers, Toth (n 6) 278.

[99] M Poiares Maduro, *How Constitutional Can the European Union Be? The Tension Between Intergovernmentalism and Constitutionalism in the European Union* (2004) NYU School of Law, Jean Monnet Working Paper 5/04, 45.

The constant and ongoing nature of conflicts implies that the Recast Proposals must be reviewed each time, as the idea of European *positive liberty* they embody will change together with their substance and circumstance.[100] The reversal of the presumption in favour of Union action makes perfect sense under the republican model: if legitimation is based on *positive liberty* instead of *non-interference*, then the ability to further a shared idea of *positive liberty* must prevail over *non-interference* with the national ideas thereof. Under the republican model, legitimacy of Union powers stems not from the vertical balance of powers but from the ability to identify and further an idea of *positive liberty* shared by the peoples of Europe.

Systemically, the demise of the vertical balance of powers is consistent with the republican legitimation and the openness of policy choice to politics. Understood in terms of the vertical division of power, subsidiarity does not advance legitimacy of republican policies while, without functional Treaty objectives, proportionality review is reduced to a statement that proportionality is satisfied because the instrument proposed is a directive.[101] Perhaps for this reason, both principles are reviewed only summarily by the EU institutions, which tend to operate under the presumption of the liberal model of subsidiarity review, eg the reasoning in terms of the internal market. Nevertheless, elements of a republican conception emerge. Union institutions and national parliaments use subsidiarity review to identify and describe interdependence and the conflicts to address. Subsidiarity is often substituted with the examination of substantive choices or the problems that they address. Cross-polity conflicts of ideas about *positive liberty* are revealed in the course of this examination, for instance in the discussion about 'unwanted' migration flows driven by welfare shopping, the levels of rights and procedural guarantees.

The changing role of subsidiarity under the republican model from a tool for the vertical division of powers into a tool of policy choice—ie from a tool for regulating conflicts of interests into a tool for identifying and negotiating conflicts of ideas—explains disinterest towards the principle in the CJEU. In all the immigration and asylum cases to date, subsidiarity is discussed by the Court only twice, both times briefly, reiterating the language of secondary acts, while the word itself is never mentioned. So, in a Visa Code case, the Court found that its aim, 'to establish the conditions for the issue of uniform visas', 'cannot be sufficiently achieved by the Member States and can therefore be better achieved at European Union level'.[102] From this, the Court concluded:

> The interpretation that the Visa Code does no more than govern the procedures for the issue of visas and oblige the Member States to refuse to issue visas in certain specific situations, without thereby harmonising the conditions for the issue of visas, is therefore incompatible with the very objective of that code.[103]

[100] Regulation of illegal immigration and crime could be an exception to this since, as pointed out earlier, liberal legitimation for these policies is impossible due to the absence of a mechanism to enforce *non-interference* without reliance on powers of the state.

[101] As stated in the recitals to all immigration directives to date.

[102] Case C-84/12 *Koushkaki* §49.

[103] ibid §50.

In a Schengen Borders Code case, the subsidiarity statement was again limited to reiterating the wording of secondary act: 'the objective of the code is to establish the conditions, criteria and detailed rules applicable to the control of external borders of the European Union, which cannot be satisfactorily achieved by the Member States acting alone'.[104] The conclusion that directly followed is identical in wording and effect to the previous case.[105] This time, however, the Court incorporated an element of interdependence between Member States into its reasoning:

> Recital 6 to the Schengen Borders Code states, moreover, that border control is in the interests not only of the Member State at whose external borders it is carried out but of all Member States which have abolished internal border controls—a statement that implies a common definition of the entry conditions.[106]

These two cases are interesting because they involve two different types of conflict. As concerns the external borders, interests of different Member States permanently differ. This is not the same for visa policy, where the potential conflict concerns ideas about substantive policy choice. In both cases, the Court accepted policy objectives as stated not only in primary but also in secondary law, without examining the policy choice declared by the legislator nor the level at which this policy choice is made.

5. FROM BALANCE OF POWERS TO BALANCE OF POLITIES

This chapter explored how the move towards the republican conception of Europe affected the general principles of Union law that legitimate the Union in terms of the federal division of powers. Grounding legitimacy in shared European *positive liberty* (republican Europe) spells the demise of the vertical division of powers. For policies characterised by cross-polity conflicts of ideas about *positive liberty*, the vertical balance of powers between Member States and the Union appears to have lost significance for legitimising Union acts. Identification of the level of power that is the most suitable to advance a policy choice is unimportant when this choice is not made in primary law. The liberty roots of legitimacy of Union law go deeper than the federal balance of powers. Once Union Treaties leave policy choice open to politics, identification of the nature of conflict necessarily precedes the shaping and implementation of policy. The liberal and republican models now must be distinguished in order to advance legitimacy of European policy choice. Under the liberal model, Union law is legitimate because it can limit the political process; under the republican model, Union law is legitimate because of its capacity to advance it. This fundamental difference in the structure of legitimacy shifts

[104] Case C-575/12 *AirBaltic* §65.
[105] ibid §66.
[106] ibid §65.

the process of legitimating Union law one stage earlier than was the case under the liberal model. Instead of identifying the level of power that best advances a policy choice, the process of legitimising Union law begins with the identification of the nature of conflict.

The institutions recognise this implicitly by refocusing subsidiarity review from the vertical balance of powers to the conflict to be addressed in Union law. Subsidiarity review by national parliaments and EU institutions tends to reveal the nature of potential conflict and interference between Member States.

Once republican legitimation is chosen, proportionality review of Union law cannot follow the familiar (liberal) EU-law-limited-to-its-objectives test. On the one hand, under the republican model, European *positive liberty* prevails over national policy choice and over *non-interference* between the national polities in the EU. The distinction between more or less restrictive legal instruments (regulations or directives) for the advancement of policy choice makes no sense when legitimacy is based on the ability to elaborate and advance a shared idea about *positive liberty*. On the other hand, without functional Treaty objectives, national ideas about *positive liberty* may now be subject to majoritarian political process in the European political space. Where national policy choice preferences are shaped by their immutable characteristics such as geography or size, a permanent cross-polity interest cleavage risks being subjected to majoritarian policy choice. This could create insular minority polities that permanently lose out to other polities in the European political space. This is a problem under the republican model because the legitimacy of European policy choice relies on each national polity internalising it as its own. Permanently losing out to other polities will, on the contrary, result in learning from disappointment, frustration and a desire to Exit. Counter-majoritarian guarantees are needed for such polities in Union law.

Two questions are relevant:

- What is the nature of conflict? This will determine the constitutional role of Union law: to prevent conflicts by limiting the political process or to solve conflicts by enabling it.
- How is its solution enforced? Are there individuals with *locus standi* to enforce Union law in court? This will determine the institutional arrangements. For conflicts of interest, where the role of Union law is to limit the political process, policies that regulate individuals whose interests are situated outside the system of reciprocity established in law can only be enforced by the Commission, eg competition policy or illegal migration. For conflicts of ideas, where the role of Union law is to advance the political process, policies that regulate individuals whose interests are situated outside the system of reciprocity established in law can be enforced by Member State nationals in the course of the political process, eg criminal law. The latter case involves particularly strong mutual reliance of Member States on each other's political process and constitutional guarantees that secure interest representation and accountability.

This is summarised in Table 4.1.

Table 4.1: Liberal and republican models of legitimation

	EU law regulates interests situated within the law	**EU law regulates interests situated outside the law**
Conflict of interests	Example: free movement of Union citizens Enforced by the individual in court	Example: illegal immigration Enforced by the Commission or otherwise based on international law
Conflict of ideas	Example: legal migration Enforced by the individual in court	Example: criminal law Enforced by the individual in the political process

Republican legitimation requires safeguards for *liberty from dependence*: constitutional review of the national political process when it is part of the European political space. This could be done as comparative constitutional analysis[107] where the Court would examine the constitutional guarantees in Union law that ensure interest representation in the political process by comparison to a situation when the policy choice is made in the national political space. Comparative constitutional analysis would ensure that accountability of power in the national political process is not jeopardised by making the policy choice in Europe. Without a unified political community on the level of the EU, preserving accountability on the national level is fundamental for Europe's legitimacy. Self-perception of being part of a single political community is important: there will be no incentive for polity members to hold politicians accountable for failing to advance a policy choice that is perceived as being made by 'others'. It is when 'I am a genuine member of a political community, its act is in some pertinent sense my act. Even when I argued and voted against it'.[108] A further step would be to subject interest representation and accountability in the national political process to constitutional guarantees in Union law.

The next chapter tests the hypothesis presented in Table 4.1 by examining how proportionality and constitutional guarantees of Union law are being used and adjusted by the CJEU in order to ensure interest representation in the European political space. The reluctance of the CJEU to engage in review of counter-majoritarian and counter-minoritarian guarantees forces the Court to manoeuvre between solidarity and mutual trust.

[107] By analogy with comparative institutional analysis, see N Komesar, *Imperfect Alternatives* (Chicago, IL, University of Chicago Press, 1994).

[108] R Dworkin, *Freedom's Law: The Moral Reading of the American Constitution* (Cambridge, MA, Harvard University Press, 1996) 22.

5

The EU Court and Liberty from Dependence

The final political end of society is to become fully just and stable for the right reasons.
John Rawls, *The Law of Peoples*[1]

1. THE TRIUMPH OF *POSITIVE LIBERTY*

ONCE REPUBLICAN LEGITIMACY is found suitable to legitimate a European policy choice, proportionality review needs to adjust. With the demise of the vertical balance of powers, vertical limits on the exercise of power through proportionality do not further legitimacy. The principle needs to acquire a new role in order to further legitimacy of republican policies.

Three lines of AFSJ cases emerge from the case law of the CJEU. Both the demise of the vertical balance of powers and the blurring between the liberal and republican models are traceable in these cases. In the first line, effectiveness of Union law is balanced against national discretion, resulting in strict review of Member State acts. In the second line, effectiveness of Union law is balanced against the rights of the individual, and the Court follows the ECtHR standard of review. In the third line, effectiveness of Union law is balanced against national Constitutions. In all cases, the Court protects the idea of European *positive liberty* as expressed in secondary law. Conflicting national ideas of *positive liberty* and interests of the individual give way. The third line of cases reveals the problem with this approach: the Court is using the liberal model to enforce a republican policy.

Line 1: European Positive Liberty > National Positive Liberty

This line of cases at first appears as a conventional rights-based approach characteristic of liberal legitimation. Striving to ensure effectiveness of Union law, the Court upheld rights of the individual secured in secondary law, scrutinised national discretion strictly, and gave uniform interpretation to open and undefined

[1] J Rawls, *The Law of Peoples* (Cambridge, MA, Harvard University Press, 1999) 119.

provisions of secondary law. The cases falling into this category are: C-575/12 *Air-Baltic* (borders); C-508/10 *Commission v Netherlands*, C–502/10 *Singh*, C-571/10 *Kamberaj*, C-491/13 *Ben Alaya* (legal immigration); C-357/09 PPU *Kadzoev*, C-61/11 PPU *El Dridi*, C-329/11 *Achughbabian*, C-430/11 *Sagor*, C-47/15 *Affum*, Joined Cases C-473 and 514/13 *Bero*, C-146/14 *Mahdi* (illegal immigration); C-465/07 *Elgafaji* and C-285/12 *Diakite*. The message from these cases is unequivocal. Policy choice contained in secondary Union law (the idea of *positive liberty* shared by the peoples of Europe as it emerges from the European political process) prevails over the national ideas of *positive liberty*; the rights of the individuals secured in secondary Union law serve to further this shared idea.

In the policy on *legal immigration*, most cases centred on Directive 2003/109/EC. The first case concerned the fees charged by the national authorities for the long-term residence permit. None of EU directives under the AFSJ regulates fees to be charged for permits nor contains indications of what their amounts might be. This was pointed out by the Netherlands[2] and accepted by the Court.[3] Nevertheless, the Court found that the discretion left to the Member States 'is not unlimited' and they 'may not apply national rules which are liable to jeopardise the achievement of the objectives pursued by a directive and, therefore, deprive it of its effectiveness'.[4] The Court accepted the objectives of the directive as stated in its recitals:

> [T]he principal purpose of [Directive 2003/109/EC] is the integration of third-country nationals who are settled on a long-term basis in the Member States. The right of residence of long-term residents and members of their family in another Member State, provided for by Chapter III of that directive, also aims to contribute to the effective attainment of an internal market as an area in which the free movement of persons is ensured.[5]

It then declared:

> Charges which have a significant financial impact on third-country nationals who satisfy the conditions laid down by Directive 2003/109 for the grant of those residence permits could prevent them from claiming the rights conferred by that directive, contrary to recital 10 to that directive.[6]
>
> … in so far as the high amount of the charges levied on third-country nationals by the Kingdom of the Netherlands is liable to create an obstacle to the exercise of the rights

[2] Case C-508/10 *Commission v Netherlands* §63: 'while the Commission's Proposal for a Directive provided for the issue of a residence permit free of charge or against payment of a sum not exceeding the charges required of nationals of the Member State concerned for the issue of identity cards, the EU legislature, by adopting Directive 2003/109, decided not to include such a provision in the directive'.

[3] ibid §64: 'It is thus undisputed … that Member States may make the issue of the residence permits … subject to the payment of charges and that, in fixing the amount of those charges, they enjoy a margin of discretion'.

[4] ibid §65.

[5] ibid §66.

[6] ibid §70.

> conferred by Directive 2003/109, the Netherlands legislation undermines the objective pursued by that directive and deprives it of its effectiveness.[7]

The Court further found that the amount of fees was 'disproportionate and liable to create an obstacle to the exercise of the rights conferred by that directive'[8] because the charges

> vary within a range in which the lowest amount is about seven times higher than the amount to be paid to obtain a national identity card. Even if [EU] citizens and third-country nationals and the members of their families to whom Directive 2003/109 relates are not in identical situations, such a variation illustrates the disproportionate nature of the charges claimed.[9]

A similar test of proportionality that borders the rule of law was employed in two recent cases that concerned fees for integration tests.[10]

In the second case, the Court was asked whether Member States could exclude a specific group of third-country nationals from the scope of the directive by granting them 'a fixed-period residence permit … the validity of which may be extended indefinitely'.[11] Although Article 3(2)(e) 'excludes from the scope of Directive 2003/109 third-country nationals who reside in a Member State on the basis of a formally limited residence permit',[12] and the directive 'does not define either the concept of "legal residence" or the conditions or rights pertaining to that residence, which fall within the competence of the Member States',[13] the Court proceeded to interpret the concept of 'formally limited residence permits' contained in Article 3(2)(e) 'as otherwise the achievement of the objectives pursued by the Directive would be jeopardised and, therefore, it would be deprived of its effectiveness'.[14] The objective declared in the directive's recitals were accepted by the Court without examination:

> [T]he principal objective of [Directive 2003/109/EC Long-Term Residents] is the integration of third-country nationals who are settled on a long-term basis in the Member States … the Directive seeks, by granting the status of long-term resident to such third-country nationals, to approximate the legal status of third-country nationals to that of Member States' nationals.[15]

[7] ibid §73.
[8] ibid §72.
[9] ibid §77.
[10] Case C-579/13 *P&S* and Case C-153/14 *K&A*. It is regrettable that although the substance of the Court's reasoning clearly pertains to coherence and the rule of law, this is not explicitly stated and instead the Court insists that its analysis is proportionality (§§64–70 Case C-153/14 *K&A*) and effectiveness (§§50–45 Case C-579/13 *P&S*).
[11] Case C-502/10 *Singh* §29.
[12] ibid §49.
[13] ibid §39.
[14] ibid §51.
[15] ibid §47.

The Court adopted a factual approach reminiscent of the internal market[16] rather than the permit-based approach characteristic of its case law on third-country nationals under the mixed external agreements analysed in Chapter 2:

> [T]he fact that a residence permit contains a formal restriction does not in itself give any indication as to whether that third-country national might settle on a long-term basis in the Member State, notwithstanding the existence of such a restriction.[17]

It reached an unexpected conclusion that:

> Thus, a formally limited residence permit within the meaning of national law, but whose formal limitation does not prevent the long-term residence of the third-country national concerned, cannot be classified as a formally limited residence permit within the meaning of Article 3(2)(e) of Directive 2003/109, as otherwise the achievement of the objectives pursued by the Directive would be jeopardised and, therefore, it would be deprived of its effectiveness.[18]

This argument is linked to the coherence of action by the national authorities:

> [T]he fact that the validity of a residence permit can be extended for successive periods, including beyond a five-year period, and, in certain cases, indefinitely, may be a strong indication from which it can be concluded that the formal limitation attached to that permit does not prevent the long-term residence of the third-country national in the Member State concerned.[19]

The third case on the same directive concerned equal treatment of third-country national long-term residents in the allocation of housing benefits. Although the third-country national in question held 'a residence permit for an indefinite period' in Italy and not the EU long-term residence permit, the Court proceeded to answer the question on substance. Once again, uniform interpretation of a 'may' clause of the directive turned on the effectiveness of Union law:

> 77 … when the European Union legislature has made an express reference to national law … it is not for the Court to give the terms concerned an autonomous and uniform definition under European Union law. … Such a reference means that the European Union legislature wished to respect the differences between the Member States concerning the meaning and exact scope of the concepts in question.
>
> 78 However, the absence of such an autonomous and uniform definition under European Union law … and the reference to national law [in the EU directive] concerning those concepts do not mean that the Member States may undermine the effectiveness of [the directive].[20]

The Court concluded that:

> [S]ince the integration of third-country nationals who are long-term residents in the Member States and the right of those nationals to equal treatment … is the general rule,

16 Where the decision to engage in economic activity triggers a right to enter and reside in another Member State as a worker, Case 344/87 *Bettray*, Case C-3/90 *Bernini*.
17 Case C-502/10 *Singh* §50.
18 ibid §51.
19 ibid *Singh* §54.
20 Case C-571/10 *Kamberaj* §§77–78.

> the derogation provided for in Article 11(4) [Directive 2003/109/EC] must be interpreted strictly.[21]

The last in this line of cases centred on the admission of third-country national students under Directive 2004/114/EC Students. The Court again accepted objectives as stated in the directive's recitals[22] and concluded:

> To allow a Member State to introduce, in relation to the admission of third-country nationals for study purposes, conditions additional to those laid down in Articles 6 and 7 of Directive 2004/114 would be contrary to the objective pursued by that directive of promoting the mobility of such nationals.[23]

The Court conceded that national authorities may require 'all the evidence necessary to assess the coherence of the application for admission, in order to fight against abuse and misuse of the procedure set out in that directive'.[24] However, since the applicant complied with all the requirements of the directive and none of the grounds for refusal allowed by the directive were raised against the applicant by the national authorities, the latter were required to issue the residence permit.

In *asylum* policy, the cases centred on the subsidiarity protection status introduced by Directive 2004/83/EC. Under Article 2(e) of the Directive, a third-country national who does not qualify as a refugee is eligible for subsidiary protection if there are

> substantial grounds … for believing that the person concerned, if returned to his or her country of origin, or in the case of a stateless person, to his or her country of former habitual residence, would face a real risk of suffering serious harm as defined in Article 15 … and is unable, or, owing to such risk, unwilling to avail himself or herself of the protection of that country.

Article 15(c) defines 'serious harm' as 'serious and *individual* threat to a civilian's life or person by reason of *indiscriminate* violence in situations of international or internal armed conflict'.[25] Despite political disagreement over the phrasing and meaning of the latter provision at the time of its adoption, with the majority of the Member States in the Council insisting on the wording 'individual threat',[26] the Court gave a broad interpretation to its scope. It began by distinguishing between 'the three types of "serious harm" defined in Article 15 of the Directive, which

[21] ibid §86.

[22] Case C-491/13 *Ben Alaya* §29: 'recital 6 to the directive states that the approximation of the national legislation of the Member States relating to the conditions of entry and residence is part of that objective'.

[23] ibid §30.

[24] Compare Case C-84/12 *Koushkaki* §§56–62 on the Visa Code, where the Court recognised a wide margin of appreciation to the national authorities that need to assess the 'risk of illegal immigration' presented by the applicant even where she otherwise fulfils all the requirements for the issuing of a visa.

[25] Emphasis added.

[26] For an analysis of Member State positions on this article see H Storey, 'EU Refugee Qualification Directive: A Brave New World?' (2008) 20(1) *International Journal of Refugee Law* 33–34.

constitute the qualification for subsidiary protection'[27] and found that whereas points (a) and (b) of this article refer to 'the risk of a particular type of harm' (death penalty, execution and torture being specifically mentioned in the article),[28] point (c) 'covers a more general risk of harm'[29] without mentioning any 'specific acts of violence'.[30] It followed that subsidiary protection is created in EU law in addition to and above the protection offered to refugees under international law, thus requiring an independent interpretation.[31] Although effectiveness was not directly mentioned in the judgments, the Court opted for 'interpretation, which is likely to ensure that Article 15(c) of the Directive has its own field of application',[32] thus giving this provision a self-standing *effet utile*.

In the field of *illegal immigration*, preliminary references to the CJEU concerned detention of illegal immigrants pending their return under Directive 2008/115/EC. Although the 18-month detention ceiling for the purposes of removal set out in Article 15 was a 'reply' to the cases before the ECtHR,[33] the strict interpretation by the CJEU is much more limiting of the Member States than the standard of the ECtHR. The Court equated substantial provisions of the directive with its objective,[34] and, relying on 'the principles of proportionality and effectiveness with regard to the means used and objectives pursued',[35] found that '[Member] States may not apply rules, even criminal law rules, which are liable to jeopardise the achievement of the objectives pursued by a directive and, therefore, deprive it of its effectiveness'.[36] As a result, Member States 'cannot provide for a term of imprisonment for illegally-staying third-country nationals in situations in which the latter must, by virtue of the common standards and procedures established by that directive, be removed'.[37] Nor can imprisonment be permitted 'merely on account of illegal entry, resulting in an illegal stay, as such imprisonment is liable to thwart the application of that procedure and delay return, thereby undermining

[27] Case C-465/07 *Elgafaji* §31.

[28] ibid §32.

[29] ibid §33.

[30] ibid §34.

[31] ibid §28; Case C-285/12 *Diakite* §§21–24.

[32] Case C-465/07 *Elgafaji* §36; see also Case C-285/12 *Diakite* §26.

[33] In particular §113 Case *Chahal v UK* (15.11.1996) ECtHR, Reports 1996-V and §§67–74 Case *Saadi v UK* (29.01.2008) ECtHR Application no 13229/03—compare §§64–65 Case C-357/09 PPU *Kadzoev*; see also §43 Case C-61/11 PPU *El Dridi*.

[34] Case C-357/09 PPU *Kadzoev* §37: 'the objective of [Article 15(5) and (6)] of Directive 2008/115 [are] to guarantee in any event that detention for the purpose of removal does not exceed 18 months', as opposed to Recital 20 Directive 2008/115/EC, which only speaks of establishing 'common rules concerning return, removal, use of coercive measures, detention and entry bans', the maximum length of detention being the result of the European political process, not the reason legitimating it.

[35] Case C-61/11 PPU *El Dridi* §57.

[36] ibid §55 and §59: Member States cannot use their exclusive powers in such a way that risks 'jeopardising the attainment of the objective pursued by that directive, namely, the establishment of an effective policy of removal and repatriation of illegally staying third-country nationals'; Case C-329/11 *Achughbabian* §33 and §39; Case C-430/11 *Sagor* §32.

[37] Case C-329/11 *Achughbabian* §46.

the directive's effectiveness'.[38] Effectiveness of the 'removal and repatriation policy'[39] not only trumps detention as a sanction for illegal stay in national criminal law, but also imposes an obligation on Member States to carry out the removal 'as soon as possible'.[40] Objectives of secondary Union law, or the European ideas of *positive liberty* limit the Member States in the exercise of their retained powers.

In each of the policy domains examined, the European idea of *positive liberty* developed by the peoples of Europe in the Union and advanced through secondary Union law binds their national political processes against making a different policy choice. Although the binding nature of secondary Union law is similar to the liberal model, the policy choice is made at the Union level,[41] giving these policies a republican form of legitimacy. National polities are restrained not by the rules of *non-interference* with other polities but by the idea of *positive liberty* that they develop jointly in the EU.

Line 2: European Positive Liberty > Fundamental Rights

The second line of cases concerns a balance between European policy choice as set out in secondary law and the rights of the individual as they result from other sources, in particular the ECHR and the Charter of Fundamental Rights of the European Union. The European idea of *positive liberty* identified in secondary law differed from the interest that the individual sought to protect. The cases falling into this category include: C-540/03 *EP v Council* (legal immigration); C-69/10 *Samba Diouf*, C–277/11 *MM* (asylum); C-534/11 *Arslan*, C-383/13 PPU *G&R*, C-166/13 *Mukarubega*, C-249/13 *Boudjlida* (illegal immigration). In these cases, the Court balanced the European idea of *positive liberty* as expressed in objectives contained in secondary law against fundamental rights. The standard of review employed by the Court is markedly lower than in the first line of cases.

In the policy on *legal migration*, the case concerned the right to family life. The EP challenged the Council in the adoption of Directive 2003/86/EC Family Reunification on the grounds, inter alia, that the directive limited the right to family reunification of minors. Although the last part of the case was argued by all the parties on proportionality,[42] the Court in its assessment focused on whether the secondary act breached the standard set by the ECtHR. It found that the contested

[38] Case C-47/15 *Affum* §63.

[39] Case C-146/14 *Mahdi* §38.

[40] Case C-329/11 *Achughbabian* §45 and Case C-430/11 *Sagor* §43: 'It follows both from the duty of loyalty of the Member States and from the requirements of effectiveness referred to in Directive 2008/115/EC that the obligation imposed on the Member States by Article 8 of that directive to carry out the removal must be fulfilled as soon as possible', although Article 8 does not specify any period of return nor any time-related criteria for determining such period.

[41] With the exception of the objective to fight illegal migration, all the other policy choices are made in secondary Union law as opposed to Treaty rights and objectives.

[42] Case C-540/03 *EP v Council* §§91–96.

provision did not 'run counter to the right to respect for family life set out in particular in Article 8 of the ECHR as interpreted by the European Court of Human Rights' because it did not 'have the effect of precluding any family reunification, but preserves a limited margin of appreciation for the Member States'.[43] The Court concluded:

> In the final analysis, while the Directive leaves the Member States a margin of appreciation, it is sufficiently wide to enable them to apply the Directive's rules in a manner consistent with the requirements flowing from the protection of fundamental rights.[44]

The Court dismissed the action as 'not well founded': above the threshold of the ECHR, the Court would not review the policy choice of the legislator.[45]

In *asylum* and *illegal immigration* policies, which are convenient to discuss together, the cases concerned the right to an effective remedy. This right is established inter alia in Article 41(2) EU Charter, Article 13 ECHR, Article 39 Directive 2005/85/EC, as well as other immigration directives under the AFSJ. Having reiterated the fundamental importance of this right in the EU legal order,[46] the Court concluded that 'it is for the referring court to determine' whether the right was infringed in the course of the national procedure in question.[47]

Some guidance to the national courts was given. First, *the nature of the right to an effective remedy was clarified*. So, as regards recourse to an accelerated procedure for the examination of asylum claims under Directive 2005/85/EC, the Court found:

> What is important, therefore, is that the reasons justifying the use of an accelerated procedure may be effectively challenged at a later stage before the national court and reviewed by it within the framework of the action that may be brought against the final decision closing the procedure relating to the application for asylum.[48]

As regards detention of illegal immigrants, all decisions concerning detention and its extension 'must be ordered in writing with reasons being given in fact and in law'.[49]

As regards return of illegal immigrants, the purpose of the right to be heard in all proceedings is

> to enable [the person concerned] to correct an error or submit such information relating to his or her personal circumstances as will argue in favour of the adoption or non-adoption of the decision, or in favour of its having a specific content.[50]

[43] ibid §98.

[44] ibid §104 citing Case 5/88 *Wachauf* §22.

[45] No party argued—and the Court did not review—the lack of Community powers to adopt the directive, although under Article 63 EC prior to the Lisbon Treaty it could have been done.

[46] Case C-146/14 *Mahdi* §46, Case C-166/13 *Mukarubega* §42, Case C-249/13 *Boudjlida* §§34, 36 and 39–40, Case C-383/13 PPU *G&R* §35.

[47] Case C-383/13 PPU *G&R* §44.

[48] Case C-69/10 *Samba Diouf* §58.

[49] Case C-146/14 *Mahdi* §44.

[50] Case C-249/13 *Boudjlida* §37.

When examining compliance of the national authorities with the right to be heard, the referring judge is to consider

> whether the infringement at issue actually deprived the party relying thereon of the possibility of arguing his defence better, to the extent that the outcome of that administrative procedure could have been different.[51]

Arguing *a contrario*, a national administrative procedure would not be invalidated for a failure to comply with the right to be heard unless compliance with such a right would lead to substantive changes in the decision of the national administrative authorities. But how can the referring court know this *before* the right to be heard is actually exercised?

Second, the Court reaffirmed that fundamental rights

> do not constitute unfettered prerogatives and may be restricted, provided that the restrictions in fact correspond to objectives of general interest pursued by the measure in question and that they do not involve, with regard to the objectives pursued, a disproportionate and intolerable interference which infringes upon the very substance of the rights guaranteed.[52]

The effective attainment of the objective pursued by secondary Union law may thus justify restrictions of fundamental rights. In the context of Directive 2008/115/EC Return, for example:

> The detailed rules made to ensure that illegally staying third-country nationals are able to exercise their right to be heard prior to the adoption of a return decision must be assessed in the light of the objective of Directive 2008/115, namely, the effective return of illegally-staying third-country nationals to their countries of origin.[53]

Several conclusions followed. First, the right to an effective remedy only arises *after* the decision is taken. This is true both for asylum and return decisions. So, the duty of cooperation between the national authorities and the applicant established in Article 4(1) of Directive 2004/83/EC

> cannot be interpreted as meaning that, where a foreign national requests subsidiary protection status after he has been refused refugee status and the competent national authority is minded to reject that second application as well, the authority is on that basis obliged—before adopting its decision—to inform the applicant that it proposes to reject his application and notify him of the arguments on which it intends to base its rejection, so as to enable him to make known his views in that regard.[54]

[51] Case C-383/13 PPU *G&R* §44; for analysis see P De Bruycker and S Mananashvili, 'Audi Alteram Partem in Immigration Detention Procedures, Between the CJEU, the ECtHR and Member States: G & R' (2015) 52 *CML Rev*.

[52] Case C-249/13 *Boudjlida* §43; see also Case C-383/13 PPU *G&R* §33, Case C-166/13 *Mukarubega* §53.

[53] Case C-329/11 *Achughbabian* §39; Case C-166/13 *Mukarubega* §43; Case C-383/13 PPU *G&R* §42–43.

[54] Case C-277/11 *MM* §95.

Similarly, in the context of Directive 2008/115/EC, the right to be heard

> does not require a competent national authority to warn the third-country national, prior to the interview arranged with a view to that adoption, that it is contemplating adopting a return decision with respect to him, or to disclose to him the information on which it intends to rely as justification for that decision, or to allow him a period of reflection before seeking his observations, provided that the third-country national has the opportunity effectively to present his point of view on the subject of the illegality of his stay and the reasons which might, under national law, justify that authority refraining from adopting a return decision.[55]

Indeed, 'prior to the adoption by the competent national authority of a return decision' even the right to be assisted by a lawyer is subject to a condition that 'the exercise of that right does not affect the due progress of the return procedure and does not undermine the effective implementation of Directive 2008/115'.[56]

Second, the right to an effective remedy does not require the presence of the individual in the EU, so that while Member States' may criminalise illegal immigration,[57] 'The return … may be achieved regardless of that criminal prosecution, without requiring that prosecution to have come to an end'.[58] Nor does it require giving more than 15 days for appeal:

> With regard to abbreviated procedures, a 15-day time limit for bringing an action does not seem, generally, to be insufficient in practical terms to prepare and bring an effective action and appears reasonable and proportionate in relation to the rights and interests involved.[59]

Third, it is not necessary to hear the applicant twice if two decisions are made in the same procedure (refusal of asylum and return, or finding of illegal stay and return). Although, in the context of Directive 2004/83/EC,

> when a Member State has chosen to establish two separate procedures, one following upon the other, for examining asylum applications and applications for subsidiary protection, it is important that the applicant's right to be heard, in view of its fundamental nature, be fully guaranteed in each of those two procedures.[60]

However, when a return decision was adopted together with a rejection of an asylum application, 'the principle of effective judicial protection affords an individual a right of access to a court but not to a number of levels of jurisdiction'[61] so that no separate review procedure is necessary for the former if the national law allows to challenge the latter. On the contrary,

[55] Case C-249/13 *Boudjlida* §69.
[56] ibid §70.
[57] Case C-329/11 *Achughbabian* §28.
[58] Case C-430/11 *Sagor* §35.
[59] Case C-69/10 *Samba Diouf* §67; but see Case C-429/15 *Danqua* as concerns subsidiary protection.
[60] Case C-277/11 *MM* §91.
[61] Case C-168/13 PPU *Jeremy F* §44, Case C-69/10 *Samba Diouf* §69.

> the obligation to hear [the applicant] specifically on the subject of the return decision before the adoption of that decision would needlessly prolong the administrative procedure, without adding to the legal protection of the person concerned.[62]

It is not clear whether and to what extent such an arrangement would allow review of alternative grounds (other than asylum) capable of reversing a return decision, for instance family ties that could develop with a Union citizen or a lawfully resident third-country national during consideration of an asylum application (33 months in this case).

2. LIBERAL REVIEW OF A REPUBLICAN POLICY

The two lines of cases presented above appear contradictory: in the first line, rights of the individual trump national discretion; in the second line, the opposite takes place. The rights that trump national discretion are found in secondary law, while the rights that yield to it are found in the Charter and the ECHR. This leads to an apparent paradox: under the republican model, secondary law is enforced against national law more consistently than primary law.[63]

In order to reconcile the two lines of cases, the function of the rights-based approach identified in Chapter 2 needs to be revisited. In the internal market, rights of the individual served to enforce rules between Member States, these rules amounting to a deregulation secured through directly effective rights. Rights of the individual in Union law provided a mechanism to enforce reciprocity between the peoples of Europe without relying on the power of the state. This is true both for *non-interference* between the European polities in the internal market and a shared idea of *positive liberty* sealed by Member States in mixed external agreements. This mechanism of enforcement through directly effective rights of the individual enabled the abolition of retaliation and power politics between Member States.[64] In the internal market, the making of policy choices thus shifted from the national polities to the individual polity members; as concerns mixed external agreements, the liberty of both European polities and their polity members was thereby partially lost.[65]

The same instrumentality is traceable in the AFSJ. The characteristic of secondary EU law as rules that regulate relations between Member States is explicitly emphasised by the Court in the third line of AFSJ cases. As early as in its first asylum case, the Court reiterated that one of the key objectives pursued by

[62] Case C-166/13 *Mukarubega* §70.

[63] NB: (1) the Charter does not create any new rights per se while (2) the ECHR is not primary Union law at least until the Union accedes to the ECHR, but it is mentioned in the EU Treaties and secondary law specifically, with an explicit reference to the jurisprudence of the ECtHR, so what is at stake is the interpretation of the rights contained in secondary law in accordance with the Charter and the ECHR.

[64] Chapter 2, Section 3 and the references therein.

[65] Chapter 2, Section 5.

Regulation 343/2003/EC is 'to allow the Member States' a six-month period for arranging transfers of asylum seekers between them.[66] Should Member States, in the exercise of their powers, choose to grant individuals additional rights above those required by Union law, this choice may not prejudice their interest vis-a-vis other Member States as regards responsibility for asylum seekers.[67] The objective of 'expedition in processing asylum applications' pursued by secondary Union law and linked to guaranteeing 'effective access to the procedures for determining refugee status'[68] was not to place such Member States 'in a less favourable situation'.[69] The Court observed:

> Thus, a Member State which, in the context of transfer procedures, has decided to introduce various appeal remedies, including ones having suspensive effect, and for that reason had the time available to it to proceed with deportation of the asylum seeker reduced by the amount of time necessary for the domestic courts to rule on the merits of the case, would be placed in an awkward position, since, if it is unable to organise the transfer of the asylum seeker within the very brief period between the judicial decision on the merits of the case and the expiry of the time-limit for implementation of the transfer, it runs the risk, pursuant to Article 20(2) of Regulation No 343/2003—under which the acceptance of its responsibility by the requested Member States lapses once the time-limit for implementation of the transfer has expired—of becoming definitively the Member State responsible for processing the asylum application.[70]

In later cases the Court was even more explicit:

> Furthermore, certain provisions of Regulations Nos 343/2003 and 1560/2003 attest to an intention on the part of the EU legislature to lay down, as regards the determination of the Member State responsible for examining an asylum application, organisational rules governing the relations between the Member States, like the Dublin Convention.[71]

Specific provisions of secondary law preserving national powers to establish bilateral administrative arrangements, to have recourse 'to a conciliation procedure in which members of a committee representing three Member States not connected with the matter participate, but in which it is not envisaged that the applicant for asylum will even be heard',[72] and to 'exercise the right to grant asylum'[73] or the 'right to send an applicant to a safe third country'[74] were adduced as evidence of this. It is these rules between states or polities, their commitment to the European policy choice fleshed out in secondary law, that are enforced by the CJEU. As one author put it in relation to a broader set of CJEU cases:

> [M]ost of the great judgments which led to a constitutionalization of the Treaties are not meant to implement substantive principles, but focus instead on furthering integration

[66] Case C-19/08 *Petrosian* §§40, 41, 44.
[67] ibid §§48–50.
[68] Recital 4 Regulation 343/2003/EC.
[69] Case C-19/08 *Petrosian* §49.
[70] ibid §59.
[71] Case C-394/12 *Abdullahi* §56.
[72] ibid §58.
[73] ibid §57.
[74] Case C-695/15 PPU *Mirza* §48, see also §56 on the obligations between Member States.

through ensuring that the results of the political process, i.e. primary or secondary law, are enforced.[75]

What the CJEU enforces is not a rights-based approach but rules between the peoples of Europe. By enacting Union law, the European polities commit to a European idea of *positive liberty* expressed either in secondary (regulation of third-country nationals under the AFSJ) or primary (regulation of third-country nationals under the mixed external agreements) law. The CJEU enforces this commitment. To the extent that the rights of the individual further this idea—and enforce the commitment between the European polities—they command enforcement of an individual's rights against the actions of national authorities.[76] However, when the interest of the individual is balanced against the idea of European *positive liberty*, the latter prevails.

Priority to enforcement of European commitment is evident in review of the *residual powers of Member States*. In an EAW case, the 'objective of accelerating judicial cooperation'[77] prompted the Court to disregard the difference in wording between Article 17 Framework Decision on the one hand, and Articles 27(4) and 28(3)(c) on the other hand, finding that although the maximum time period of 90 days for making a surrender decision set out in Article 17 refers specifically to the *final* decision, while no such reference is present in Articles 27(4) and 28(3)(c), where 'the time-limit they lay down relates only to the original decision and does not concern cases in which such an appeal is brought',[78]

> [i]t would, however, be contrary to the underlying logic of the Framework Decision and to its objectives of accelerating surrender procedures if the periods for adoption of a final decision under Articles 27(4) and 28(3)(c) of the Framework Decision were longer than those laid down in Article 17.[79]

Consequently, any suspensive effect of the appeal provisions in national law 'must, in any event, comply with the time limits laid down in Article 17 of the Framework Decision for making a final Decision'.[80] The exercise of Member States' residual powers was reviewed strictly, even at the expense of the interest of the individual.

As concerns the return of illegal immigrants, from recital 17 Directive 2008/115/EC 'it is apparent that the conditions for the initial arrest of third-country nationals suspected of staying in a Member State illegally remain governed by

[75] A Von Bogdandy, 'The European Union as a Human Rights Organization? Human Rights and the Core of the European Union' (2000) 37 *CML Rev* 1325, citing J Gerkrath, *L'emergence d'un droit constitutionnel pour l'Europe* (University of Brussels, 1997) 214 et seq; R Dehousse, *The European Court of Justice* (London, Palgrave MacMillan, 1998) 36 et seq.

[76] Case C-63/15 *Ghezelbash* and Case C-115/15 *Karim*.

[77] Case C-168/13 PPU *Jeremy F* §58.

[78] ibid §72.

[79] ibid §73.

[80] ibid §74.

national law'.[81] The directive thus does not prevent detention for the purposes of identification of third-country nationals:

> [T]he objective of Directive 2008/115, namely the effective return of illegally-staying third-country nationals, would be undermined if it were impossible for Member States, by deprivation of liberty such as police custody, to prevent a person suspected of staying illegally from fleeing before his situation has even been able to be clarified.[82]

The same also applies in asylum policy, where 'neither Directive 2003/9 nor Directive 2005/85 carries out, at the present stage, a harmonisation of the grounds on which the detention of an asylum seeker may be ordered',[83] so that:

> [F]or the time being it is for Member States to establish, in full compliance with their obligations arising from both international law and European Union law, the grounds on which an asylum seeker may be detained or kept in detention.[84]

Member States may continue to detain, under the provisions of national law, third-country nationals against whom a return decision had been issued and who subsequently applied for asylum

> where it appears, after an assessment on a case-by-case basis of all the relevant circumstances, that the application was made solely to delay or jeopardise the enforcement of the return decision and that it is objectively necessary to maintain detention to prevent the person concerned from permanently evading his return.[85]

Indeed, the Court pointed to the synergies between the asylum and return directives:

> Article 23(4)(j) of Directive 2005/85 expressively provides that the fact that the applicant is making an application merely in order to delay or frustrate the enforcement of an earlier or imminent decision which would result in his removal may also be taken into account in the procedure in which that application is examined, since that fact may justify an accelerated or prioritised examination of the application. Directive 2005/85 thus ensures that Member States have the necessary instruments at their disposal to ensure the effectiveness of the return procedure by avoiding suspension of the procedure beyond what is necessary to process the application properly.[86]

Two requirements are imposed on Member States when they exercise their retained powers in the context of pursuing European *positive liberty*:

> Where neither the conditions under which observance of the rights of defence of illegally staying third-country nationals is to be ensured, nor the consequences of the infringement of those rights, are laid down by EU law, those conditions and consequences *fall within the scope of national law*, provided that *the rules* adopted to that effect *are the*

[81] Case C-329/11 *Achughbabian* §30.
[82] ibid §30.
[83] Case C-534/11 *Arslan* §55.
[84] ibid §56.
[85] ibid§63.
[86] ibid §61.

> *same as those to which individuals in comparable situations under national law are subject* (the principle of *equivalence*) and that they do not make it impossible in practice or excessively difficult to exercise the *rights conferred by the European Union legal order* (the principle of *effectiveness*).[87]

The combination of the two principles (equivalence and effectiveness) ensures that national law does not 'discriminate' between the procedure established in Union law and the procedures established in national law. A failure to respect both principles places the conditions and consequences of national rules within the scope of Union law. On the one hand, Member States enjoy a broad discretion in the exercise of their retained powers when this contributes to furthering the European idea of *positive liberty*; on the other hand, primacy of Union law is preserved and the European idea of *positive liberty* is enforced against the deviating state. This way, the Court acts as a guardian of the European idea of *positive liberty* both against external interests and against non-compliant Member States.[88] So, in the context of the EAW:

> [A]n obligation for the issuing judicial authorities to hear the requested person before such a European arrest warrant is issued would inevitably lead to the failure of the very system of surrender provided for by Framework Decision 2002/584 and, consequently, prevent the achievement of the area of freedom, security and justice, in so far as such an arrest warrant must have a certain element of surprise, in particular in order to stop the person concerned from taking flight.[89]

In another EAW case, the Court concluded that the effective attainment of the AFSJ through the establishment of forced migration schemes may prevent the national authorities from releasing a criminal suspect pending a decision on the execution of a EAW[90] even despite an explicit reference to national law.[91] While the Court recognised the ECtHR standard for the protection of liberty and security of person, the principle of effectiveness of Union law might prevent Member States from exceeding this standard.

Compliance with the commitment to *European positive liberty* is so important that it *prevails over the national constitutional structure*. In a case concerning conditions of detention for the purposes of removal of illegal immigrants, the Court found that the obligation imposed on Member States by Directive 2008/113/EC[92]

[87] Case C-249/13 *Boudjlida* §41, emphasis added; see also Case C-166/13 *Mukarubega* §51, Case C-383/13 PPU *G&R* §35.

[88] Chapter 3, Section 4, 'The Liberal and Republican Models of Legitimation in Europe'.

[89] Case C-396/11 *Radu* §40.

[90] Case C-237/15 PPU *Lanigan* § 50 and §28.

[91] Article 12 EAW.

[92] Article 16(1) Directive 2008/113/EC: 'Detention shall take place as a rule in specialised detention facilities. Where a Member State cannot provide accommodation in a specialised detention facility and is obliged to resort to prison accommodation, the third-country nationals in detention shall be kept separated from ordinary prisoners'. The CJEU interpreted the first sentence as a rule and the second sentence as a narrowly construed exception from it, concluding that 'The national authorities responsible for applying the national legislation transposing Article 16 of Directive 2008/115 must therefore be able to detain third-country nationals in specialised detention facilities'. See Joined Cases C-473 and 514/13 *Bero* §§24–29.

has precedence over their internal federal structure and division of tasks.[93] This approach to the horizontal balance between federal entities of a Member State can be contrasted with protection of the horizontal balance between Member States in the Union, as discussed above.[94]

The *European* idea of *positive liberty* also *prevails over national Constitutions*. In *Melloni*, the Court found that the objective of the Framework Decision—to establish a system of surrender based on the principles of mutual recognition and mutual trust—trumped national constitutional guarantees, such as the right to a fair trial and the rights of defence when 'the standard of protection of fundamental rights guaranteed by [a Member State] constitution ... is higher than that deriving from the Charter'.[95] The case concerned surrender of a Union citizen for the purposes of detention following his trial *in absentia* in the requesting Member State; the national authorities of the executing Member State wanted to condition the surrender 'upon the conviction being open to review in the issuing Member State, in order to avoid an adverse effect on the right to a fair trial and the rights of the defence guaranteed by its constitution'.[96] The Court disagreed and argued this decision on primacy and effectiveness: 'rules of national law, even of a constitutional order, cannot be allowed to undermine the effectiveness of EU law on the territory of that State'.[97] Casting doubt on the standard of protection of fundamental rights secured in Constitutions of other Member States and in the Charter would undermine EU systems of forced migration:

> Consequently, allowing a Member State to avail itself of Article 53 of the Charter to make the surrender of a person convicted *in absentia* conditional upon the conviction being open to review in the issuing Member State, a possibility not provided for under Framework Decision 2009/299, in order to avoid an adverse effect on the right to a fair trial and the rights of the defence guaranteed by the constitution of the executing Member State, by casting doubt on the uniformity of the standard of protection of fundamental rights as defined in that framework decision, would undermine the principles of mutual trust and recognition which that decision purports to uphold and would, therefore, compromise the efficacy of that framework decision.[98]

European positive liberty even *retracts the principles of Union citizenship in the internal market*. This is the case with the concept of integration into the host society of Union citizens. In the internal market, integration benefits Union citizens by

[93] Joined Cases C-473 and 514/13 *Bero* §§31–32.

[94] Case C-19/08 *Petrosian* §49: 'Those Member States which wished to introduce appeal remedies liable to lead to decisions having suspensive effect in the context of transfer procedures may not, for the sake of meeting the requirement of expedition, be placed in a less favourable situation than those Member States which did not deem it necessary to do so'.

[95] Case C-399/11 *Melloni* §56; For analysis see N de Boer, 'Addressing Rights Divergences under the Charter: Melloni' (2013) *CML Rev* 50: 1083–1104; LFM Besselink, 'The parameters of constitutional conflict after Melloni' (2014) 39(4) *European Law Review*.

[96] Case C-399/11 *Melloni* §55.

[97] ibid §§58–59.

[98] ibid §63.

granting them progressive rights.[99] This concept is echoed under the EAW Decision, which allows a Member State to invoke an exception from its obligation[100] to execute an EAW, subjecting the surrender 'to the condition that the person, after being heard, is returned to the executing Member State in order to serve there the custodial sentence or detention order passed against him in the issuing Member State'.[101] Although the objective of this exception is to 'increas[e] the requested person's chances of reintegrating into society',[102]

> the fact that it may be impossible for a requested person to serve his sentence in the Member State of which he is a national or resident, or even in which he is staying, is inherent in the very wording of those provisions.[103]

The establishment of a system of surrender 'for the good of the area of freedom, security and justice'[104] requires that, in cases of chain surrender, the first executing Member State 'be deprived of the possibility of relying, for the benefit of a person who is a national or resident of that State, on Articles 4(6) and 5(3) of the Framework Decision'.[105]

Such unconditional *primacy of secondary law*—policy choice made in the European political process—*is incompatible with republican legitimation.* Liberal and republican legitimation must be distinguished. Under the liberal model, legitimacy derives from the ability of Union law to secure *non-interference* through binding reciprocal deregulation (free movement in the internal market); substantive rules of Union law abolish national regulatory powers and decouple enforcement of reciprocity from the power of national polities and power politics between Member States. Secondary Union law advances Treaty objectives and rights thus contributing to *non-interference* between the national polities: it regulates national political processes securing *negative liberty* of each polity; this is its constitutional function. Under the republican model, substantive European policy choice does not have any constitutional function: it is the result of the political process but does not impose a limit on it. Legitimacy derives not from the commitment to the substance of European policy choice, which is constantly subject to change, but from the ideas of *positive liberty* of each national polity, leading each polity to accept the European policy choice as its own. Internalisation of European policy choice as every polity's own *positive liberty* ensures legitimacy and compliance with Union law. This is particularly important where the mechanism for enforcing Union law in cross-polity situations without reliance on power politics between the states is absent due to the abolition of Member State powers on the one hand

[99] eg progressive rights after five years of residence: Article 16 Directive 2004/38/EC Union Citizens.
[100] Article 4(6) EAW.
[101] Article 5(3) EAW; Case C-306/09 *I.B.* §§50–51.
[102] Case C-306/09 *I.B.* §52, Case C-123/08 *Wolzenburg* §62.
[103] Case C-192/12 PPU *West* §74.
[104] ibid §62.
[105] ibid §69.

and no concomitance of interest between the individual with *locus standi* and any European polity on the other. For policies that regulate interests thus external to Union law, enforcement of European *positive liberty* must be internal to each polity and take place through the political process rather than merely through law.

More consistent enforcement by the CJEU of European policy choice by comparison to EU primary law and enforcement of secondary law over the national Constitutions shows the focus of the CJEU on the relations between Member States. This is a clearly liberal conception of the constitutional function of Union law: by enforcing substantive EU policy choice, EU law regulates the national political process by limiting its capacity to interfere with the other Union polities. The next section shows why, under the republican model, *liberty from dependence* of each national polity falls within the scope of Union law and why the CJEU needs to refocus from the enforcement of European policy choice on to reviewing the political process in the course of which this choice is made.

3. DOMINATION OF MUTUAL TRUST AND THE FAUX VIRTUE OF SOLIDARITY

The liberal and republican models outlined above and throughout this work are ideal types, while the reality is often mixed. For instance, as regards illegal immigration, there may be a conflict of ideas at the stage of adoption (a preference for forced or voluntary return) and a conflict of interests at the stage of enforcement (such as where one polity abstains from implementing Directive 2008/115/EC Return in the expectation that illegal immigrants will instead cross the internal border into another polity). This reality points to two sources of interdependence between the European polities in the AFSJ. In both cases, legitimacy of one national polity is dependent on the legitimacy of others.[106]

The first source of interdependence between the European polities in the AFSJ is the abolition of internal borders, which leads to the conflict of interests of different polities in the EU. A policy pursued by one European polity will affect the policy pursued by the others. The abolition of internal borders results in *policy interdependence*. To the extent that the interests of different polities conflict, this interdependence is similar to the internal market and, to the extent that the interest of the individual with *locus standi* coincides with European policy choice, this conflict can be resolved under the liberal model. This interdependence is logistical: reinstitute the internal borders and it is removed. The systems of forced migration and residence permits valid for only one Member State eliminate this interdependence by virtually reinstating the internal borders.

The second source of interdependence between the European polities in the AFSJ is revealed in the systems for forced migration. The limits that these systems set on the liberty of the individual require that each participating Member State

[106] For the concept of legitimacy that is based on the three aspects of liberty that result in Loyalty see Chapter 1.

respect international human rights law, the Geneva Convention and the ECHR.[107] EU Member States are thus deemed safe countries of origin and destination for people.[108] Lawfulness and legitimacy of the entire system and of each national polity in it is premised on the respect by each participating polity for the norms that constitute and validate its polity and legal order internally and externally. This creates *constitutional interdependence*, similar to the interdependence between the national political processes in the European political space, where legitimacy of one polity, its legal order and policy choice is linked to securing Voice or representation of interests in each political process that composes the European political space.[109] It is not merely logistical interdependence that can be remedied by closing the internal borders: eliminating this interdependence would require dismantling of the three systems of forced migration created in Union law. Indeed, it would require dismantling of all republican policies of the Union.

The CJEU approached constitutional interdependence in the AFSJ through the same *mutual recognition* lens as logistical interdependence in the internal market. The principle of mutual recognition originated in the internal market with the free movement of goods and the famous judgment in *Cassis de Dijon*.[110] In this case, the Court established that there was 'no valid reason why' goods 'lawfully produced and marketed in one of the Member States ... should not be introduced into any other Member State' and that the sale of such goods could not be subject to a legal prohibition on their marketing across Member States. The Court rejected the claim advanced by Germany that its prohibition to market a French liquor with alcohol content below what was provided in German law was based on a twofold consideration of the need to protect consumers and the need to protect public health. Once national authorities of one Member State allowed the product onto its market, other Member States could not jeopardise 'the free movement of goods, which constitutes one of the fundamental rules of the Community' by placing additional requirements on the marketing of these products. Thus, mutual recognition amounted to partial deregulation pending a shared standard set in the EU. As for complete deregulation in the internal market, any exceptions to the principle of mutual recognition must serve 'the general interest' and be

[107] As regards immigration, *The Stockholm Programme* (3.3.2010) Council doc 5731/10, 109; *Communication on Migration* (4.5.2011) COM (2011) 248 final, 9; Council Directive 2001/40/EC on the mutual recognition of decisions on the expulsion of third country nationals. As regards criminal law, Framework Decision 2002/584/JHA on the European Arrest Warrant, discussed below. As regards asylum, Protocol 24 to the Lisbon Treaty institutes a presumption of a high level of protection of fundamental rights and freedoms in all Member States, which are thus deemed to constitute safe countries of origin for the purposes of the 1951 Refugee Convention.

[108] It is not possible for a national of one Member State to claim asylum in another Member State: Protocol 24 TFEU and Case C-306/09 *I.B.* §44.

[109] Chapter 3, Section 5.

[110] Case 120/78 *Cassis de Dijon*. See also C Janssens, *The Development of the Principle of Mutual Recognition in the Secondary Legislation* (Oxford, Oxford University Press, 2014) and F Kostoris and P Schioppa (eds), *The Principle of Mutual Recognition in the European Integration Process* (Basingstoke, Palgrave Macmillan, 2005).

proportionate to the aim they pursue. Without harmonising national rules on product specifications, mutual recognition buttressed the effectiveness of the internal market and primacy of Union law; the requirement of aiming to serve the general interest and proportionality to this aim also provided the necessary buffer against the under-representation problem faced by out-of-state producers and importers—it is a constitutional guarantee in EU law that regulates the national political process. The principle of mutual recognition was extended to free movement of persons, with an obligation of Member States to recognise each other's nationality decisions.[111]

In the internal market, mutual recognition operates in relation to the regulatory choices, ie the ideas about *positive liberty* that result from the national political processes, and is based on a twofold presumption that (1) each European polity is subdivided into identical or similar interest groups, and (2) all the groups are represented in each national political process. This allowed for 'virtual representation'[112] of mobile Union citizens in their host polity, while EU law protected from the political process the interests that were not so represented. This mechanism of 'virtual representation' enjoyed not only formal legitimacy on the level of polities who ratified the Treaties but an additional consent on the level of each individual to whom it applied: virtual representation is triggered by voluntary migration to another polity. The exercise of free movement thus constitutes an implicit consent to virtual representation: it is internalised, a part of the individual's idea of *positive liberty*.[113] Liberty and legitimacy are safeguarded despite the interdependence.

Mutual recognition under the AFSJ imposes a requirement more restrictive of liberty that risks undermining legitimacy of both the EU and national legal orders. Three elements contribute to this. First, differently from the internal market, under the AFSJ mutual recognition applies not (only) to the outcomes of the political process but (also) to the norms of constitutional law, ie rules of the political process that are constitutive of the national political communities. Union law does not offer rules that regulate the national political process under the AFSJ in a way that would be similar to the requirement of aiming to serve the general interest and the proportionality to this aim in EU free movement law. Under the principle of mutual recognition as pronounced in *Melloni*, the peoples of Europe are not only obliged to respect each other's national constitutional identities but to substitute their own constitutional identity for a shared identity developed in secondary law. A crucial element of the national political identity—one of the fundamental rights[114]—can be harmonised at Union level through secondary law,

[111] Chapter 2, Section 1; Case C-369/90 *Micheletti* and Case C-135/08 *Rottmann*.

[112] A Somek, *The Cosmopolitan Constitution* (Oxford, Oxford University Press, 2014) 26–27.

[113] This is not so for goods and services provided from other Member States; EU competition and state aids law compensated for this, see Section 4 below.

[114] Fundamental rights are constitutive of national political identities inasmuch as they enable a certain type of interest representation in and protection from the political process; while some fundamental rights are absolute under the system of the Council of Europe, eg abolition of the death

an equivalent to changing the Constitution by ordinary law.[115] An obvious risk of minoritarian bias occurs: by shifting law making to Europe, national governments can not only circumvent accountability in their national political processes in the course of making unpopular policy choices but de facto change the national Constitutions, creating a risk of *domination* of national polities by vested interests and by their own political elites.

Second, constitutional interdependence is created whereby the legitimacy of shared rules and of each national legal order that incorporates them depends on compliance by each national polity. For instance, Article 5(1) EAW requires that Member States rely on a statement by a requesting Member State that the European level of protection of constitutional guarantees has been observed. Similarly, the CEAS 'was conceived in a context making it possible to assume that all the participating States, whether Member States or third States, observe fundamental rights'[116] and 'maintain the credibility of the protection system'.[117] Requiring a political community to rely on another polity for the elements of its constitutional identity refutes and suppresses differences between them. This conception of mutual recognition is based on the assumption of equivalence and interchangeability in the eyes of polity members internally and as perceived by the interlocutors of the EU and its polities externally. Beyond mere equivalence of interests for the purpose of virtual representation, this is an equivalence of identities of all the peoples of Europe as polities: equivalence in the extent the interests of individual polity members are represented in the national political process—the constitutional identity of each European polity.[118] In a long line of cases, the CJEU confirmed that the AFSJ

> is based on the fundamental premiss [*sic*] that each Member State shares with all the other Member States, and recognises that they share with it, a set of common values on which the EU is founded, as stated in Article 2 TEU. That premiss [*sic*] implies and justifies the existence of mutual trust between the Member States that those values will be recognised and, therefore, that the law of the EU that implements them will be respected.[119]

The Court thus requires 'yielding to the authority of another "so long as" this other respects a threshold level of constitutional decency'.[120] Reliance on another

penalty, most of them allow a variety of interpretations and it is these interpretations that constitute the identity of each national polity, eg ECtHR Case *Lautsi v Italy* (18.3.2011) and ECtHR Case *SAS v France* (1.7.2014).

[115] Case C-399/11 *Melloni* §§62–63: the Court took for granted constitutionality of Article 2 Framework Decision 2009/299 and enforced this standard not only as a shared minimum but as a maximum of protection afforded by the right to a fair trial.

[116] Case C-394/12 *Abdullahi* §52.

[117] Joined Cases C-57 and 101/09 *B&D* §115.

[118] For more on identity and the different aspects thereof see G Gasser and M Stefan (eds), *Personal Identity: Complex or Simple?* (Cambridge, Cambridge University Press, 2012); H Harris (ed), *Identity* (Oxford, Oxford University Press, 1995).

[119] Opinion 2/13 ECHR §168.

[120] Somek (n 112) 19. Somek calls it 'mutual embedding' between legal orders, see pp 196, 200–01.

polity for one's own constitutional identity can only be legitimate if all the national polities perceive themselves as being 'of the same kind' or 'substantively homogeneous'[121]—in other words, if differences between them either do not exist or are immaterial for polity members. These differences pertain not to the national language or typical cuisine but to the structure and functioning of the national political process. Accepting the constitutional identity of another people as its own implies equivalence in the structure of interest representation: there is a presumption 'that all EU Member States are equally democratic'.[122] Requiring the renunciation of one's own identity as a political community goes against the letter of the Treaties, which guarantee continuity of the peoples of Europe as distinct political communities.[123] Furthermore, this requirement goes against the spirit of the Treaties inasmuch as legitimacy of the European political process is premised on the continuous legitimacy of the national political processes and on the ability to internalise a shared European idea of *positive liberty* through them. Engaging in meaningful relationships with others without one's own sense of identity will merely lead to *dependence* as opposed to Loyalty based on liberty.

Third, there is no mechanism to enforce such equivalence. In the internal market, mutual recognition of policy choices made in the national political processes and the principles of mutual trust related to it were buttressed by a mechanism in EU law that corrected three situations of under-representation of cross-polity interests in the national political process.[124] No similar mechanism is in place under the AFSJ. While EU law creates a situation where legitimacy of each national polity is intertwined with the legitimacy of others, there is no mechanism in Union law to ensure that the polity shift from Member States to the EU does not diminish liberty in the Union.[125] The obligation of mutual recognition based on trust thus collapses into dependence and introduces power politics back into relations between Member States.[126] EU free movement law promoted mutual trust by securing a certainty of expectation—the expectation that power politics between Member States was abolished. Without abolishing power politics, enforcing mutual reliance

[121] ibid 21.

[122] C Closa, 'Supranational Citizenship and Democracy: Normative and Empirical Dimensions' in M La Torre (ed), *European Citizenship. An Institutional Challenge* (The Hague, Kluwer Law International, 1998) 432.

[123] Article 4(2) TEU (respect for political and constitutional identities of Member States) and Article 67(1) TFEU ('respect of fundamental rights and the different legal systems and traditions of the Member States' in the AFSJ): these articles are about *non-interference* with the national constitutional guarantees; yet, *non-interference* is impossible under the republican model.

[124] Chapter 2, Section 1.

[125] For instance, Article 5(1) EAW expressly rules out any possibility of review where the requesting Member State merely 'states' that the criteria for the right to a fair trial have been respected; where the decision is final, this may mean no possibility of review either on the initiative of the person concerned or of the Member State that executes the EAW.

[126] Somek (n 112) 197: 'The "constitution" of the interaction between and among internally monistic systems is political in the sense that it comprises merely political processes whose patterns may actually reflect power differentials'.

in EU law promotes dependence and domination, not trust. Crucially, the deficit in the political autonomy of individual European polities between each other (dependence) is likely to be replicated in relations with non-EU polities resulting in external dependence of the peoples of Europe.

Following a number of warnings from the European peoples and constitutional courts,[127] the extent of *constitutional dependence* created under the AFSJ was accentuated by a body external to the system of Union law.[128] The ECtHR found that, because Greece did not respect the ECHR prohibition of inhuman and degrading treatment, Belgium breached its ECHR obligations of *non-refoulement* by returning an asylum seeker to Greece under the CEAS.[129] Following this judgment, two options were available to the CJEU for preserving legitimacy of the Union and Member States: (1) suspend the provisions of the CEAS incompatible with the ECHR (in particular, forced migration) leaving the rest of EU asylum law intact or (2) invalidate the CEAS in its entirety. In line with its previous case law, where the CJEU understood its role of the guardian of the Treaties[130] as protecting the idea of *positive liberty* contained in EU primary and secondary law, the CJEU chose the former option. Faced with the eventuality that the CEAS could be invalidated entirely,[131] the CJEU conceded that the presumption of compliance by all Member States with fundamental rights, on which the CEAS is founded, 'must be regarded as rebuttable'.[132] Where it is so rebutted, Member States are now obliged not to transfer asylum seekers between them:

> [T]o ensure compliance by the European Union and its Member States with their obligations concerning the protection of the fundamental rights of asylum seekers, the Member States, including the national courts, may not transfer an asylum seeker to the 'Member State responsible' within the meaning of Regulation No 343/2003 where they cannot be unaware that systemic deficiencies in the asylum procedure and in the reception

[127] Failed constitutional referenda, falling turnout in EP elections, cases from the national constitutional courts, in particular the BVG, see eg the Lisbon Judgment, Judgment of 30 June 2009, 2 BvE 2/08, 2 BvE 5/08, 2 BvR 1010/08, 2 BvR 1022/08, 2 BvR 1259/08 and 2 BvR 182/09. Somek (n 112) 204, 214: 'Widespread low voter turnout is a smart reaction to the de facto dethronement of politics'.

[128] This is coherent with the position of the ECtHR to recognise and even emphasise the importance of national constitutional identity: ECtHR Case *Lautsi v Italy* (18.3.2011), ECtHR Case *SAS v France* (1.7.2014).

[129] ECtHR Case *MSS v Belgium and Greece* (21 January 2011) Application no 30696/09; Joined Cases C-411 and 493/10 *NS*; see also M den Heijer, 'Joined Cases C-411 & 493/10, *N.S. v. Secretary of State for the Home Department and M.E. and Others v. Refugee Applications Commissioner, Minister for Justice, Equality and Law Reform*, Judgment of the Court (Grand Chamber) of 21 December 2011, nyr.' (2012) 49 *CML Rev*; F Billing, 'The Parallel Between Non-removal of Asylum Seekers and Non-execution of a European Arrest Warrant on Human Rights Grounds: The CJEU Case of N.S. v Secretary of State for the Home Department' (2012) 1 *European Constitutional Law Review*.

[130] Article 19(1) TEU: 'The Court of Justice of the European Union … shall ensure that in the interpretation and application of the Treaties the law is observed'.

[131] Joined Cases C-411 and 493/10 *NS* §100: 'could itself be regarded as undermining the safeguards which are intended to ensure compliance with fundamental rights by the European Union and its Member States'.

[132] ibid §104.

> conditions of asylum seekers in that Member State amount to substantial grounds for believing that the asylum seeker would face a real risk of being subjected to inhuman or degrading treatment within the meaning of Article 4 of the Charter.[133]

The extent of 'systemic deficiencies'[134] and the absence of any unconditional obligation to assume responsibility for asylum seekers by the Member State where they are present[135] are only secondary. The principle of mutual recognition that denied national constitutional identity was dismantled:

> [A]n application of Regulation No 343/2003 on the basis of the conclusive presumption that the asylum seeker's fundamental rights will be observed in the Member State primarily responsible for his application is incompatible with the duty of the Member States to interpret and apply Regulation No 343/2003 in a manner consistent with fundamental rights.[136]

This partial suspension of the CEAS was enabled by a disconnect in its structure. The CEAS contains two types of rules: (1) a commitment by all European polities to an idea of *positive liberty* concerning the status and rights of third-country nationals and (2) rules pertaining to forced migration the purpose of which is to ensure *non-interference* between the European polities by limiting their logistical interdependence created by the abolition of internal borders. This structure of Union law was inherited from the internal market, where legitimacy of (2) depends on there being (1): legitimacy of the limits on the national political process in Union law was buffered by rights of the individual that secured 'virtual representation'. However, under the republican model, legitimacy of (2) is not related to (1): the limits placed on the political process cannot be legitimated by its outcome. The two types of rules are disconnected. (2) can be suspended while (1) is preserved.

The system for the transfer of people between Member States under the CEAS addressed logistical interdependence between the peoples of Europe that resulted from the abolition of internal borders; simultaneously, this system of forced migration created constitutional interdependence. Now, this constitutional interdependence was removed by suspending transfers of asylum seekers; logistical interdependence was reinstated and Member States once again could not insulate themselves from each other's regulatory choices. However, now it is not merely factual but by virtue of Union law. A Member State may be *required by Union law* to take charge of asylum seekers who enter the Union through other Member States.

[133] ibid §94.

[134] Severely limited by the Court to situations where the other Member States 'cannot be unaware' of 'systemic deficiencies' that would 'amount to substantial grounds for believing' that the Member State does not respect the ECHR, ibid §106.

[135] Case C-4/11 *Puid* §29 and §§33–34.

[136] Joined Cases C-411 and 493/10 *NS* §99.

This principle of co-responsibility or solidarity, once established, quickly spread into other cases. In a case concerning the financial burden for the reception of asylum seekers under Directive 2003/9/EC, the Court found that:

> a Member State in receipt of an application for asylum is obliged to grant the minimum conditions for reception of asylum seekers laid down in Directive 2003/09 even to an asylum seeker in respect of whom it decides, under Regulation No 343/2003, to call upon another Member State, as the Member State responsible for examining his application for asylum, to take charge of or take back that applicant.[137]

This obligation 'ceases when that same applicant is actually transferred by the requesting Member State, and the financial burden of granting those minimum conditions is to be assumed by that requesting Member State, which is subject to that obligation'.[138] This can be contrasted with the *non-interference* position taken by the Court in free movement cases, ensuring that Union citizens do not become 'an unreasonable burden on the social assistance system of the host Member State'[139] even where the host Member State issues the Union citizen 'a residence certificate of unlimited duration (*unbefristete Freizügigkeits-bescheinigung*) for EU nationals'.[140]

Solidarity between Member States arises not only as a result of shortcomings in the protection of human rights by the state, but also due to the factual situation of the asylum seeker. Thus, in two cases humanitarian considerations led the Court to give a broad interpretation to the rules on assigning responsibility between Member States for examination of asylum claims under Regulation 343/2003/EC. In the first case, an asylum seeker who illegally entered Poland and then illegally moved to Austria claimed that her daughter-in-law and grandchildren, all lawfully resident in Austria, depended on her care for them due to a serious illness and handicap of the daughter-in-law. The case turned on the interpretation of Article 15(1), (2) and (4) Regulation 343/2003/EC. Three issues arose: first, whether the term 'another relative' in Article 15(2) was to be interpreted more broadly than the term 'family members' defined in Article 2(i): the Court stated that it was;[141] second, whether Article 15(2) only concerned situations where asylum seeker was dependent on the relative or also vice versa: the Court found that both cases were covered;[142] third, whether Article 15(2) was a mandatory obligation on the national authorities, or whether it required, pursuant to Article 15(1), a request from the Member State where the first application for asylum was made and/or, pursuant to Article 15(4), an agreement of the national authorities to assume responsibility: the Court found that Article 15(2) was mandatory and neither a request nor agreement of the national authorities were needed. As a result,

[137] Case C-179/11 *Cimade* §50.
[138] ibid §61.
[139] Case C-333/13 *Dano* §74.
[140] ibid §36.
[141] Case C-245/11 *K* §§38–43.
[142] ibid §§32–37.

> Article 15(2) of Regulation No 343/2003 must be interpreted as meaning that a Member State which is not responsible for examining an application for asylum pursuant to the criteria laid down in Chapter III of that regulation becomes so responsible. It is for the Member State which has become the responsible Member State within the meaning of that regulation to assume the obligations which go along with that responsibility.[143]

The second case concerned an unaccompanied minor without any relatives in the EU who submitted two asylum applications in different Member States and a question arose as to whether Regulation 343/2003/EC allowed the second Member State to send the minor back to the first Member State. The Court found that it did not:

> Since unaccompanied minors form a category of particularly vulnerable persons, it is important not to prolong more than is strictly necessary the procedure for determining the Member State responsible, which means that, as a rule, unaccompanied minors should not be transferred to another Member State.[144]

This, however, was not apparent from the Regulation, where the second paragraph of Article 6 simply states: 'In the absence of a family member, the Member State responsible for examining the application shall be that where the minor has lodged his or her application for asylum'. Two aspects contributed to this interpretation. First, the Court considered the intent of the Union legislature[145] and, second, the best interests of the child.[146] In both cases, humanitarian considerations trumped rules between Member States on responsibility for asylum seekers. Rules of secondary Union law on forced transfers of people were suspended when their application could infringe human rights—an external norm legitimating each European people as a polity.

These cases reveal that *constitutional dependence* takes place on two levels. First, Member States rely on each other for interest representation in their national political processes. As discussed in the previous chapter, the European political process is necessarily composed of the national political processes, whereby legitimacy of the European idea of *positive liberty* is tied to the ability of each national political process to represent and protect the interests that compose its polity. This creates constitutional interdependence *internal* to the Union: it concerns the national constitutional identity of each European polity and compatibility between them. Second, Member States rely on each other for compliance with international obligations that determine their external legitimacy, in particular international human rights law. The EU systems of forced migration might lose legitimacy and be outlawed by a court that does not belong to EU legal order if any of the participating Member States fails to respect these international law constraints. This constitutional interdependence is *external* to the Union: it concerns the international constitutional identity of each European polity and the Union

143 ibid §54.
144 Case C-648/11 *MA* §55.
145 ibid §§52–53: this is a very basic textual analysis without recourse to the *travaux preparatoires*.
146 ibid §§59–61.

as a whole. In both internal and external dimensions, constitutional interdependence thus affects the very ability of the polity to identify and pursue its own idea of *positive liberty*. It is a problem of political culture, interest representation, ability to take charge of one's own future: 'things that shape a society's political will'.[147]

Yet, solidarity as developed by the CJEU does not solve these problems of interdependence nor does it require any solutions: it merely shifts responsibility from one polity to the next. This conception of solidarity is not about constitutional structures, political autonomy and interest representation but about redistribution of costs and benefits between polities. Such redistribution at Union level could only be legitimised if each people of Europe internalised this particular conception of justice through its national political process. Without a European political process in the course of which to debate, develop and constantly readjust the European conception of solidarity,

> there can be no true social contract capable of legitimising the emerging European polity and the consequences would be either a return to a less advanced form of integration (including a reduction of majoritarian decision-making and stricter limits on European competences) or, if the current model continues to be stretched, a crisis of social legitimacy which may manifest itself in increased national challenges to European policies (whose redistributive effects are not understood and accepted).[148]

In the choice between these two options, the CJEU favoured the latter. Solidarity as defined and dictated by the Court undermines the political autonomy of the peoples of Europe in two fundamental ways. First, by identifying what constitutes solidarity, the Court denies each polity's political autonomy as the ability to identify and internalise the European idea of *positive liberty*. Each European polity's own identity and capacity to identify and pursue its own idea of *positive liberty* without domination and interference by others is needed in order to accept European policy choice as its own. Only those peoples who are able to identify and pursue their own idea of *positive liberty* can engage in reciprocal cooperation with others, internalise shared choices and 'become willing to make sacrifices for each other'.[149] Lack of ability to identify one's own idea of *positive liberty* results in *dependence* on others for policy choice; lack of ability to further one's own idea of *positive liberty* results in *domination* of polity. Aside from the permanent cross-polity conflicts of interests regulated through *non-interference* under the liberal model, the protection of one specific policy choice or conception of fundamental rights in Union law interferes with the choices made in the national political processes, undermining interest representation and political autonomy of the peoples of Europe. 'As a result, the use of the political process would become largely superfluous'.[150]

147 Rawls (n 1) 106.

148 M Poiares Maduro, 'Europe's Social Self: "The Sickness unto Death"' in J Shaw (ed), *Social Law and Policy in an Evolving EU* (Oxford, Hart Publishing, 2000) 347.

149 Rawls (n 1) 113. Rawls talks about well-ordered peoples, by which he means political autonomy and adherence to the principles of justice within each polity.

150 A Somek, 'From Workers to Migrants, from Distributive Justice to Inclusion: Exploring the Changing Social Democratic Imagination' (2012) 18(5) *European Law Journal*. Somek argues this in

Second, the substance of the principle of solidarity as conceived in the above-surveyed case law reintroduces power politics between the peoples of Europe. This weakens Peace as non-domination of peoples composing the Union. EU law not only fails to secure *non-interference* between the peoples of Europe but, on the contrary, now requires it. However, this is not a return to the point of departure, when abolition of internal borders created a de facto interdependence between the national polities. A very important step is taken and it concerns primacy of Union law. When constitutional interdependence is present (and it is of the kind that may question the legitimacy of Union law), secondary law is suspended: constitutional *dependence* between national polities and their loss of external legitimacy is avoided at the cost of reinstating their logistical interdependence and power politics between Member States. Secondary law can be suspended—it no longer enjoys unconditional primacy—in the face of norms that define a polity. This is inevitable under republican legitimation: *rules that result from the political process cannot have primacy over the rules that enable it.*

Reliance of the republican model for Europe on each European people as a political community dismantles unconditional primacy of Union law. The composite nature of the European political process and the need to internalise European policy choice as a part of the national idea of *positive liberty* require political autonomy of each European polity. This autonomy is pursued in the national political process defined and enabled by the constitutional norms that legitimate each polity internally and externally. It follows that the outcome of the European political process—a process that is composed of the national political processes—cannot have primacy over the national Constitutions and validating norms of international law. The principle of *primacy* of Union law must be adjusted to the republican model allowing secondary Union law be set aside in the face of norms that constitute each national polity. Although judgments of the CJEU have been contradictory, the recent precedents confirm that norms constitutive of external legitimacy (the ECHR) trump secondary Union law.[151] Under the republican model of legitimacy, norms that constitute each European people as a political community will need to prevail over EU policy choice.

In the next and last section, I argue that in its development of the solidarity principle, the Court has been choosing between the wrong options. Solidarity in relation to EU migration law is contained in Article 80 TFEU. The broad formulation of this principle in the Treaty clearly indicates the need for a political process to establish the content for the principle (policy choice). The alternative to balancing between less integration and less legitimacy—the constitutional choice made by the CJEU—is to use EU constitutional law for advancing *liberty from dependence* in the course of the political process.

the context of collective action (*Viking* and *Laval*) cases but the same could be the case for immigration rules connected to Union citizenship (*Metock* and *Zambrano*).

[151] Joined Cases C-411 and 493/10 *NS* and Joined Cases C-404/15 and C-659/15 PPU *Aranyosi and Căldăraru*.

4. THE INVISIBLE LIBERTY

Political autonomy—*liberty from dependence*—of the peoples of Europe lies at the foundation of Europe's constitutional construct. As a matter internal to each national polity, it is an 'invisible liberty' in Union law. Yet, this is not a liberty that Union law ignores—quite the opposite. The Treaties safeguard the political identity of each people of Europe[152]—and so does the structure of Union law. Political autonomy of each national polity is an element of the republican Europe that entered EC law when the principles of primacy and direct effect introduced by the CJEU were accepted in national polities. Primacy and direct effect foreclosed Exit based on voluntary acceptance, which implies sharing the idea of *positive liberty* as life together under the rules of EC law.[153] This is an instance of Loyalty premised on the ability of each European polity to identify and pursue its own idea of 'ideal life'. Since then, hardly any Union policy does not present elements of republican legitimation.

Indeed, *liberty from dependence* was advanced by the Court long before the Treaty of Lisbon. Cases such as *Schmidberger*,[154] *Omega*,[155] *Sunday Trading*,[156] *ERT*,[157] *Viking*[158] and *Laval*[159] highlight clearly republican issues in EU internal market law. On the one hand, these cases present a tension between each polity's national conception of values and fundamental rights—ideas and norms that constitute and define each polity—and the pursuit of *non-interference* in Union law (1).[160] On the other hand, they underscore how Union law opens up Exit for vested minority interests from the national political process to the EU, which could undermine legitimacy of the national and European policies (2). The *Schmidberger* and *Omega* cases belong to the first group, *Sunday trading* and *ERT* to the second, while *Viking* and *Laval* exhibit a trade-off between the liberal and the republican conceptions of Europe: *non-interference* with the interests of other polities versus the Exit from the national political process of vested interests

[152] Articles 9–12 TEU; Article 7 TFEU requires enforcement by Member States thus reintroducing power politics in relations between polities in the Union.

[153] This, however, is not what made EC law different and unique by comparison to international law, see B de Witte, 'The European Union as an International Legal Experiment' in G de Burca and JHH Weiler (eds), *The Worlds of European Constitutionalism* (Cambridge, Cambridge University Press, 2012). What made EC law stronger than other forms of international law is the *locus standi* for individuals as a tool of reciprocal abolition of powers of the state, see E Guild, *European Community Law from a Migrant's Perspective* (The Hague, Kluwer Law International, 2000).

[154] Case C-112/00 *Schmidberger.*

[155] Case C-36/02 *Omega.*

[156] Case 145/88 *Torfaen Borough Council* and Case 169/91 *Stoke-on-Trent City Council.*

[157] Case C-260/89 *ERT.*

[158] Case C-438/05 *Viking Line.*

[159] Case C-341/05 *Laval.*

[160] J Rawls and P van Parijs 'Three Letters on *The Law of Peoples* and the European Union' (2003) 7(1) *Revue de Philosophie Économique*: 'Isn't there a conflict between a large free and open market comprising all of Europe and the individual nation-states, each with its separate political and social institutions, historical memories, and forms and traditions of social policy. Surely these are great value to the citizens of these countries and give meaning to their life'.

(*Viking*) and the ability of every polity to pursue its idea of 'ideal life' (*Laval*). This trade-off between the two conceptions of legitimacy in Europe render the latter two cases particularly controversial.

These two dangers to *liberty from dependence* were addressed by the Court by adjusting the *scope of Union law*. In situations where *non-interference* is balanced against *liberty from dependence*, the scope of Union law is restricted: *liberty from dependence* prevails. So, in the context of EU free movement law, the Court conceded that the abolition of nobility titles in national constitutional law 'as an element of national identity, may be taken into consideration when a balance is struck between legitimate interests [of national polities] and the right of free movement of persons recognised under European Union law'.[161] In a similar manner, derogations from free movement of goods are allowed where the national constitutional norm seeks to guarantee 'the level of protection of human dignity'[162] or 'freedom of expression and freedom of assembly'[163] in the national polity and is proportionate to this goal. These and many more cases[164] accord with the ECtHR case law where, while setting some absolute rights (eg the abolition of the death penalty or prohibition of torture), significant leeway is given for variation between the constitutive elements of peoples as polities, leaving issues of constitutional choice such as access to the national territory,[165] religious expression[166] and 'indispensable element[s] of community life within the society in question'[167] that ensure the 'minimum requirement of civility that is necessary for social interaction'[168] to the autonomy of each national polity.

Conversely, in cases where Union law applies against private interests (undertakings or states acting as such),[169] the scope of Union law is extended. So, in the context of market freedoms, the Court examined whether the national law respected 'the general principle of freedom of expression embodied in Article 10 [ECHR]'.[170] In the context of EC competition law,[171] the Court engaged in an

[161] Case C-208/09 *Sayn-Wittgenstein* §83; see also Case C-438/14 *Bogendorff von Wolffersdorff.*

[162] Case C-36/02 *Omega* §39.

[163] Case C-112/00 *Schmidberger* §69.

[164] *Ex multis* Case C-348/09 *I* §21, Case C-268/99 *Jany* §60: 'European Union law does not impose on Member States a uniform scale of values as regards the assessment of conduct which may be considered to be contrary to public security'. Case C-36/02 *Omega* §37: 'It is not indispensable in that respect for the restrictive measure issued by the authorities of a Member State to correspond to a conception shared by all Member States as regards the precise way in which the fundamental right or legitimate interest in question is to be protected'.

[165] ECtHR Case *Abdulaziz, Cabales and Balkandali v UK* (28.05.1985) §67; ECtHR Case *Chahal v UK* (15.11.1996) §73; ECtHR Case *Hode and Abdi v UK* (6.11.2012) §43.

[166] ECtHR Case *Lautsi v Italy* (18.3.2011).

[167] ECtHR Case *SAS v France* (1.7.2014) §122.

[168] ibid §141.

[169] This is a regulatory element typical of the republican model (based on shared *positive liberty*) as opposed to free movement law that regulates states (based on *non-interference*).

[170] Case C-260/89 *ERT.*

[171] *Ex multis*, Case C-35/99 *Arduino*; Joined Cases C-94/04 and C-202/04 *Cipolla and Macrino*; Joined Cases C-264,306,354 and 355/01 *AOK Bundesverband*; Joined Cases C-367/98, C-483/99 and C-503/99 *Golden Shares.*

inquiry as to 'whether the state's legislative process is dominated by a concern to protect the public interest, or, conversely, whether the degree to which private interests are being taken into account is likely to alter the overriding objective of the state measure'.[172] The Court thus reviewed the *national* political process, not merely compliance with substantive Union law. Similarly, though perhaps less surprisingly, in external relations, the CJEU accords significant freedom of action to Union institutions in the making of policy choices, reviewing instead the process with which this choice is made.[173] For policies characterised by strong republican features, the Court is increasingly willing to refocus from enforcing compliance with the substance of European policy choice, interpreted strictly, to reviewing the political process with which the policy choice is made. Considering the composite nature of the European political process, where accountability and internalisation of policy choice remain grounded in the national political space, interest representation in the national political process necessarily becomes subject of constitutional review in Union law.

The same approach used by the Court for ensuring *non-interference* in the internal market can be used to secure *liberty from dependence* in Europe's political union. Review by the Court of constitutional safeguards for interest representation in the national political process can be developed into a comprehensive system of basic constitutional guarantees. In republican policies that address conflicts of ideas between the peoples of Europe, departure from unconditional primacy of secondary Union law must be accompanied by the extension in the scope of EU law's constitutional provisions—rules that secure Voice in the political process—to the national political process, including actions brought by Union citizens against own polity (so-called purely internal situations). Such constitutional review in Union law of the political process would ensure against capture by vested interests, complementing *non-interference* between the national polities. EU constitutional law would secure liberty in the European political space by providing counter-minoritarian and counter-majoritarian guarantees of *liberty from dependence* that cannot the secured in national constitutional laws (in situations where the political process extends beyond any single polity). Together, the liberal and republican constitutional guarantees would advance liberty as non-domination for every polity in the EU and thus build Loyalty among the peoples of Europe.

[172] M Poiares Maduro, 'The Chameleon State. EU Law and the Blurring of the Private/Public Distinction in the Market' in R Nickel (ed), *Conflict of Laws and Laws of Conflict in Europe and Beyond* (Antwerp, Intersentia, 2010) 286.

[173] See M Cremona, 'A Reticent Court? Policy Objectives and the Court of Justice' in M Cremona and A Thies (eds), *The European Court of Justice and External Relations Law: Constitutional Challenges* (Oxford, Hart Publishing, 2014) 15.

6

Conclusion

Union Law as the Pacifier of Conflicts

The release of atomic power has changed everything except our way of thinking.
Albert Einstein (1945)

CONSTITUTIONAL ORDERS CONSTITUTE political communities—and international orders deriving from them—by managing conflicts that threaten Peace. In his book *The Shield of Achilles*, Philip Bobbitt showed how constitutional structures and institutions that are developed in one era give birth to a new world where the role of these institutions is either diminished or has to undergo a drastic change.[1] Successful constitutional order reduces the threat to Peace posed by the conflicts it was designed to manage and brings about a world where these conflicts grow relatively less important. Together with their importance, the relevance of the constitutional order declines. Other types of conflict emerge and begin to threaten Peace. The constitutional order needs to adjust if it is to manage these newly important conflicts. A failure to adjust will lead to the order's demise and its replacement by another order, the one better suited for managing the type of conflicts relevant in the world generated by the outgoing order. A similar evolution takes place in a 'society of states' whose Constitutions 'are always written at peace conferences, which occur at the end of epochal wars'.[2] This book has traced the evolution of conflicts and adjustments to them in EU constitutional law.

The EU legal order was established with the promise of Peace between the peoples of Europe. Europe had been torn apart in conflicts resulting from domination attempts of one European people by another. To paraphrase another author, the essential element of the notion of Union power in Community law was not to secure centralisation in the Community but to secure independence of each

[1] P Bobbitt, *The Shield of Achilles: War, Peace and the Course of History* (New York, Knopf, 2002).
[2] D Patterson, 'The New Leviathan' (2003) 101 *Michigan Law Review* 1715, fn 16.

European people from others.[3] Today, 70 years later, domination no longer implies a war. The ability of a people to govern, make policy choices and pursue its own goals can be vanquished without the military. Domination can be imposed by different means. Both the nature of conquest and sources of domination have changed. Liberty of polities is closely linked to governance, which can be undermined from three different sources: (1) domination between polities in the Union, (2) domination of EU polities by external interests, and (3) domination of each polity by vested interests. Between the peoples of Europe, there is a potential for interference of one European polity with the interests and political autonomy of another. This is the original EC law understanding of Peace. Vis-a-vis interests that are external to the system of Union law, the peoples of Europe, jointly and individually, need to advance their own idea of 'ideal life', requiring development of shared European policy choices. In order to develop shared policy choices, all peoples of Europe need to adhere to key constitutive elements of the political process and democratic culture (key constitutional guarantees) so that no polity is dominated by vested interests. Peace in Europe relies on three aspects of liberty—*negative liberty*, *positive liberty* and *non-domination*—while the changing nature and source of threats to Peace mean that the constitutional aspects of Union law need be adjusted to advance each of the three aspects of liberty for each national polity. This is the ultimate role for EU constitutional law.

Community law advanced liberty as *non-interference* through reciprocal deregulation of cross-border interests, withdrawing them from the national political process. This approach to Peace was rooted in disabling politics through reciprocal deregulation in binding supranational law. Functional deregulatory choice fixed in the Treaties via objectives and rights of the individual disarmed national political processes and bound polities to a unanimous policy choice. Conflict between the interests composing different national polities was pre-empted by the binding nature of this policy choice. Thus, European policies bore a constitutional function, rendering them unlike policies of a state. Citizens of national polities received a right of membership in other European polities through 'virtual representation' under EU free movement law. National polities were presumed to be structurally equivalent in terms of the interests represented within each. Free movement of Union citizens opened an Exit option for members of national polities, advancing not only legitimacy of EU legal order thanks to this additional liberty, but also Loyalty to national polities. For only a free individual who has other options can be truly loyal.

The very success of Community law opened a new chapter in conquest. As the Member State powers declined through deregulation—based on reciprocity in EU

[3] S Griller, 'Is This a Constitution?' in S Griller and J Ziller (eds), *The Lisbon Treaty. EU Constitutionalism Without a Constitutional Treaty?* (Vienna, Springer, 2008) 39. The original reads: 'the essential element of the notion of state power, at least in international law, is not to secure a certain element of centralisation within a polity but to secure—in addition to validity and efficacy—independence from outside powers'.

law—their position vis-a-vis external interests weakened. An interest is external not due to physical absence from the territory of any one state or lack of polity membership but as defined by reference to Union law. Interests are external when they (1) do not belong to the system of binding reciprocity in Union law (non-EU polities), (2) Exit the law by breaking it (illegal activities and crime) and/or (3) Exit by moving to another jurisdiction (transnational business and finance). Comparison of free movement with mixed external agreements revealed a tension between, on the one hand, *non-interference* between European polities and, on the other hand, their ability to advance *positive liberty* vis-a-vis interests not bound by Union law.

This tension provoked a reconsideration of Europe's promise of Peace. Reciprocal *non-interference* between Member States through deregulation does nothing to advance Peace externally. This is better achieved by pursuing one's own *positive liberty*—in other words, regulation. The essential element in Europe's promise of Peace shifted from securing *non-interference* between Member States to advancing *positive liberty*. A series of Treaty reforms endowed the Union with new powers, including in immigration and criminal law. These powers are not defined by functional result-based objectives: their purpose is not abolishing regulatory powers of the state but shifting them to Union level.

This change opened Union law to politics. A new type of cross-polity conflict surfaced. Previously, Community law had neutralised permanent cross-polity *conflicts of interest* by fixing policy choice in the Treaties, thereby limiting national politics. This ensured *non-interference* between national political processes. Legitimacy of Union law was based on the vertical division of powers and closure of Exit from Union law (primacy, direct effect, and the role of the CJEU). This was—and remains—the liberal model for Europe: liberty of the individual trumps the political process. EU law put in place counter-majoritarian guarantees. With the opening of Union law to politics, *conflicts of ideas* arise. This new type of conflict requires adjustments in EU constitutional law. Unlike permanent conflicts of interest, ideas are subject to change—and so are the conflicts between them. Policy choices play no role in regulating the political process but, on the contrary, result from it. With legitimacy of Europe now based on the ability to develop and constantly renegotiate a European idea of *positive liberty*, vertical division of powers between Member States and the Union no longer legitimates Union law. This is the republican model for Europe: liberty of the individual depends on the political process. EU law needs to secure counter-minoritarian guarantees.

The emergence of two types of conflict changed subsidiarity and proportionality *qua* tools of legitimating substantive Union law. Once politics are enabled and relevant, legitimacy of Union policies is no longer linked to the vertical division of powers but starts with identification of the type of conflict to be addressed in Union law. The nature of conflict not only legitimates the shift in regulatory powers from Member States to the Union but also determines the mechanism of review and enforcement. There are four possible combinations as shown in Figure 6.1.

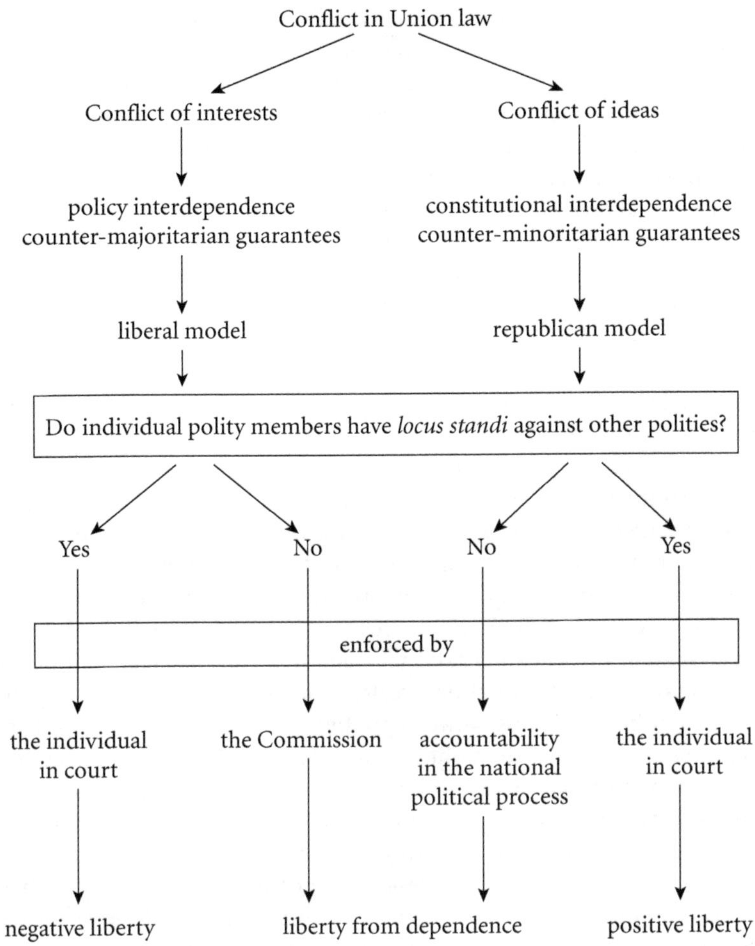

Figure 6.1: Conflict in Union law and the mechanism of enforcement

In the liberal model, the policy choice set in the Treaties regulates politics by limiting it. In the republican model, EU rules of the political process determine *how* a European policy choice is made. In each model, two mechanisms for enforcement are possible: enforcement by the individual through rights in Union law or alternative enforcement by the Union (the Commission, other EU institutions or Member States) or through the political process. At the two extremes belong those policies that can be enforced by the individual in court: here, the interest of the individual in enforcement coincides with the idea of *positive liberty* fixed in Union law (policy choice). On the left, there are conflicts of interest between polities in the Union, such as free movement of workers and services in the internal market, discussed in Chapter 2. To the extent that there is a permanent conflict of interest (own market protectionism), it can be solved by reciprocal deregulation between the polities. On the right, there are cross-polity conflicts of ideas about *positive liberty*, legal immigration being an example of this: preferences as regards policy choice will vary with historical ties, economic situation and culture. Such a conflict can be solved by regulation that embodies a shared policy choice. This policy can also be enforced by the individual against her host polity. The CJEU enforces European policy choice strictly for this policy choice pertains to the maintenance of the Union legal order by foreclosing Exit.

In the middle belong two types of conflict where the solution in Union law cannot be enforced by the individual, either due to the absence of *locus standi* or because the individual is not interested in enforcing the law. For such conflicts, Union law can be enforced either in Union law by the states or EU institutions, or through accountability of power in the national political process and national constitutional review. This distinction is relevant for legitimacy for, under international law, the rule must be ratified by each polity bound thereby. Policy choices set in the Treaties are more difficult to change, rendering this solution suitable for permanent conflicts of interest between polities. Different interests lead to different policy preferences, creating a potential for conflict that is unlikely to change. Conflicts of immutable interests are best solved by unanimously adopted binding supranational law. For example, immutable interest differences between polities relate to their geography, such as whether a polity has external borders through which migrants transit or international trade flows. Subjecting such permanent interests to constant renegotiation creates instability, while subjecting them to majoritarian political process between polities or not solving these conflicts at all risks domination between the polities. The effects of the Dublin system on Italy and EU sanctions against Russia on Finland are good examples of this.

Conversely, when the reason for conflict lies in ideas that vary with time and circumstance, a permanent policy choice only perpetuates conflict potential. Ideas change and require changes in policies—and therefore rules for making new policy choices. Conflicts of ideas entail renegotiation between polities as the circumstances and ideas change. In the course of this renegotiation, European polities are interdependent at the constitutional level. To be perceived as legitimate, renegotiation needs to follow established rules for the political process that advance *liberty from dependence* between and within each polity. The policy choice resulting from thus construed European political process are then enforced within the national constitutional system: through accountability in the national political process and by national constitutional courts. Criminal law tends to be such a policy: the Union has created a system for forced migration (surrender) based on mutual recognition, while substance of criminal law remains determined by each national polity, subject to its Constitution and the validating norms of international law.

Republican legitimation is relevant for all Union policies. Virtually every policy presents mixed conflict potential where both interests and ideas could clash. Cases such as *Schmidberger*, *ERT*, *Omega*, *Wittgenstein*, *Viking* and *Laval* highlight clearly republican issues in the internal market; cases such as *Melloni* and *NS* expose elements of liberal conflicts and reasoning in the AFSJ. The need to ensure *liberty from dependence* of each national polity through constitutional principles of Union law emerges much more strongly with the opening of Union law to politics. A republican conception of Europe addresses policy interdependence between the European peoples by creating a space for the elaboration of a European idea of *positive liberty*—but this in turn intensifies constitutional interdependence between them as polities. The ability of each polity to identify and pursue its own idea of *positive liberty* directly affects legitimacy of European policy choice. Only a people that can take charge of its own political life can internalise a policy choice made together with others and can therefore engage in a Union with them. Vice versa, a people that cannot take charge of its own political life is dependent on others for its idea of *positive liberty* and relies on external assistance for re-acquiring *liberty from dependence*.[4] Union law can provide such a constitutional safeguard. Once legitimacy in the Union is linked to *positive liberty*, interest representation in the national political process is no longer a 'purely internal' matter for each national polity. Rules that regulate the national political processes cannot remain outside the scope of constitutional norms of Union law.

Two problems arise for *liberty from dependence*. The shift of policy making to Europe could enable national governments and vested minority interests to dominate their polities—'the heads of State … assembled in the European Council … could be equipped with competences … that annul the … prerogative of the national parliaments'[5]—and circumvent accountability mechanisms currently available only in the national political process. A semi-permanent Exit from accountability would be open: once policy choice is made at Union level, 'there is no way for a majority of citizens in one country, after having learned about a legal act supported by their government in the Council, to have the decision repealed without the support of majorities of other Member States'.[6] Crucially, this could undermine legitimacy of both national polities and of the Union as a whole. EU law cannot reply on a mere presumption that each national political process is and remains equivalent in democratic terms. Constitutional safeguards in Union law are needed.

Republican policy components require that Union law engage with transparency and accountability, procedural and substantive review of policies, and two-way passage of powers. The scope of Union law must be expanded to include situations that, in policy terms, are purely internal but where nevertheless constitutional interdependence between Union polities ensues. One way to achieve this is by extending the scope of proportionality review to include interest representation in

[4] J Rawls, 'The Law of Peoples' (1993) Autumn, *Critical Inquiry* 63, who speaks of liberty generally without distinction between the three aspects of liberty.

[5] J Habermas, 'Bringing the Integration of Citizens into Line with the Integration of States' (2012) 18(4) *European Law Journal*. In the context of economic, monetary, and constitutional crises, see HJ Trenz, 'Mediated Representative Politics. The Euro-crisis and the Politicization of the EU' in S Kroger (ed), *Political Representation in the European Union. Still Democratic in Times of Crisis?* (Abingdon, Routledge, 2014) 182.

[6] A Somek, *Individualism* (Oxford, Oxford University Press, 2008) 150.

the national political process. Another option is comparative constitutional analysis to identify the most legitimate level for making policy choices by comparing national and European political processes in terms of counter-majoritarian and counter-minoritarian guarantees. Rights of the individual in Union law cannot dismantle national polities for it would render people little more than slaves: 'The truth about human individuals is that they are social products, not independent atoms capable of constituting society through a voluntary coming together. We are as much constituted by our society as it is by us'.[7]

Primacy of Union law cannot be unconditional but yields to the norms constitutive of European polities: the outcome of the political process cannot have primacy over the norms that enable politics. Beyond constitutional elements, Europe needs rules to prevent Exit of the ruling elites from national polities (from polities to multinationals, from the national to the European), stronger protection for polities with permanent minority interests, and opening of expert-based policies to the political process.[8] Together, these measures promote Union citizens not as consumers of rights and policies but as political actors, members of their national polities.[9] Strengthening national democracy will strengthen Europe. This is a return to Europe's essence, albeit in contemporary, twenty-first-century mode.

[7] N MacCormick, *Questioning Sovereignty: Law, State, and Nation in the European Commonwealth* (Oxford, Oxford University Press, 1999) 163.

[8] The emergence of new political conflicts and the challenge for Union law with the introduction of the single currency—often presented as a technocratic policy independently managed by the European Central Bank—was correctly predicted by M Feldstein, 'EMU and International Conflict' (1997) November/December, *Foreign Affairs*.

[9] For an explanation and defence of 'republican virtue' of citizens and rulers, see P Pettit, 'Republican Theory and Political Trust' in M Levi and V Braithwaite (eds), *Trust and Governance* (New York, Russell Sage Foundation, 1998) 295–314.

Bibliography

Books

Alexy, R, *A Theory of Constitutional Rights* (Oxford, Oxford University Press, 2002)
Arendt, H, *Between Past and Future* (New York, Penguin Books, 1968)
St Augustine, *The City of God* (XIX, 24)
Barak, A, *The Judge in a Democracy* (Princeton, NJ, Princeton University Press, 2006)
Barnard, C, *The Substantive Law of the EU. The Four Freedoms* (Oxford, Oxford University Press, 2013)
—— and S Peers, *European Union Law* (Oxford, Oxford University Press, 2014)
Bauböck, R, *Stakeholder Citizenship: An Idea Whose Time Has Come?* (Migration Policy Institute, 2008)
Bellamy, R, *Political Constitutionalism: A Republican Defence of the Constitutionality of Democracy* (Cambridge, Cambridge University Press, 2007)
Bobbitt, P, *The Shield of Achilles: War, Peace and the Course of History* (New York, Knopf, 2002)
Bobek, M, *Comparative Reasoning in European Supreme Courts* (Oxford, Oxford University Press, 2013)
Boeles, P, M den Heijer, G Lodder and K Wouters, *European Migration Law* (Antwerp, Intersentia, 2009)
Cartabia, M and A Simoncini, *La Legge di Re Salomone. Ragione e diritto nei discorsi di Benedetto XVI* (Edizioni Rizzoli BUR, 2013)
Cholewinski, R, *The Legal Status of Migrants Admitted for Employment* (Council of Europe Publishing, 2004)
Cicero, *The Republic and The Laws* (Oxford, Oxford University Press, 1998)
Condinanzi, M, A Lang and B Nascimbene, *Citizenship of the Union and Free Movement of Persons* (Leiden, Brill, 2008)
Craig, P, *EU Administrative Law* (Oxford, Oxford University Press, 2006)
—— *The Lisbon Treaty* (Oxford, Oxford University Press, 2010)
—— *The Lisbon Treaty, Revised Edition: Law, Politics, and Treaty Reform* (Oxford, Oxford University Press, 2013)
Curtin, DM, *Postnational Democracy* (The Hague, Kluwer Law International, 1997)
Dashwood, A, *Reviewing Maastricht, Issues for the 1996 IGC* (London, Sweet & Maxwell, 1996)
Dehousse, R, *The European Court of Justice* (Basingstoke, Palgrave Macmillan, 1998)
Dollard, J, NE Miller, LW Doob, OH Mowrer and RR Sears, *Frustration and Aggression* (Newhaven, CT, Yale University Press, 1939)
Dworkin, R, *Freedom's Law: The Moral Reading of the American Constitution* (Cambridge, MA, Harvard University Press, 1996)
Eisele, K, *The External Dimension of the EU's Migration Policy. Different Legal Positions of Third-Country Nationals in the EU: A Comparative Perspective* (Leiden, Brill Nijhoff, 2014)

Ely, JH, *Democracy and Distrust* (Cambridge, MA, Harvard University Press, 1980)
Emiliou, N, *The Principle of Proportionality in European Law* (London, Kluwer Law International, 1996)
Eriksen, EO and JE Possum, *Rethinking Democracy in the European Union* (London, Routledge, 2012)
Estrella, A, *The EU Principle of Subsidiarity and Its Critique* (Oxford, University Press, 2002)
Favell, A, *Eurostars and Eurocities. Free Movement and Mobility in an Integrating Europe* (Oxford, Blackwell Publishing, 2008)
Galipeau, CJ, *Isaiah Berlin's Liberalism* (Oxford, Clarendon Press, 1994)
Greenhill, KM, *Weapons of Mass Migration. Forced Displacement, Coercion, and Foreign Policy* (Ithaca, NY, Cornell University Press, 2010)
Guild, E, *European Community Law from a Migrant's Perspective* (The Hague, Kluwer Law International, 2000)
Habermas, J, *The Postnational Constellation* (Cambridge, Polity Press, 1998)
Hewstone, M, W Stroebe and K Jonas, *An Introduction to Social Psychology* (British Psychological Society and John Wiley & Sons Ltd, 2012)
Hirschman, AO, *Voice, Exit, Loyalty* (Cambridge, MA, Harvard University Press, 1970)
Hübner Mendes, C, *Constitutional Courts and Deliberative Democracy* (Oxford, Oxford University Press, 2014)
Janssens, C, *The Development of the Principle of Mutual Recognition in the Secondary Legislation* (Oxford, Oxford University Press, 2014)
Kant, I, *Political Writings* (Cambridge University Press, 1991)
Kiiver, P, *The Early Warning System for the Principle of Subsidiarity: Constitutional Theory and Empirical Reality* (London, Routledge, 2012)
Klamert, M, *The Principle of Loyalty in EU Law* (Oxford, Oxford University Press, 2014)
Klatt, M and M Meister, *The Constitutional Structure of Proportionality* (Oxford, Oxford University Press, 2012)
Komesar, N, *Imperfect Alternatives. Choosing Institutions in Law, Economics, and Public Policy* (Chicago, IL, University of Chicago Press, 1994)
Luhmann, N, *Law as a Social System* (Oxford, Oxford University Press, 2004)
MacCormick, N, *Questioning Sovereignty: Law, State, and Nation in the European Commonwealth* (Oxford, Oxford University Press, 1999)
Madison, J, *The Federalist No 10* (1787)
Majone, G, *Dilemmas of European Integration* (Oxford, Oxford University Press, 2005)
Mill, JS, *Considerations on Representative Government* (New York, Harper & Brothers, 1862)
Monnet, J, *Mémoires. Nous ne coalisons pas des etats, nous unissons des hommes* (Paris, Fayard, 1976)
Muniz-Fraticelli, VM, *The Structure of Pluralism* (Oxford, Oxford University Press, 2014)
Nozick, R, *The Examined Life* (New York, Simon and Schuster, 1989)
Papagianni, G, *Institutional and Policy Dynamics of EU Migration Law* (The Hague, Martinus Nijhoff Publishers, 2006)
Parent, J, *Voluntary Union in World Politics* (Oxford, Oxford University Press, 2011)
Peers, S, *EU Justice and Home Affairs Law* (Oxford, Oxford University Press, 2006)
—— *EU Justice and Home Affairs Law* (Oxford, Oxford University Press, 2011)
Pettit, P, *Republicanism: A Theory of Freedom and Government* (Oxford, Oxford University Press, 1999)
—— *Theory of Freedom. From the Psychology to the Politics of Agency* (Cambridge, Polity Press, 2001)

Piris, JC, *The Lisbon Treaty. A Legal and Political Analysis* (Cambridge Cambridge University Press, 2010)
Poiares Maduro, M, *We the Court* (Oxford, Hart Publishing, 1998)
Rawls, J, *A Theory of Justice* (Cambridge, Harvard University Press, 1999)
—— *The Law of Peoples* (Cambridge, Harvard University Press, 1999)
Rosas, A and L Armati, *EU Constitutional Law. An Introduction* (Oxford, Oxford University Press, 2010)
—— and —— *EU Constitutional Law* (Oxford, Hart Publishing, 2012)
Sajó, A, *Constitutional Sentiments* (Newhaven, CT, Yale University Press, 2011)
Schütze, R, *From Dual to Cooperative Federalism* (Oxford Oxford University Press, 2011)
—— *European Constitutional Law* (Cambridge Cambridge University Press, 2012)
Somek, A, *Individualism: An Essay on the Authority of the European Union* (Oxford, Oxford University Press, 2008)
—— *Engineering Equality: An Essay on European Anti-Discrimination Law* (Oxford, Oxford University Press, 2011)
—— *The Cosmopolitan Constitution* (Oxford, Oxford University Press, 2014)
Soros, G, *The Tragedy of the European Union* (New York, NY Public Affairs, 2014)
Spinelli, A and E Rossi, *The Ventotene Manifesto* (Ventotene: The Altiero Spinelli Institute for Federalist Studies, 1941)
Sternberg, RJ and K Sternberg, *The Nature of Hate* (Cambridge, Cambridge University Press, 2008)
Stone Sweet, A, *Governing with Judges: Constitutional Politics in Europe* (Oxford, Oxford University Press, 2004)
—— *The Judicial Construction of Europe* (Oxford, Oxford University Press, 2004)
Tekin, F, *Differentiated Integration at Work. The Institutionalization and Implementation of Opt-Outs from European Integration in the Area of Freedom, Security and Justice* (Baden-Baden, Nomos, 2012)
Tuori, K, *Critical Legal Positivism* (Aldershot, Ashgate, 2002)
—— and S Sankari, *The Many Constitutions of Europe* (Aldershot, Ashgate, 2010)
Vermeule, A, *Law and the Limits of Reason* (Oxford, Oxford University Press, 2008)
Waldron, J, *Law and Disagreement* (Oxford, Oxford University Press, 1999)
Weiler, JHH, *The Constitution of Europe: "Do the New Clothes Have an Emperor?" and Other Essays on European Integration* (Cambridge, Cambridge University Press, 1999)
Wittgenstein, L, *Philosophical Investigations* (Oxford, Basil Blackwell Ltd, 1958)
Yuen, DMC, *Deciphering Sun Tzu* (Oxford, Oxford University Press, 2014)

Edited Volumes

de Angelis, G and P Barcelos (eds), *The Long Quest for Identity: Political Identity and Fundamental Rights Protection in the European Union* (Bern, Peter Lang, 2013)
Arnull, A, C Barnard, M Dougan and E Spaventa (eds), *A Constitutional Order of States? Essays in EU Law in Honour of Alan Dashwood* (Oxford, Hart Publishing, 2011)
Avbelj, M and J Komarek (eds), *Constitutional Pluralism in the European Union and Beyond* (Oxford, Hart Publishing, 2012)
Biondi, A, P Eeckhout and S Ripley (eds), *EU Law after Lisbon* (Oxford Oxford University Press, 2012)

Boeles, P, M Den Heijer, G Lodder and K Wouters (eds), *European Migration Law* (Cambridge, Intersentia, 2009)
de Bruycker, P (ed), *The Emergence of a European Immigration Policy* (Brussels, Bruylant, 2003)
de Burca, G and JHH Weiler (eds), *The Worlds of European Constitutionalism* (Cambridge, Cambridge University Press, 2012)
Cartabia, M, N Lupo and A Simoncini (eds), *Democracy and Subsidiarity in the EU* (Bologna, Il Mulino, 2013)
Ellis, E (ed), *The Principle of Proportionality in the Laws of Europe* (Oxford, Hart Publishing, 1999)
Eriksen, EO (ed), *Making the European Polity* (London, Routledge, 2005)
Fleming, JE and JT Levy (eds), *Federalism and Subsidiarity* (New York, NYU Press, 2014)
Gasser, G and M Stefan (eds), *Personal Identity: Complex or Simple?* (Cambridge, Cambridge University Press, 2012)
Harmless, W (ed), *Augustine in His Own Words* (Washington, DC, Catholic University of America Press, 2010)
Harris, H (ed), *Identity* (Oxford, Oxford University Press, 1995)
Isin, EF and M Saward (eds), *Enacting European Citizenship* (Cambridge, Cambridge University Press, 2013)
Kostoris, F and P Schioppa (eds), *The Principle of Mutual Recognition in the European Integration Process* (Basingstoke, Palgrave Macmillan, 2005)
Laursen, F (ed), *The FU's Lisbon Treaty. Institutional Choices and Implementation* (Aldershot, Ashgate, 2012)
Maes, M, MC Foblets and P De Bruycker (eds), *External Dimensions of EU Migration and Asylum Law and Policy* (Brussels, Bruylant, 2011)
Martenczuk, B and S Van Thiel (eds), *Justice, Liberty, Security: New Challenges for EU External Relations* (Brussels, ASP-VUB Press, 2010)
Minderhoud, P and N Trimikliniotis (eds), *Rethinking the Free Movement of Workers: The European Challenges Ahead* (Nijmegen, Wolf Legal Publishers, 2009)
Peers, S and N Rogers (eds), *EU Immigration and Asylum Law* (The Hague, Martinus Nijhof, 2006)
Schmidt, SK and RD Kelemen (eds), *The Power of the European Court of Justice* (London, Routledge, 2013)
de Vries, S, U Bernitz and S Weatherill (eds), *The Protection of Fundamental Rights in the EU after Lisbon* (Oxford, Hart Publishing, 2013)
Weiler, JHH and M Wind (eds), *European Constitutionalism Beyond the State* (Cambridge, Cambridge University Press, 2003)
de Witte, B and HW Micklitz (eds), *The European Court of Justice and the Autonomy of Member States* (Antwerp, Intersentia, 2012)

Chapters in Edited Volumes

Almestad, K, 'The Essentials' in The EFTA Court (ed), *The EEA and the EFTA Court* (London, Bloomsbury Publishing, 2014)
Amato, G, 'Foreword' in HJ Blanke and S Mangiameli (eds), *The Treaty on European Union, A Commentary* (Berlin, Springer, 2013)

Baldaccini, A and H Toner, 'From Amsterdam and Tampere to the Hague: An Overview of Five Years of EC Immigration and Asylum Law' in A Baldaccini, E Guild and H Toner (eds), *Whose Freedom, Security and Justice? EU Immigration and Asylum Law and Policy* (Oxford, Hart Publishing, 2007)

Barbou, S des Places, 'Droit communautaire de la liberté de circulation et droit des migrations ou est la frontier?' in C Boutayeb, JC Muscatel, S Rodrigues and H Ruiz-Fabri (eds), *Mélanges en l'honneur de Philippe Manin. L'Union européenne: union de droit, union des droits* (Paris, Pedone, 2010)

Bartolini, S, 'Should the Union Be "Politicised"? Prospects and Risks' in S Hix and S Bartolini (eds), *Politics: The Right or the Wrong Sort of Medicine for the EU?* Policy Paper No 19 (Paris, Notre Europe, 2006)

Bellamy, R and C Attucci, 'Normative Theory and the EU: between Contract and Community in European Integration Theory' in A Wiener and T Diez (eds), *European Integration Theory* (Oxford, Oxford University Press, 2009)

Bermann, GA, 'Proportionality and Subsidiarity' in C Barnard and J Scott (eds), *The Law of the Single European Market: Unpacking the Premises* (Oxford, Hart Publishing, 2002)

Biondi, A, 'Subsidiarity in the Courtroom' in A Biondi, P Eeckhout and S Ripley (eds), *EU Law After Lisbon* (Oxford, Oxford University Press, 2012)

von Bogdandy, A and J Bast, 'The Federal Order of Competences' in A von Bogdandy and J Bast (eds), *Principles of European Constitutional Law* (London, Hart/CH Beck/Nomos, 2010)

Borrell Fontelles, J, 'The Future Role of the European Parliament' in L Tsoukalis and JA Emmanouilidis (eds), *The Delphic Oracle on Europe: Is There a Future for the European Union?* (Oxford, Oxford University Press, 2011)

van den Brink, T, 'The Substance of Subsidiarity: The Interpretation and Meaning of the Principle after Lisbon' in M Trybus and L Rubini (eds), *The Treaty of Lisbon and the Future of European Law and Policy* (Cheltenham, Edward Elgar, 2012)

de Bruycker, P, 'Legislative Harmonisation in European Immigration Policy' in R Cholewinski, R Perruchoud and E MacDonald (eds), *International Migration Law: Developing Paradigms and Key Challenges* (The Hague, TMC Asser Press, 2007)

Cassese, S, 'Is There Really a "Democratic Deficit"?' in S Cassese and G della Cananea (eds), *Institutional Reforms in the European Union: Memorandum for the Convention* (EuropEos, 2002)

Closa, C, 'Supranational Citizenship and Democracy: Normative and Empirical Dimensions' in M La Torre (ed), *European Citizenship. An Institutional Challenge* (The Hague, Kluwer Law International, 1998)

Craig, P, 'Integration, Democracy and Legitimacy' in P Craig and G De Burca (eds), *Evolution of EU Law* (Oxford, Oxford University Press, 2011)

Cremona, M, 'A Reticent Court? Policy Objectives and the Court of Justice' in M Cremona and A Thies (eds), *The European Court of Justice and External Relations Law: Constitutional Challenges* (Oxford, Hart Publishing, 2014)

Cygan, A, '"Collective" Subsidiarity Monitoring by National Parliaments After Lisbon: The Operation of the Early Warning Mechanism' in M Trybus and L Rubini (eds), *The Treaty of Lisbon and the Future of European Law and Policy* (Cheltenham, Edward Elgar, 2012)

Edward, D, 'Subsidiarity as a Legal Concept' in P Cardonnel, A Rosas and N Wahl (eds), *Constitutionalizing the EU Judicial System* (Oxford, Hart Publishing, 2012)

Favell, A and E Recchi, 'Social Mobility and Spatial Mobility' in A Favell and V Guiraudon (eds), *Sociology of the European Union* (London, Palgrave, 2011)

Gibbs, A, 'Taking Agency Seriously: An Examination of Legal Integration and Constitutionalism' in D Augenstein (ed), *Integration Through Law Revisited: The Making of the European Polity* (Aldershot, Ashgate, 2012)

Griller, S, 'Is This a Constitution?' in S Griller and J Ziller (eds), *The Lisbon Treaty. EU Constitutionalism without a Constitutional Treaty?* (Vienna, Springer, 2008)

Groenendijk, K, 'Access of Third-country Nationals to Employment under the New EC Migration Law' in F Julien-Laferrière, H Labaye and Ö Edström (eds), *The European Immigration and Asylum Policy: Critical Assessment Five Years After the Amsterdam Treaty* (Brussels, Bruylant, 2005)

Guild, E, 'The Europe Agreements: The Right to Establishment in the Central and Eastern European Agreements' in E Guild (ed), *The Legal Framework and Social Consequences of Free Movement of Persons in the European Union* (The Hague, Kluwer Law International, 1999)

—— and H Staples, 'Labour Migration in the European Union', in P De Bruycker (ed), *The Emergence of a European Migration Policy* (Brussels, Bruylant, 2003)

Habermas, J, 'Citizenship and National Identity: Some Reflections on the Future of Europe' in B van Steenbergen (ed), *The Condition of Citizenship* (London, Sage Publications, 1994)

Halberstam, D, 'Constitutional Heterarchy: The Centrality of Conflict in the European Union and the United States' in J Dunoff and J Trachtman (eds), *Ruling the World? Constitutionalism, International Law, and Global Governance* (Cambridge, Cambridge University Press, 2009)

Halberstam, D, 'Systems Pluralism and Institutional Pluralism in Constitutional Law: National, Supranational and Global Governance' in M Avbelj and J Komarek (eds), *Constitutional Pluralism in the European Union and Beyond* (Oxford, Hart Publishing, 2012)

Kocharov, A, 'Subsidiarity after Lisbon: Federalism without a Purpose?' in L Azoulai, L Boucon and FX Millet (eds), *Deconstructing EU Federalism through Competences*, EUI Working Paper LAW 2012/06

—— 'In the Image of State: Constitutional Complexities of Engineering a European Democracy' in F Fabbrini, E Hirsch Ballin and H Somsen (eds), *What Form of Government for the European Union and the Eurozone?* (Oxford, Hart Publishing, 2015)

Komárek, J, 'The Institutional Dimension of Constitutional Pluralism' in M Avbelj and J Komárek (eds), *Constitutional Pluralism in the European Union and Beyond* (Oxford, Hart Publishing, 2012)

Lebeck, C, 'General Principles' in The EFTA Court (ed), *The EEA and the EFTA Court* (Oxford, Hart Publishing, 2014)

Nic Shuibhne, N, 'EU citizenship after Lisbon' in D Ashiagbor, N Countouris and I Lianos (eds), *The European Union after the Treaty of Lisbon* (Cambridge Cambridge University Press, 2012)

Olmstead, RE and PM Bentler, 'Structural Equations Modeling: A New Friend?' in FB Bryant, J Edwards, RS Tindale, EJ Posavac, L Heath, E Henderson-King and Y Suarez-Balcazar (eds), *Methodological Issues in Applied Social Psychology* (Berlin, Springer, 1992)

Patterson, D, 'Methodology and Theoretical Disagreement' in U Neergaard, R Nielsen and L Roseberry (eds), *European Legal Method Paradoxes and Revitalization* (Copenhagen, DJOF Publishing, 2011)

Pech, L, 'The Institutional Development of the EU Post-Lisbon: A case of Plus Ça Change…?' in D Ashiagbor, N Countouris and I Lianos (eds), *The European Union After the Treaty of Lisbon* (Cambridge Cambridge University Press, 2012)

Peers, S, 'The EU Institutions and Title IV' in S Peers and N Rogers (eds), *EU Immigration and Asylum Law* (The Hague, Martinus Nijhoff Publishers, 2006)

—— 'EU Migration Law and Association Agreements' in B Martenczuk and S Van Thiel (eds), *Justice, Liberty, Security: New Challenges for EU External Relations* (Brussels, ASP-VUB Press, 2010)

Peters, A, 'Membership in the Global Constitutional Community' in J Klabbers, A Peters and G Ulfstein (eds), *The Constitutionalization of International Law* (Oxford, Oxford University Press, 2009)

Pettit, P, 'Love and its Place in Moral Discourse' in R Lamb (ed), *Love Analyzed* (Boulder, CO, Westview Press, 1997)

—— 'Republican Theory and Political Trust' in M Levi and V Braithwaite (eds), *Trust and Governance* (New York, Russell Sage Foundation, 1998)

Poiares Maduro, M, 'Europe's Social Self: "The Sickness unto Death"' in J Shaw (ed), *Social Law and Policy in an Evolving EU* (Oxford, Hart Publishing, 2000)

—— 'Where to Look for Legitimacy?' in EO Eriksen, JE Fossum and AJ Menéndez (eds), *Constitution Making and Democratic Legitimacy* (ARENA Report No 5, 2002)

—— 'Contrapunctual Law: Europe's Constitutional Pluralism in Action' in N Walker (ed), *Sovereignty in Transition* (Oxford, Hart Publishing, 2003)

—— 'Sovereignty in Europe: the European Court of Justice and the Creation of European Political Community' in ML Volcansek and JF Stack Jr (eds), *Courts Crossing Borders. Blurring the Lines of Sovereignty* (Durham, NC, Carolina Academic Press, 2005)

—— 'The Chameleon State. EU Law and the Blurring of the Private/Public Distinction in the Market' in R Nickel (ed), *Conflict of Laws and Laws of Conflict in Europe and Beyond* (Antwerp, Intersentia, 2010)

—— 'Introduction' in M Poiares Maduro, B De Witte and M Kumm (organizers) *The Democratic Governance of the Euro* (2012) European University Institute, RSCAS working paper 2012/08

—— 'Three Claims of Constitutional Pluralism' in M Avbelj and J Komárek (eds), *Constitutional Pluralism in the European Union and Beyond* (Oxford, Hart Publishing, 2012)

—— 'Rendre plus visible le sentiment d'appartenance à un espace européen' in J Jappert and S Landa (eds), *Favoriser l'émergence d'une identité européenne grâce au sport: réalité ou utopie?* (Think Tank Sport et Citoyenneté, 2013)

Post, R, 'Constructing the European Polity: AETR and the Open Skies Judgments' in M Poiares Maduro and L Azoulai (eds), *The Past and Future of EU Law* (Oxford, Hart Publishing, 2010)

Ryan, B, 'The EU and Labour Migration: Regulating Admission or Treatment?' in A Baldaccini, E Guild and H Toner (eds), *Whose Freedom, Security and Justice?* (Oxford, Hart Publishing, 2007)

Schmidt, VA, 'Identity and Legitimacy in the European Union: Is More Politics the Answer?' in S Lucarelli, F Cerutti and V Schmidt (eds), *Debating Political Identity and Legitimacy in the European Union* (London, Routledge, 2011)

Somek, A, 'Monism—A Tale of the Undead' in M Avbelj and J Komárek (eds), *Constitutional Pluralism in the European Union and Beyond* (Oxford, Hart Publishing, 2012)

Sternberg, RJ, 'Triangulating Love' in RJ Sternberg and ML Barnes (eds), *The Psychology of Love* (Newhaven, CT, Yale University Press, 1988)

Toner, H, 'Impact Assessments: A Useful Tool for "Better Lawmaking" in EU Migration Policy?' in A Baldaccini, E Guild and H Toner (eds), *Whose Freedom, Security and Justice?* (Oxford, Hart Publishing, 2007)

Trenz, HJ, 'Mediated Representative Politics. The Euro-crisis and the Politicization of the EU' in S Kroger (ed), *Political Representation in the European Union. Still Democratic in Times of Crisis?* (Abingdon, Routledge, 2014)

Tridimas, T, 'The Rule of Reason and Its Relation to Proportionality and Subsidiarity' in A Schrauwen (ed), *Rule of Reason. Rethinking Another Classic of European Legal Doctrine* (Groningen, Europa Law Publishing, 2005)

Weiler, JHH, 'European Citizenship—Identity and Differentity' in M La Torre (ed), *European Citizenship. An Institutional Challenge* (The Hague, Kluwer Law International, 1998)

—— 'Challenges to Electoral Participation in the European Elections of 2014. Restoring Electoral Faith: Prospects and Risks' in *Strengthening European Democracy: Citizens' Participation. Which Challenges Do We Face at the European Elections of 2014?* (Brussels, European Parliament AFCO Report doc. PE 493.036, 2013)

Wiener, A and T Diez, 'Introducing the Mosaic of Integration Theory' in A Wiener and T Diez (eds), *European Integration Theory* (Oxford, Oxford University Press, 2009)

de Witte, B, 'The European Union as an International Legal Experiment' in G de Burca and JHH Weiler (eds), *The Worlds of European Constitutionalism* (Cambridge, Cambridge University Press, 2012)

Wolff, S and G Mounier, 'The External Dimension of JHA: a New Dimension of EU Diplomacy' in S Wolff, F Goudappel and J De Zwaan (eds), *Freedom, Security and Justice after Lisbon and Stockholm* (The Hague, TMC Asser Press, 2011)

Articles

Abramst, K and H Kerentt, 'Who's Afraid of Law and the Emotions?' (2009–2010) 94 *Minnesota Law Review*

Amar, AR, 'Of Sovereignty and Federalism' (1987) 96 *Yale Law Journal*

Apap, J, 'Shaping Europe's Migration Policy. New Regimes for the Employment of Third Country Nationals: A Comparison of Strategies in Germany, Sweden, the Netherlands and the UK' (2002) 4 *European Journal of Migration and Law*

Arkush, DJ, 'Situating Emotion: A Critical Realist View of Emotion and Nonconscious Cognitive Processes for Law and Legal Theory' [2008] *Brigham Young University Law Review*

Avbelj, M, 'Supremacy or Primacy of EU Law—(Why) Does it Matter?' (2011) 17(6) *European Law Journal*

Barber, NW, 'The Limited Modesty of Subsidiarity' (2005) 11(3) *European Law Journal*

Barbou Des Places, S and H Oger, 'Making the European Migration Regime: Decoding Member States' Legal Strategies' (2005) 6 *European Journal of Migration and Law*

Beck, G, 'The Lisbon Judgment of the German Constitutional Court, the Primacy of EU Law and the Problem of Kompetenz-Kompetenz: A Conflict between Right and Right in Which There is No Praetor' (2011) 17(4) *European Law Journal*

Bellamy, R, '"An Ever Closer Union Among the Peoples of Europe": Republican Intergovernmentalism and Demoicratic Representation within the EU' (2013) 35(5) *Journal of European Integration*

—— 'A European Republic of Sovereign States: Sovereignty, Republicanism and the European Union' [2016] *European Journal of Political Theory*

Bensson, S, 'Europe as a Demoi-cratic Polity' (2007) 30(1) *Jurist-og Økonomforbundets Forlag* Retfaerd Årgang
Besselink, LFM, 'The Parameters of Constitutional Conflict after Melloni' (2014) 39(4) *European Law Review*
Billing, F, 'The Parallel Between Non-removal of Asylum Seekers and Non-execution of a European Arrest Warrant on Human Rights Grounds: The CJEU Case of N.S. v Secretary of State for the Home Department' (2012) 1 *European Constitutional Law Review*
de Boer, N, 'Addressing Rights Divergences under the Charter: Melloni' (2013) 50 *CML Rev*
von Bogdandy, A, 'The European Union as a Human Rights Organization? Human Rights and the Core of the European Union' (2000) 37 *CML Rev*
—— 'Constitutionalism in International Law: Comment on a Proposal from Germany' (2006) 47(1) *Harvard International Law Journal*
—— 'Founding Principles of EU Law: A Theoretical and Doctrinal Sketch' (2010) 16(2) *European Law Journal*
Boelaert-Suominen, S, 'Non-EU Nationals and Council Directive 2003/109/EC on the Status of Third-Country Nationals Who Are Long-Term Residents: Five Paces Forward and Possibly Three Paces Back' (2005) 42 *CML Rev*
Brinkmann, G, 'The Immigration and Asylum Agenda' (2004) 10(2) *European Law Journal*
de Bruycker, P and S Mananashvili, 'Audi Alteram Partem in Immigration Detention Procedures Between the CJEU, the ECtHR and Member States: G & R' (2015) 52 *CML Rev*
de Burca, G, 'The Quest for Legitimacy in the European Union' (1996) 59(3) *MLR*
—— and O Gerstenberg, 'The Denationalization of Constitutional Law' (2006) 47(1) *Harvard International Law Journal*
Cambien, N, 'Case C-127/08, Blaise Baheten Metock and Others v Minister for Justice, Equality and Law Reform' (2009) 15 *Columbia Journal of European Law*
Castello, C, 'Metock: Free Movement and "Normal Family Life" in the Union' (2009) 46 *CML Rev*
Constant, A and KF Zimmermann, 'Immigrant Performance and Selective Immigration Policy: a European Perspective' (2005) 195 *National Institute Economic Review*
Cooter, R, 'Do Good Laws Make Good Citizens? An Economic Analysis of Internalized Norms' (2000) 86(8) *Virginia Law Review*
Cox, AB, 'Immigration Law's Organizing Principles' (2008) 157(2) *University of Pennsylvania Law Review*
Cremona, M, 'The "dynamic and homogeneous" EEA: Byzantine Structures and Various Geometry' (1994) 19(5) *European Law Review*
Cuesta Lopez, V, 'The Lisbon Treaty's Provisions on Democratic Principles: A Legal Framework for Participatory Democracy' (2010) 16(1) *European Public Law*
Currie, S, 'Accelerated Justice or a Step Too Far?' (2009) 34(2) *European Law Review*
Dani, M, 'Rehabilitating Social Conflicts in European Public Law' (2012) 18(5) *European Law Journal*
Davies, G, 'Democracy and Legitimacy in the Shadow of Purposive Competence' (2015) 21(1) *European Law Journal*
Delaney, EF, 'Justifying Power: Federalism, Immigration, and "Foreign Affairs"' (2013) 8(1) *Duke Journal of Constitutional Law & Public Policy*
Desomer, M and K Lenaerts, 'Bricks for a Constitutional Treaty of the European Union: Values, Objectives and Means' (2002) 27(4) *European Law Review*

Dougan, M, 'When Worlds Collide! Competing Visions of the Relationship between Direct Effect and Supremacy' (2007) 44 *CML Rev*

Eilstrup-Sangiovanni, M and D Verdier, 'European Integration as a Solution to War' (2005) 11(1) *European Journal of International Relations*

Eriksen, EO and JE Fossum, 'Bringing European Democracy Back In—Or How to Read the German Constitutional Court's Lisbon Treaty Ruling' (2011) 17(2) *European Law Journal*

Evans, A, 'Third Country Nationals and the Treaty on European Union' (1994) 5 *European Journal of International Law*

Feldstein, M, 'EMU and International Conflict' (1997) November/December, *Foreign Affairs*

Forman, J, 'The EEA Agreement Five Years On: Dynamic Homogeneity in Practice and Its Implementation by the Two EEA Courts' (1999) 36 *CML Rev*

Garcia Andrade, P, 'The Legal Feasibility of the EU's External Action on Legal Migration: The Internal and the External Intertwined' (2013) 15 *European Journal of Migration and Law*

van Gerven, W, 'The Genesis of EEA Law' [1992] *Fordham International Law Journal*

van Gestel, R and HW Micklitz, 'Why Methods Matter in European Legal Scholarship' (2014) 20(3) *European Law Journal*

Gonzales, JM, 'Comment: The Interstate Privileges and Immunities: Fundamental Rights or Federalism' (1986) 15 *Capital University Law Review*

Goucha Soares, A, 'Pre-Emption, Conflicts of Powers and Subsidiarity' (1998) 23(2) *European Law Review*

Graver, HP, 'Mission Impossible: Supranationality and National Legal Autonomy in the EEA Agreement' (2001) 7 *European Foreign Affairs Review*

Guild, E, 'Discretion, Competence and Migration in the European Union' (1999) *European Journal of Migration and Law* 1

Guliyeva, G, 'Lost in Transition: Russian-speaking Non-citizens in Latvia and the Protection of Minority Rights in the European Union' (2008) 33 *European Law Review*

Habermas, J, 'Why Europe Needs a Constitution' (2001) 11 *New Left Review*

—— 'Bringing the Integration of Citizens into Line with the Integration of States' (2012) 18(4) *European Law Journal*

Hailbronner, K and J Polakiewicz, 'Non-EC Nationals in the European Community: the Need for a Coordinated Approach' (1992–1993) 3 *Duke Journal of Comparative International Law*

—— 'European Immigration and Asylum Law under the Amsterdam Treaty' (1998) 35 *CML Review*

Haukeland Fredriksen, H, 'One Market, Two Courts: Legal Pluralism vs. Homogeneity in the European Economic Area' (2010) 79 *Nordic Journal of International Law*

—— 'Bridging the Widening Gap between the EU Treaties and the Agreement on the European Economic Area' (2012) 18(6) *European Law Journal*

den Heijer, M, 'Joined Cases C-411 & 493/10, *N.S. v Secretary of State for the Home Department and M.E. and Others v Refugee Applications Commissioner, Minister for Justice, Equality and Law Reform*, Judgment of the Court (Grand Chamber) of 21 December 2011, nyr.' (2012) 49 *CML Rev*

Iglesias Sanches, S, 'Free Movement of Third-Country Nationals in the European Union?' (2009) 15(6) *European Law Journal*

Jacobs, F, 'European Parliament Elections in Times of Crisis' (2014) 1 *Intereconomics*

Jacobs, FG, 'Citizenship of the European Union—A Legal Analysis' (2007) 13(5) *European Law Journal*

Jiménez Lobeira, PC, 'EU Citizenship and Political Identity: The Demos and Telos Problems' (2012) 18(4) *European Law Journal*

Kiiver, P, 'The Lisbon Judgment of the German Constitutional Court: A Court-Ordered Strengthening of the National Legislature in the EU' (2010) 16(5) *European Law Journal*

Kirchner, C, 'Competence Catalogues and the Principle of Subsidiarity in a European Constitution' (1997) 8 *Constitutional Political Economy*

Kocharov, A, 'What Intra-Community Mobility for Third-Country Workers?' (2008) 6 *European Law Review*

—— 'Regulation that Defies Gravity. Policy, Economics and Law of Legal Immigration in Europe' (2011) 4(2) *European Journal of Legal Studies*

—— 'Governance of Migration in the EU: Home Affairs or Foreign Policy?' (2013) 15 *European Journal of Migration and Law*

—— 'Constitutional Complexities of European Democracy in Light of the 2014 EP Elections' (2014) 4 *Europa-Institut der Universität des Saarlandes, Zeitschrift für Europarechtliche Studien*

Komárek, J, 'Czech Constitutional Court Playing with Matches: The Czech Constitutional Court Declares a Judgment of the Court of Justice of the EU Ultra Vires' (2012) 8(2) *European Constitutional Law Review*

Kumm, M, 'Constitutionalising Subsidiarity in Integrated Markets: The Case of Tobacco Regulation in the European Union' (2006) 12(4) *European Law Journal*

Lenaerts, K and M Desomer, 'New Models of Constitution-Making in Europe: The Quest for Legitimacy' (2002) 39 *CML Rev*

Li Feldman, H, 'Foreword: Law, Psychology, and the Emotions' (2000) 74 *Chicago-Kent Law Review*

Lindseth, PL, 'Equilibrium, Demoi-cracy, and Delegation in the Crisis of European Integration' (2014) 15(4) *German Law Journal*

MacCormick, N, 'Democracy, Subsidiarity, and Citizenship in the "European Commonwealth"' (1997) 16 *Law and Philosophy*

Magnusson, S, 'Judicial Homogeneity in the European Economic Area and the Authority of the EFTA Court' (2011) 80 *Nordic Journal of International Law*

—— and O Hannesson, 'State Liability in EEA Law: Towards Parallelism or Homogeneity?' (2013) (38)2 *European Law Review*

Mahroum, S, 'Europe and the Immigration of Highly Skilled Labour' (2001) 39(5) *International Migration*

Mala Corbin, C, 'Emotional Compelled Disclosures' (2014) 127 *Harvard Law Review*

Martin, D, 'Comments on Förster (Case C-158/07 of 18 November 2008), Metock (Case C-127/08 of 25 July 2008) and Huber (Case C-524/06 of 16 December 2008)' (2009) 11 *European Journal of Migration and Law*

Mills, A, 'Federalism in the European Union and the United States: Subsidiarity, Private Law, and the Conflict of Laws' (2010) 32(2) *University of Pennsylvania Journal of International Law*

Nicolaidis, K, 'The New Constitution as European Demoi-cracy?' (2004) 7(1) *Critical Review of International Social and Political Philosophy*

Niessen, J, 'Overlapping Interests and Conflicting Agendas: The Knocking into Shape of EU Immigration Policies' (2001) 3 *European Journal of Migration and Law*

Orcalli, G, 'Constitutional Choice and European Immigration Policy' (2007) 18(9) *Constitutional Political Economy*

Palombella, G, 'Whose Europe? After the Constitution: A Goal-based Citizenship' (2005) 3(2–3) *International Journal of Constitutional Law*

Patterson, D, 'The New Leviathan' (2003) 101 *Michigan Law Review*

Peers, S, 'Living in Sin: Legal Integration Under the EC-Turkey Customs Union' (1996) 7 *European Journal of International Law*

—— 'Implementing Equality? The Directive on Long-Term Resident Third-Country Nationals' (2004) 29 *European Law Review*

—— 'EU Immigration and Asylum Competence and Decision-Making in the Treaty of Lisbon' (2008) 10 *European Journal of Migration and Law*

Pettit, P, 'The Paradox of Loyalty' (1988) 25(2) *American Philosophical Quarterly*

Phelan, W, 'The Troika: The Interlocking Roles of *Commission v Luxembourg and Belgium, Van Gend en Loos* and *Costa v ENEL* in the Creation of the European Legal Order' (2015) 21(1) *European Law Journal*

Poiares Maduro, M, 'O superavit democrático europeu' (2001) XXXVI *Análise Social*

—— 'In Search of A Meaning and Not in Search of The Meaning: Judicial Review and the Constitution in Times of Pluralism' [2013] *Wisconsin Law Review*

Posner, EA, 'Law and the Emotions' (2001) 89 *Georgetown Law Journal*

Priban, J, 'The Self-Referential European Polity, its Legal Context and Systemic Differentiation: Theoretical Reflections on the Emergence of the EU's Political and Legal Autopoiesis' (2009) 15(4) *European Law Journal*

Rawls, J, 'The Law of Peoples' (1993) Autumn, *Critical Inquiry*

—— and P van Parijs, 'Three letters on *The Law of Peoples* and the European Union' (2003) 7(1) *Revue de Philosophie Économique*

Reif, K and H Schmitt, 'Nine Second-order Elections' (1980) 8(3) *European Journal of Political Research*

Ruhs, M and P Martin, 'Numbers vs. Rights: Trade-Offs and Guest Worker Programs' (2008) 42(1) *International Migration Review*

Sajó, A, 'Emotions in Constitutional Design' (2010) 8(3) *International Journal of Constitutional Law*

Sangiovanni, A, 'Global Justice, Reciprocity and the State' (2007) 35(1) *Philosophy & Public Affairs*

Scharpf, FW, 'The Joint-Decision Trap: Lessons from German Federalism and European Integration' (1988) 66 *Public Administration*

Schoebi, D, BM Way, BR Karney and TN Bradbury, 'Genetic Moderation of Sensitivity to Positive and Negative Affect in Marriage' (2012) 12(2) *Emotion*

Schütze, R, 'Subsidiarity after Lisbon: Reinforcing the Safeguards of Federalism?' (2009) 68(3) *Cambridge Law Journal*

Shachar, A, 'The Race for Talent: Highly-Skilled Migrants and Competitive Immigration Regimes' (2006) 18 *NYU Law Review*

Shaw, J, 'The Political Representation of Europe's Citizens: Developments. Court of Justice of the European Communities' (2008) 4 *European Constitutional Law Review*

Sieberson, SC, 'The Treaty of Lisbon and Its Impact on the European Union's Democratic Deficit' (2008) 14 *Columbia Journal of European Law*

Skordas, A, 'Immigration and the Market: The Long-Term Residents Directive' (2006) 13 *Columbia Journal of European Law*

Somek, A, 'From Workers to Migrants, from Distributive Justice to Inclusion: Exploring the Changing Social Democratic Imagination' (2012) 18(5) *European Law Journal*

von Staden, A, 'The Democratic Legitimacy of Judicial Review Beyond the State: Normative Subsidiarity and Judicial Standards of Review' (2012) 10(4) *International Journal of Constitutional Law*

Stein, E, 'Lawyers, Judges, and the Making of a Transnational Constitution' (1981) 75 *American Journal of International Law*

Sternberg, RJ, 'A Triangular Theory of Love' (1986) 93(2) *Psychological Review*

—— 'Construct Validation of a Triangular Love Scale' (1997) 27 *European Journal of Social Psychology*

Storey, H, 'EU Refugee Qualification Directive: A Brave New World?' (2008) 20(1) *International Journal of Refugee Law*

Szewczyk, BMJ, 'European Citizenship and National Democracy: Contemporary Sources of Legitimacy of the European Union' (2011) 17 *Columbia Journal of European Law*

Thym, D, 'EU Migration Policy and Its Constitutional Rationale: A Cosmopolitan Outlook' (2013) 50 *CML Rev*

Toth, AG, 'Is Subsidiarity Justiciable?' (1994) 19(3) *European Law Review*

Tushnet, R, 'More Than a Feeling: Emotion and the First Amendment' (2014) 127 *Harvard Law Review*

Vasileva, K, 'Population and Social Conditions: Nearly two-thirds of the Foreigners Living in EU Member States are Citizens of Countries Outside the EU-27' (2012) 31 *Eurostat: Statistics in Focus*

Vauchez, A, 'The Transnational Politics of Judicialization. Van Gend en Loos and the Making of EU Polity' (2010) 16(1) *European Law Journal*

Walker, N, 'Constitutionalising Enlargement, Enlarging Constitutionalism' (2003) 9(3) *European Law Journal*

—— 'Europe's Constitutional Momentum and the Search for Polity Legitimacy' (2005) 3(2 and 3) *International Journal of Constitutional Law*

Weiler, JHH, 'The Transformation of Europe' (1991) 100 *Yale Law Journal*

—— '60 Years since the First European Community—Reflections on Political Messianism' (2011) 22(2) *European Journal of International Law*

—— 'The Political and Legal Culture of European Integration: An Exploratory Essay' (2011) 9 *International Journal of Constitutional Law*

—— 'Europe in Crisis—On "Political Messianism", "Legitimacy" and the "Rule of Law"' (2012) *Singapore Journal of Legal Studies*

—— 'Van Gend en Loos: The Individual as Subject and Object and the Dilemma of European Legitimacy' (2014) 12(1) *International Journal of Constitutional Law*

—— and JP Trachtman, 'European Constitutionalism and Its Discontents' (1997) 17(1) *Northwestern Journal of International Law and Business*

Wille, A, 'The Politicization of the EU Commission: Democratic Control and the Dynamics of Executive Selection' (2012) 78(3) *International Review of Administrative Sciences*

Wollenschläger, F, 'A New Fundamental Freedom Beyond Market Integration: Union Citizenship and Its Dynamics for Shifting the Economic Paradigm of European Integration' (2011) 17(1) *European Law Journal*

Newspaper Articles

'"Vote for Schulz to Ensure a German Commission President", Says Ad' (23.05.2014) *EU Observer*

Mahony, H, 'EU Election Turnout at Record Low After All' (6.8.2014) *EU Observer*

Working Papers and Lectures

Bartolini, S, 'Taking "Constitutionalism" and "Legitimacy" Seriously' (2008) *European Governance Discussion Paper* 2008/01

de Burca, G, *Reappraising Subsidiarity's Significance after Amsterdam* (2000) Harvard Jean Monnet Working Paper 7/99

Habermas, J, *Democracy, Solidarity and the European Crisis*, Lecture delivered on 26 April 2013 in Leuven

Kocharov, A (ed), *Another Legal Monster? An EUI Debate on the Fiscal Compact Treaty* (2012) European University Institute working paper LAW 2012/09

Mair, P, *Popular Democracy and the European Union Polity* (2005) European Governance Papers (EUROGOV) No C-05-03

Piedrafita, S and V Renman, *The 'Personalisation' of the European Elections: A Half-hearted Attempt to Increase Turnout and Democratic Legitimacy?* (April 2014) EPIN Paper No 37

Poiares Maduro, M, *How Constitutional Can the European Union Be? The Tension Between Intergovernmentalism and Constitutionalism in the European Union* (2004) NYU School of Law, Jean Monnet Working Paper 5/04

—— *Passion and Reason in European Integration* (2010) Vortrag an der Humboldt-Universität zu Berlin am 10. Februar 2010, Walter Hallstein-Institut für Europäisches Verfassungsrecht (FCE 03/10)

—— 'Europe's Democratic Deficit Lies in its Member States' (2013) in Foundation for European Progressive Studies, Italiani Europei, Fondation Jean-Jaurès, Friedrich Ebert Stiftung, *Renaissance for Europe—A Democratic Union of Peace, Prosperity and Progress*

Ponzano, P, C Hermanin, D Corona, *The Power of Initiative of the European Commission: A Progressive Erosion?* (2012) Notre Europe

Raunio, T, *Destined for Irrelevance? Subsidiarity Control by National Parliaments* (19/11/2010) Elcano Royal Institute Madrid—Spain Working Paper 36/2010

Scharpf, FW, *Interdependence and Democratic Legitimation* (1998) MPIfG Working Paper No 98/2

—— 'Legitimate Diversity: The New Challenge of European Integration' (2002) *Les Cahiers européens de Sciences Po* 1 Centre d'études européennes, Sciences Po.

—— *Legitimacy Intermediation in the Multilevel European Polity* (October 2012) Max Planck Institute for the Study of Societies, Cologne, MPIfG Discussion Paper 12/6

—— *Political Legitimacy in a Non-optimal Currency Area* (2013) MPIfG Discussion Paper 13/15

Skinner, Q, *A Third Concept of Liberty* (2002) Proceedings of the British Academy 117

Vergés Bausili, A, *Rethinking the Methods of Dividing and Exercising Powers in the EU: Reforming Subsidiarity and National Parliaments* (2002) NYU School of Law, Jean Monnet Working Paper 9/02

Walker, N, *After Finalité? The Future of the European Constitutional Idea* (2007) EUI Working Paper LAW No 2007/16

Weiler, JHH, U Haltern, F Mayer, *European Democracy and its Critique Five Uneasy Pieces* (1995) EUI Working Paper RSC No 95/11

—— 'On the Distinction between Values and Virtues in the Process of European Integration' (3 March 2010, unpublished) Institute for International Law and Justice, International Legal Theory Colloquium, *The Turn to Governance: The Exercise of Power in the International Public Space*, NYU Law School

—— *Challenges to Electoral Participation in the European Elections of 2014* (2013) European Parliament doc PE 493.036

—— *Van Ghend en Loos: The Individual as Subject and Object and the Dilemma of European Legitimacy* (2014) NYU Jean Monnet Working Paper 10/14

Zaragoza-Cristiani, J, 'Analysing the Causes of the Refugee Crisis and the Key Role of Turkey: Why Now and Why So Many?' (2015) *European University Institute Working Paper RSCAS* 2015/95

Index

www.ingramcontent.com/pod-product-compliance
Lightning Source LLC
Chambersburg PA
CBHW071257180926
51613CB00001B/60
* 9 7 8 1 5 0 9 9 1 0 7 4 8 *